No Place to Go

No Place to Go:
Local Histories of the
Battered Women's Shelter Movement
Nancy Janovicek

UBCPress·Vancouver·Toronto

16 15 14 13 12 11 10 09 08 07   5 4 3 2 1

Printed in Canada on acid-free paper ∞

Library and Archives Canada Cataloguing in Publication

Janovicek, Nancy, 1968-
    No place to go : local histories of the Battered Women's Shelter Movement / Nancy Janovicek.

    Includes bibliographical references and index.
    ISBN 978-0-7748-1421-8

    1. Women's shelters – Canada – History. 2. Abused women – Services for – Canada – History. 3. Rural women – Services for – Canada – History. 4. Women's shelters – Canada – Case studies. I. Title.

HV1448.C3J36 2007   362.82'92830971   C2007-904280-5

Canadä

UBC Press gratefully acknowledges the financial support for our publishing program of the Government of Canada through the Book Publishing Industry Development Program (BPIDP), and of the Canada Council for the Arts, and the British Columbia Arts Council.

This book has been published with the help of a grant from the Canadian Federation for the Humanities and Social Sciences, through the Aid to Scholarly Publications Programme, using funds provided by the Social Sciences and Humanities Research Council of Canada.

UBC Press
The University of British Columbia
2029 West Mall
Vancouver, BC V6T 1Z2
604-822-5959 / Fax: 604-822-6083
www.ubcpress.ca

Contents

Acknowledgments / vii

Introduction / 1

1 Assisting Our Own: Beendigen, 1972-89 / 21

2 Maybe It Wasn't the Best Way to Do It, but It Got Done: Faye Peterson Transition House, 1972-85 / 43

3 We're Here to Help: Kenora Women's Crisis Intervention Project, 1975-85 / 61

4 It's a Band-Aid Service , and It's a Damn Needed One: The Nelson Safe Home Program, 1973-89 / 79

5 It Was Never about the Money: Crossroads for Women/Carrefour pour femmes, 1979-87 / 95

Conclusion / 113

Appendix: Interviews / 119

Notes / 123

Bibliography / 153

Index / 165

Acknowledgments

I have travelled to many communities to write this book and have incurred many debts along the way. It is my pleasure to thank some of the people who have helped me.

During the early stages of this project, I benefitted from the encouragement of many people at Simon Fraser University and the University of New Brunswick. Joy Parr's respect for the people she studies remains an inspiration for my own work. Marjorie Griffin Cohen's experience as an activist and academic helped me refine my arguments about the women's movement. Mary Lynn Stewart and Yasmin Jiwani have also been supportive mentors. Gillian Walker and Mark Leier provided valuable feedback on an early version of the manuscript. Margaret Conrad gave me excellent advice about publishing and writing. I would also like to thank Gail Campbell, Linda Kealey, Bev Lemire, Bill Parenteau, and Gillian Thompson for their advice.

Transition houses and women's centres are busy places, and I am grateful to the boards of these organizations for permission to use their records. Thanks also to the staff and residents for making space for me and for inviting me to join them for meals. Audrey Gilbeau, Bobbi Harrington, Lena Horswill, Karen Newmoon, Gabrielle LeBlanc, and Gwen O'Reilly helped me find documents and answered my questions. Conversations with them about the women's movement made research days even more interesting. Lisa Bengsston, Helen Smith, and Pamela Wakewich took time to explain the politics of their communities. Huberte Gautreau introduced me to the board of Crossroads for Women/Carrefour pour femmes, and Charlotte Holm put me in touch with activists in Kenora. Special thanks to the women I interviewed for their stories and cups of tea.

For their generous hospitality, I thank Michele and Molly Sam, Harriet Reid, and Toni Smith, Jaimie Sobiski, and their daughters Karli and Tess. These families opened their homes to a stranger and made me feel comfortable by quietly setting another plate at dinnertime. Many thanks to the owners and staff at the Dancing Bear Inn in Nelson (the best hostel in the world) for taking so many messages for me. Old friends opened their homes, too; thanks are due to Anna Hunter, Laura McCoy and Murray Cooke, Tanya Smith and Nick Fabiano, and my aunt Julie Slavik.

Sarita Srivastava and Mary Jane McCallum generously shared work in progress with me. Alexander Hill, Anna Hunter, Martin L'Heureux, Katherine Sam, and Annette Timm read drafts of chapters and Sarah Carter read the entire manuscript. Their feedback helped me clarify my arguments. I would also like to thank the anonymous reviewers whose thoughtful commentaries helped me to improve the contents of this book. My colleagues at the University of Calgary have offered useful advice about publishing. I thank Elizabeth Jameson, Jewel Spangler, and Frank Towers, in particular, for their encouragement. Annette Timm and I spent many summer days at the university rewriting our manuscripts. Thanks for the advice and company.

This research was supported by graduate fellowships from Simon Fraser University, the William and Ada Isabelle Steel Memorial Scholarship, the CRIAW/ICREF Marta Danylewycz Award, and a postdoctoral fellowship funded by the Canada Research Chair Program. At UBC Press, Emily Andrew, Darcy Cullen, and Ann Macklem promptly answered my questions and skilfully guided me through the various stages of publication. Lesley Barry did an excellent job as copy editor.

For their friendship, I thank Elizabeth Blaney, Michelle Bogdan, Dawn Bourque, Theresa Lalonde, Nancy Olson, Allanah Quinn, and my brothers, Ken and Dennis, who have patiently listened to me talk about this project. My parents, John and Rosalind, have supported me in many ways, most importantly by having confidence in me. Finally, I thank Martin L'Heureux for his patience and love, and for making me laugh.

No Place to Go

Introduction

"There was no place to go." This was how many activists whom I interviewed summarized abused women's isolation and social apathy about wife battering before the women's movement made it a political issue. When feminists opened women's centres in the 1970s, they were surprised by the number of women who wanted information about domestic violence. In discussions with these women, they learned that many of them stayed in violent relationships because they did not have the resources to leave. Economic dependence on the family and a lack of affordable, safe housing gave women few choices other than staying with their abusive spouses.

Racism, unfair child welfare practices, and discrimination against women in the Indian Act made it even more difficult for Aboriginal women to leave violent families. Confusing and inconsistent jurisdiction over services for Aboriginal people restricted women's access to welfare. Even if they needed financial help, many women were reluctant to apply because they were afraid that social workers would take away their children. Many women fleeing violent families had to move to cities, and unscrupulous landlords often either took advantage of people who had recently moved from the reserve or would not rent homes to them. In addition to the racism that Aboriginal women faced in cities, leaving home had adverse ramifications for them. Under the Indian Act, women were involuntarily removed from the Indian registry when they left their communities or married outside of it. Fleeing from abusive relationships forced many Aboriginal women to choose between immediate safety and their own and their children's entitlement to treaty rights and benefits.[1]

No Place to Go is about women's campaigns to organize transition houses and services for battered women in smaller cities and towns in the 1970s and 1980s. I focus on women's groups in four communities: Thunder Bay and Kenora, Ontario; Nelson, British Columbia; and Moncton, New Brunswick. The services these groups organized were not the first in Canada.

Indeed, transition houses were already established in major urban centres in Canada when women in these smaller communities began to organize. Some scholars have assumed that services in rural areas took longer to develop and were less radical than their urban counterparts because of the inherent conservatism in the country.[2] However, the reasons for the delayed organization in these communities are more complex than the assumption that feminist ideas began in urban centres and spread to small towns. First, feminists working in rural areas first had to change the entrenched view that family violence was primarily an urban phenomenon.[3] Second, they had to compete with other community groups for the limited resources allocated to smaller municipalities. Often, feminists organizing in smaller towns made a strategic decision not to identify themselves publicly as feminists to gain community support for the transition house. This encouraged women who did not identify with the women's movement to join the group, and many of these women developed a feminist consciousness through their advocacy for abused women.

In the northwestern Ontario communities examined in this book, a significant portion of the women seeking services were Aboriginal, and many of them were from remote northern reserves. Aboriginal activists in communities across northwestern Ontario organized services that sought to rectify the legacy of the devaluation of indigenous culture, families, women, and children. As in other Canadian cities, specialized services to address family violence initially took the form of hostels that were designed to ensure that young Aboriginal women who had just moved from the reserve to the city did not become involved in harmful activities. These hostels belonged to a network of Aboriginal-run services that opposed the federal government's goal of assimilating Aboriginal peoples. Organizers of the hostels soon recognized that the majority of their clients had been abused by family members or had been victims of sexual assault, and they began to develop counselling programs for abused women that sought to develop pride in their Aboriginal ancestry as the first step toward healing.

The organizations examined in this book were part of the battered women's shelter movement, an international movement that responded to battered women's need for a safe place by organizing transition houses and safe homes.[4] These services were more than emergency hostels because the organizers' objective was to help battered women to develop the self-confidence they needed to live violence-free lives. Transition houses became the foundation of a political campaign to convince federal, provincial, and municipal governments that they had a responsibility to protect abused women.

By demonstrating the need for transition houses in their communities, anti-violence activists hoped to change social indifference toward abused women. Their immediate goal was to provide a safe place for abused women and their children, but feminists and Aboriginal women also developed theories of violence against women that reflected divergent cultural values and political histories. Feminists challenged the dominant social view that women provoked men's violence and that it was better for the family if abused women tried to make their marriages work. Because they offered safety from abusive husbands, transition houses were also a profound critique of the assumption that the family offered protection to women and children, its most vulnerable members. Aboriginal activists also developed theories of violence that conceptualized it as a social rather than an individual problem, but the programs that Aboriginal women developed sought to strengthen the family and provide services for all members of violent families, including the abusers. Feminists and Aboriginal activists had different goals, but women's needs, rather than government priorities, were the basis of their services. Even though the two groups shared the goal of ending domestic violence, the battered women's shelter movement did not integrate Aboriginal theorization of gendered violence into its strategies for change.

The battered women's shelter movement emerged from campaigns to change the laws and social practices that prevented women from controlling their own bodies. "The politics of the body" became a key theme of feminist organizing in the late 1960s, when women began to link women's equality with reproductive rights and safety from male violence.[5] In consciousness-raising groups, women began to talk about their experiences of violence. The limited evidence we have about the discussions in consciousness-raising groups suggests that women spoke more frequently about rape than about domestic abuse. Rape was the first issue taken up by feminists demanding an end to male violence against women.[6] Feminist analysis of rape underscored the centrality of male misogyny and violence to the maintenance of patriarchal power and the subordination of women. By the late 1970s, radical feminists organized political groups, such as Women against Violence against Women, that were based on an analysis of oppression that distinguished itself from liberal and socialist feminism by identifying sexism as the foundational form of oppression.[7] Early feminist analysis of wife battering followed radical feminist assertions that male violence against women sustained patriarchal power.

The silence and shame associated with family violence most likely made women reluctant to discuss abuse in consciousness-raising groups and other public venues. However, this reluctance may also have been a response to some feminists' frustration with women who would not leave abusive relationships. In the heady days of the women's liberation movement, many feminists could not understand why women stayed with violent spouses. Joan Baril, one of the founders of the Thunder Bay Women's Liberation Group, recalled that her consciousness-raising group had little sympathy for a woman who often came to the meetings with a black eye but who would not leave her husband, because members did not yet understand the systemic barriers that prevented her from doing so.[8] Some feminists were reluctant to accept that wife battering was a political issue because the helplessness of many abused women contradicted the feminist belief that women could live independently from men. Others thought that there was sufficient legislative protection for abused women. When Florence Bird chaired the Royal Commission on the Status of Women from 1967 to 1970, she did not want wife abuse discussed during the hearings because it was already covered under the criminal code.[9] Frontline workers soon learned that the law offered little real protection for battered women, but they still had to justify the need for services to feminists who asked, "Why doesn't she just leave?"[10] Lack of understanding of the complexity of woman abuse accounts for this unsympathetic attitude. In addition, there was some resistance within feminist groups to organizing services for abused women. This reluctance was linked to a broader discussion about whether feminists should use their limited resources to educate women with the goal of mobilizing them into action or to organize more costly services. I explore the various ways that feminist groups resolved this debate in some of the case studies that follow.

Safety and shelter were the basic needs of women trying to leave abusive partners. Before transition houses opened in their communities, many women's centre activists took women and their children home with them. In the early 1970s, the Vancouver Women's Centre converted the beds in its attic, which were initially intended for female travellers, into a refuge for abused women and their children. Feminists soon realized that in addition to needing protection from immediate danger, abused women needed programs to help them prepare for an independent life. Thus, the first services for abused women were ad hoc until activists acquired sufficient funding to establish more formal services. The federal and provincial governments eventually ceded to pressure from women's groups to fund these services, but the financial situation of transition houses has always been precarious.

The first Canadian transition houses opened in Toronto and Vancouver in 1972. Eight years later, when Linda MacLeod wrote *Wife Battering in Canada: The Vicious Circle*, the first report that attempted to document the incidence of woman abuse in Canada, there were sixty-three shelters for battered women.[11] There were more places to which battered women could go, but many women still lived in communities with limited services; in 1980, 45 percent of the Canadian population lived in places where abused women did not have access to an emergency shelter.[12] The 1980s witnessed a significant increase in the number of shelters for abused women and their children: by 1987 there were 264 transition houses in Canada.[13] The majority of the transition houses discussed in this book opened during this latter period. Beendigen, a shelter for Aboriginal women and children, opened in Thunder Bay in 1978; Crossroads for Women/Carrefour pour femmes opened in Moncton in 1981; and Faye Peterson Transition House opened in Thunder Bay two years later. Kenora feminists did not open a transition house because the province opened a Family Resource Centre there in 1984. Activists in Nelson operated a safe home program from 1980 until 1995, when the Aimee Beaulieu Transition House took over providing shelter for abused women. Although these transition houses opened many years after those in large cities, most of the campaigns to establish these shelters began in the mid-1970s. It often took longer for women in smaller communities to obtain funding for transition houses than it did for women in major cities because they had to prove to parsimonious government officials that specialized services in small communities were necessary.

Convincing politicians and bureaucrats that it was the community's responsibility to help abused women, and that women's groups should provide these services, was every bit as challenging. Transition houses were different from government-run social services because they based their services on women's needs and refused to impose unrealistic expectations on women.

The length of a women's stay in a shelter was often a key contention between grassroots activists and governments. Local welfare offices wanted to restrict the length of stay because they were concerned about the cost of providing per diems to shelters for indefinite periods of time. Shelter organizers usually ignored these rules and did not pressure women to leave the shelter until they were ready to do so. Some politicians were simply indifferent to the plight of battered women. The extent of this apathy became clear to the women's movement on 12 May 1982, when Member of Parliament Margaret Mitchell asked the House of Commons how it was going to respond to the Standing Committee on Health, Welfare, and Social Affairs report on wife battering, which it had tabled the day before. Some of the members of Parliament laughed in response to her question.[14]

Isolation from the government and the women's movement influenced the strategies of the organizers of the transition houses examined here. These communities were not major economic or political centres. Although they provided social services for their regions, they remained distant from provincial and federal policy-makers and, in the cases of the British Columbia and Ontario communities examined in this book, from provincial legislatures. They were also far away from the urban centres that were the home of numerous diverse feminist organizations. In most of the communities studied in this book, women who held different political views worked together because there were not enough women involved in the local women's movement to form groups based on different feminist theories. Women did, however, organize separately along race lines. The board of Beendigen cooperated with women's groups in Thunder Bay but had a stronger affiliation with the Aboriginal services and political groups in the city. Women who organized feminist services in northwestern Ontario developed a strong regional network to cope with the derision they dealt with working in small northern towns. Women working in the Kootenays, British Columbia communicated with each other, but did not develop similar networks. The Moncton shelter grew out of the vibrant network of Acadian activists in the late 1960s and early 1970s that played an important role in initiating formal feminist organizing in New Brunswick.

Resistance to the politicization of wife abuse from government officials often made activists who opened transition houses targets for ridicule by people in their community, but activists had no choice but to engage with the politicians, police, welfare officers, and municipal councillors who opposed their goals. To protect women, activists were obliged to enter into contracts with all levels of government. At the local level, advocates for battered women fought for women's right to social welfare benefits as citizens and opposed the assumption that women should be dependent upon their families. Initially, shelters relied on federal grants and per diem funding from municipal governments to cover day-to-day costs. Federal job creation programs and Status of Women grants helped women open shelters, but ultimately the federal government expected the provinces to take over the funding of these new services.

However, provincial governments were reluctant to provide permanent funding for new services, and activists negotiated between different federal and provincial agendas for women's equality. In 1983, Ottawa earmarked funds to develop transition houses by providing Canadian Mortgage and Housing Corporation loans, but guaranteed support from junior levels of government was a condition of the loans. Feminists lobbied provincial governments for stabilized funding, with varying degrees of success. The Ontario Association of Transition Houses negotiated a funding formula with the provincial government in 1983. In British Columbia, transition house activists could not convince the Social Credit government to pay for shelters because it had adopted a fiscal policy that reduced government spending and froze spending on all new social programs in 1982. New Brunswick's Conservative government also emphasized responsible spending, which again made it difficult for shelter organizers to secure provincial funding. Advocates for Aboriginal women faced another layer of bureaucracy because the federal government was responsible for services for Aboriginal people with status, and the provinces were supposed to provide social services to those without status.

Municipalities were excluded from social welfare arrangements between federal and provincial governments, but local politics mattered in the development of alternative models of social services.[15] Securing funds from senior levels of government depended on approval from municipal bureaucrats, who were generally unreceptive to criticism of their welfare practices. There were parallels among the communities examined in this book, but the relationships between feminists, anti-violence activists, and local social welfare bureaucrats were not uniform. Kenora feminists and local welfare bureaucrats developed an acrimonious relationship, and consequently the town prevented the local women's movement from managing a provincially funded shelter. However, women's success in Moncton depended on support from municipal bureaucrats who joined the lobby for increased provincial funding for the transition house. In Kenora and Thunder Bay, where Aboriginal women accessed services, organizers faced vehement resistance from municipal welfare officials, who refused to help these women because they thought that all Aboriginal people were under federal jurisdiction.

An examination of the battered women's shelter movement in smaller communities shows how the local manifestation of patriarchal relations, colonization, and hinterland economies limited women's influence in their communities and at the provincial level. Knowing these politics helps to explain the choices women made and what they could and could not change. This, in turn, accounts for the uneven development of the battered women's shelter movement in Canada. It adds complexities to existing analyses of how the state absorbed feminist agendas for change, a key theme in the literature about transition houses.[16]

Frontline workers instigated analyses of wife battering as a political issue. In the 1970s, feminists challenged gender-neutral analysis of family violence by arguing that wife battering was a manifestation of patriarchal relations. Discussions about wife battering were not new. Before the revival of the women's movement, psychologists and sociologists conceptualized abuse as a symptom of family dysfunction. The goal of their research was to identify the economic and social stresses that caused family violence so that the family units could be strengthened.[17] Feminists disagreed with this analysis because it placed equal blame on the perpetrator and the victim of violence. More importantly, such clinical analysis of family violence did not consider how women experienced abuse, and thus it conflicted with the feminist conviction that women were the experts on their own lives.

The literature on violence against women has grown exponentially since feminists put the issue on the public agenda. We know more about the social and economic reasons women remain in violent relationships. Stories about wife abuse are now common in the media, though many accounts are not feminist.[18] Collections of women's testimonials and films by the National Film Board of Canada document how women found the courage to leave violent relationships.[19] Reports by grassroots organizations continue to deepen our knowledge about violence against women through participatory action research.[20]

Historians have contributed to the movement to end violence against women by challenging the assumption that family violence is a new issue and by demonstrating how its visibility as a social issue, rather than its incidence, has varied over time. Linda Gordon's book *Heroes of Their Own Lives* has been one of the most influential histories of family violence. Her argument that "family violence is historically and politically constructed" has guided subsequent histories of violence against women.[21] Gordon examines how power struggles within families are connected to changes in the social and economic situation of women and children. Her work has inspired historians to look for the historical and local circumstances that have shaped women's ability to resist gendered violence.[22]

Current chronologies of the contemporary movement to end wife battering, however, remain generalized. Histories of the battered women's shelter movement often trace its origins to Erin Pizzey's refuge for battered wives in Chiswick, England, in 1971.[23] The Canadian literature sets Toronto's Interval House and Vancouver Transition House as the origins for all shelters. Historical examinations of the women's movement emphasize the importance of grassroots activism but are preoccupied by the development of a feminist consciousness and the growth of the national women's movement. This literature acknowledges the uniqueness of local feminist groups, but it emphasizes their similarities and casts them as foundational elements for the history of the women's movement.[24]

Political scientists have examined the early years of contemporary feminist organizing to explain how working within federal and provincial bureaucracies compromised feminist agendas for change.[25] Gillian Walker's analysis of the relationship between the battered women's shelter movement and the state examines how government agencies absorbed campaigns against wife battering to suit their own priorities, while marginalizing feminist expertise and analysis of the issue.[26] Understanding the relationship between social movements and the state is crucial for planning strategies and tactics, yet as Cindy Katz argues, an exclusive focus on the macro-analysis means that "the bodies and spaces in which citizens lived their protests" are forgotten.[27] Asking how women have understood their role in local politics deepens our knowledge of the history of the women's movement.

No Place to Go shifts the focus away from metropolitan centres and instead examines how women in smaller cities and rural communities organized women-centred services. Feminists were key players in creating services for battered women in smaller communities, but so were women and men who did not identify with the women's movement. Although they had limitations, safe home programs were important in rural areas that did not have the resources to open a transition house. This book contributes to the growing literature on the history of violence against women by examining how, in the 1970s and 1980s, anti-violence activists developed an explicitly political analysis of wife battering that made visible the connections between personal experiences of violence and the systemic barriers that made women vulnerable to abuse in their families.

Feminists argued that wife battering was an extreme manifestation of unequal patriarchal relations in the family. From the beginning of the battered women's shelter movement, activists fought against more influential community organizations to ensure that women's experiences of violence were not subsumed in the larger framework of family violence. Feminists believed that "family violence" was an inaccurate analytical framework because it was a de-gendered term that hid the fact that men were far more likely than women to be the abusers in violent families. They also resisted the family violence framework because it had the potential to put children's needs before women's needs. One example of this is a 1979 report published by the United Way, which described kicking or punching a pregnant woman as instances of "intrauterine abuse" of the child.[28] As more people began to accept that violence against women in the family was unacceptable, feminists became increasingly vigilant in defending a violence-against-women framework that demonstrated how wife battering maintained male dominance.[29]

This theorization of wife battering made it possible to talk about it as a political issue, but, ultimately, the framework was exclusive. The feminist investment in the violence-against-women framework entrenched a common experience for abused women that was based on white women's experiences and assumed that woman abuse happened only in heterosexual relationships. Those who attempted to widen the analysis of abuse, by examining how race, class, citizenship status, and sexual identity shaped women's experiences of violence in intimate relationships, felt unwelcome in the battered women's shelter movement.[30]

Aboriginal women were among those who struggled to convince feminists that the violence-against-women framework was inadequate because it prioritized the needs of white women. They argued that the theorization of violence must address the impact of the legacy of federal Indian policy, which was designed to assimilate indigenous peoples, on Aboriginal women who left violent homes. White feminists dismiss Aboriginal women's criticisms of feminist agendas less frequently now than in the 1970s and early 1980s because Aboriginal women have been insistent that white women listen to them.[31] Yet as Lee Maracle argues, the mainstream women's movement included Aboriginal women on its own terms by expecting them to sensitize white women on issues of racism and to teach them about First Nations cultures. Maracle explains that inviting Aboriginal women to speak only on these issues has homogenized the diverse experiences of Aboriginal women and denied them the opportunity to speak with authority on women in general.[32] In her study of anti-racist debates in feminist organizations, Sarita Srivastava explains that analysis of the women's movement that assumes that the issues championed by white women are the central concerns of the women's movement "recentres an implicit whiteness as constitutive of the ideal feminism."[33] Historical analysis of the women's movement cannot subsume the analysis of Aboriginal women's organizing into the established narrative of the second wave of feminism, which credits white women for initiating the revival of feminist organizing in the 1960s.[34]

Benita Roth presents a useful model for understanding the history of the current women's movement. In *Separate Roads to Feminism: Black, Chicana, and White Feminist Movements in America's Second Wave,* she conceptualizes the contemporary American women's movement as "a group of feminisms, movements made by activist women that were largely organizationally distinct from one another, and from the beginning largely organized along racial/ethnic lines."[35] These different movements were part of a broader social movement that made connections among them. Rather than looking for origin stories, Roth insists that we need to pay attention to how race, ethnicity, and class affected women's access to resources because inequalities among women meant that women's feminist consciousness emerged in different social and economic contexts. *No Place to Go* demonstrates that regional disparities also shaped these social relations and, consequently, informed feminist strategies and goals.[36]

In the battered women's shelter movement, those who posited patriarchal relations as the primary reason for spousal assault have found it difficult to accept Aboriginal activists' contention that family violence in their com-munities was grounded in the history of colonial relations. Assimilation has been the guiding principle of the governance of Aboriginal people since con-tact between Europeans and indigenous peoples. Federal policy has sought to terminate traditional Aboriginal forms of government, and decreasing women's economic and political roles has been a central feature of programs designed to achieve this goal.

Federal Indian policy also targeted the family, which was the foundation of Aboriginal government, economy, and society. Removing children from their families and communities was deemed to be the easiest way to assimi-late Aboriginal peoples, first through the residential school system and later through child welfare programs that placed children in non-Aboriginal fam-ilies. Provincial governments extended child welfare to Aboriginal communi-ties in the 1960s after the federal government began to close residential schools and introduce cost-sharing agreements with provincial governments to provide services to Aboriginal people who lived on-reserve. Social workers believed that the best way to protect Aboriginal children from poverty, poor health, and poor housing conditions in reserve communities was to remove them from their families and place them in white homes. Aboriginal activists have called this the "sixties scoop." It is not known how many children were placed in non-Aboriginal homes in the 1960s, but between 1971 and 1981, 75 percent of the children who were apprehended were placed in non-Aboriginal homes, often outside of Canada.[37] Many of these children suffered in these homes, and Patricia Monture-Angus argues that this practice was itself a form of family violence.[38] Thus, fear of losing their children informed many women's decision to leave violent relationships, particularly those who needed social assistance.

Aboriginal women's theorization of violence in their communities was not simply an adaptation of feminist analysis of violence against women. *Breaking Free: A Proposal for Change to Aboriginal Family Violence*, the first published report that dealt exclusively with violence against Aboriginal women, did not appear until 1989, but Aboriginal women began to theorize the issue earlier than this.[39] When funding proposals and minutes of meet-ings are examined, it is clear that activists' analysis of family violence was based on indigenous values and was critical of government policies and social welfare practices that targeted Aboriginal families. The Native women's movement argued that strategies to help abused women were not useful if they did not consider how this history of disempowerment shaped Aboriginal women's experiences of violence.

For these reasons, proposals for ending violence in Aboriginal communities have focused on healing the family, but they have also emphasized the urgent need for services that recognize the impact of colonization on Aboriginal women. In the 1970s, the Native women's movement began to develop programs that attempted to assuage women's isolation and loneliness when they left their home communities. Family violence disrupted many women's connections to their traditional territories, their languages, and their cultures because often the only option available for Aboriginal women in abusive relationships was to leave the reserve. In addition to dispossession from their traditional territories, Aboriginal women in cities had difficulty seeking social assistance because welfare administrators argued that status Indians were under federal jurisdiction. Provincial and municipal authorities were keener on maintaining this distinction after the release of the 1969 White Paper on Indian Policy, which they considered an attempt to off-load federal responsibilities onto junior levels of government. These policies created additional challenges for the organizers of Aboriginal-run services.

Given their differing theorization of gendered violence and the fear of creating divisions within Aboriginal communities, many Aboriginal women did not find the women's movement as meaningful as the Aboriginal movement for self-determination. Aboriginal women's activism often began in Native organizations and at friendship centres. Thunder Bay Anishinabequek and women who organized the first shelter in Kenora knew that abused women who came to town from the reserve would face racism and that programs had to acknowledge that race and gender-based discrimination were inseparable. The Ontario Native Women's Association (ONWA) did not adopt feminist strategies for change because they failed to address the social and economic inequalities emanating from the colonial relations that instigated social problems in Aboriginal communities. This is not to say that there was no collaboration between the Aboriginal women and feminist groups. Even though Aboriginal and white women in northwestern Ontario established distinct organizations, they supported each other's projects. In Kenora, the movement against violence against women united women across their cultural and racial differences for a short time.

Incorporating the diverse experiences of women has been one of the most difficult issues in the women's movement. This has been especially challenging in the battered women's shelter movement because it has so much invested in the violence-against-women framework that focuses on individual change and posits patriarchy as the primary reason for violence against women. Using this framework, the movement has promoted solutions that centre the experience of white, heterosexual women. The emphasis on the criminalization of domestic violence has been far less effective for Aboriginal women, immigrant women, and women of colour, who rely on strong connections to their communities to counter racism and exclusion from Canadian society. Women from these social groups are often reluctant to involve the police because they do not want to draw negative attention to their communities or face censure from community leaders if they do. Moreover, men from these communities have been over-represented in the criminal justice system, and women do not trust police to treat their families with respect.[40] In most of the communities discussed in this book, activists were aware of the need for services for Aboriginal women. They were less concerned with developing programs for immigrant women and women of colour in the period under study because the number of women from these groups was small.

More recently, lesbians have spoken out about lesbian partner abuse. This has been one of the greatest challenges for the battered women's shelter movement because it has forced activists to acknowledge that women can be violent. As one activist explains, "it's been easier, and safer, for the battered women's movement to say that it's only men who are violent."[41] Janice Ristock recalls that when she was first confronted with the issue in Toronto, she was worried that talking about lesbian abuse would result in more harm than help to lesbians and feminists.[42] Lesbians played an important role in the movement to end violence against women, and Becki Ross has examined the debates between heterosexual and lesbian women in Toronto groups.[43] Lesbians were involved in feminist activism in the communities examined in this book. The literature on rural attitudes toward lesbians suggests that women in small towns did not welcome lesbians, but the relationship between lesbians and heterosexual women varied.[44] The Nelson and District Women's Centre promoted lesbian rights and held lesbian drop-ins. Yet the women whom I interviewed did not connect their sexual identity with their work to end violence against women. In Kenora, women did not promote lesbian visibility in their group, in part because those who opposed their goals tried to undermine their work by calling them lesbians. Doreen Worden, a lesbian activist, explained that a small group of lesbians who organized autonomously did so because they did not feel welcome in women's groups; between 1980 and 1986 they published a newspaper called *Voices: A Survival Manual for Women*.[45] It was not until 1989 that the Kenora Rape Crisis Line sponsored a lesbian support phone line.[46] While lesbians were active in these communities, I found no evidence of discussions of abuse in lesbian relationships in the records.

Many argue that the goals and interests of middle-class women dominated the women's movement in the 1960s and 1970s, but this generalization does not capture the economic context of the small, resource-based towns examined in this book. Because of the tendency to focus on middle-class women's dominance in the women's movement, there is an assumption that middle-class women controlled the boards of shelters for battered women and that their privileged status fostered unequal relations between residents, staff, and board members in feminist organizations.[47] Many boards of transition houses comprised privileged women who often were not sympathetic to the economic situation of the staff in the shelter.[48] But this was not the case in all transition houses. Many of the activists whom I interviewed came from working-class backgrounds, were single mothers, or had themselves left violent families. Meg Luxton argues that the assertion that the women's movement in the 1960s and 1970s was largely middle class "is part of a larger pattern in which both working-class women and their organizing efforts ... get written out of, or 'hidden from history.'"[49] Luxton focuses on union activism as the key site of working-class feminism. This book shows that working-class women also contributed to the development of feminist services.

Class differences between social workers and clients is an important theme in historical studies of government-run and community-based social service agencies, but without evidence I am reluctant to assume that all of the women who stayed in these transition houses were from working-class backgrounds. Crossroads/Carrefour was the only organization discussed in this book that kept statistics about the clients' and abusers' professions. However, the records do not provide sufficient data to draw conclusions about the class backgrounds of the clients because the majority of clients did not provide this information on intake sheets.[50]

Because I have limited data about the women who stayed at these shelters, this book focuses more on women's political activities than on the experiences of the clients. One of the conditions placed on my access to the records of the organizations was that I would not look at documents about former clients, and there was no response to advertisements seeking women who used the shelters and safe home systems. Understanding the relationship between residents and staff and how women responded to feminist services will be a vital aspect of the history of the battered women's shelter movement, but, at this time, protecting the confidentiality of the women who stayed there is more important. Descriptions of the poor condition of the houses and the lack of space and privacy in the original shelters do shed light on what it was like to live there, but assessments of the effectiveness of the services are based on the perceptions of the organizers and staff.

Between 1998 and 2003, I read the privately held records of women's centres, transition houses, community services, and ONWA. The histories of the shelters are based primarily on these records. Some organizations had more complete and well-organized records than others. At Beendigen, when I expressed my surprise and dismay at how few documents the organizers had left, an employee reminded me that this kind of political organizing was new for many women. As was the case in most women's groups, keeping records was not a priority. In her overview of the history of the contemporary women's movement, Marjorie Griffin Cohen explains that "their immediate work was more absorbing than writing about it."[51] Moreover, writing the documents was a political process. Feminists often made strategic decisions about whether to record the diversity of opinion within the group, to simplify the message in order to reach a wider audience, or to exclude explicitly feminist analysis in order to ensure support for their project.[52] Thus, the complexities of the debates were rarely recorded in the documents. Local feminist newspapers (*The Northern Woman* and *Images*, published in Thunder Bay and Nelson respectively) and interviews with activists clarified some of the ambiguities in the organizational records.[53]

The first three chapters discuss communities in northwestern Ontario, where violence against women mobilized more women into political action than any other issue. Women's groups from across the region worked together to organize networks to get women to safety and to lobby for shelters in the north. Chapter 1 examines the founding of Beendigen, a shelter organized by Thunder Bay Anishinabequek, a chapter of ONWA, and the development of an analysis of family violence that defined it as a consequence of colonialism. Chapter 2 discusses the two other shelters for battered women in Thunder Bay: Community Residences, a city-run service, and Faye Peterson Transition House, a feminist service for women from across the region. Organizing the transition house taught feminists that they were politically marginalized at both the municipal and provincial level. Drawing on regional solidarity among northwestern Ontario feminists, Faye Peterson Transition House organizers transformed their weak position in provincial politics into an effective political tool. Chapter 3 tells the story of the Kenora Women's Crisis Intervention Project, founded in 1976. The Kenora case study examines a brief cross-cultural collaboration between Aboriginal women and white women. Although the coalition was short-lived, non-Aboriginal activists continued to advocate for Aboriginal women during their campaign to open a transition house. The regional movement supported Kenora feminists, but they were unsuccessful because municipal bureaucrats opposed their alternate vision for service provision.

More often than not, transition houses faced the quandary of serving women in crisis when the organization itself was in crisis.[54] The next two chapters discuss internal issues in feminist groups. Chapter 4 examines how the debates about whether or not feminists should organize services influenced feminism at the Nelson and District Women's Centre. Because feminists decided not to organize a transition house without adequate government support, they were able to establish a co-operative relationship with the organizers of the safe home program, even though one of the goals of the program was to keep families together. The final chapter discusses Crossroads for Women/Carrefour pour femmes and examines how Moncton feminists negotiated the contradiction between working for women's equality and paying transition house workers low wages.

My ethical obligations to the organizations discussed in this book and to the individuals whom I interviewed put some restrictions on the analysis. Some themes that are central issues in the women's movement today – in particular, the issue of racism in the women's movement – do not receive as much attention as I had anticipated they would when I planned the research. These activists did not record discussions about racism within the organization in their minutes, and, in interviews, both Aboriginal and non-Aboriginal women were reluctant to talk about it. Women were certainly reticent to explore these issues with an outsider. But, in retrospect, I realize that Aboriginal women who spoke to me are still active in community organizing and have developed working relationships with non-Aboriginal community groups. Speaking on record about the racism that has shaped northwestern Ontario would jeopardize this network of local services.[55] Studying very recent history obliges one to consider the impact the research will have on activists' reputations and the future work of community organizations.

This book is the first Canadian study to examine the history of the battered women's shelter movement and the first history of contemporary feminist organizing that focuses exclusively on rural communities and small cities. Because it is based on specific case studies, it cannot capture all of the complexities in the organization of feminist services in the 1970s and 1980s, and the conclusion recommends areas for future research that would advance this historiography. Feminist analysis of the politics of the battered women's shelter movement informed my reading of the documents, but I do not examine the criminalization of wife abuse, current policy debates, or the state of transition houses today. The history of the battered women's shelter movement that focuses on local histories, however, can inform these debates because it explains how women grappled with these issues at the local level. Local histories demonstrate that strategies for change can work only if the people who are strategizing pay attention to local politics and circumstances.

What this book does do is examine the struggles, disappointments, and successes of women operating under specific social and economic conditions. At the time that the women in these communities were organizing services, many feminists were lamenting the loss of the radical analysis of the early years of the women's liberation movement, the institutionalization of feminist goals, divisions among feminists along race and class lines, and the lack of visibility of the movement itself. In Toronto, the International Women's Day Coalition was a response to the lack of visibility of the women's movement. Women from different groups and organizations marched in the streets in order to disprove media assertions that the women's movement was dead and to reassure activists that the movement was still vibrant.[56] Protest marches and public celebrations of the women's movement were important, but so was the tedious day-to-day work of social movements. After delivering a lecture in Vancouver, Angela Davis commented that "what demonstrations demonstrate is the existence of a movement. What happens between demonstrations is a lot of not very exciting work."[57]

It was through mundane activities, such as fundraising, typing newsletters, reassessing the collective structure, operating a safe home, or renovating an old home into a shelter, that the women you will meet in this book learned they could create change. Some groups achieved their goals and others did not. Feminist philosopher Ruth Lister argues that political actions do not need to meet their projected aims to be successful because the act of coming together to express a political voice builds women's self-esteem and their sense of themselves as political agents.[58] These women did not end violence against women, but they did help many women understand that the abuse was not their fault. Sometimes bureaucrats and politicians who had greater control over social policy took over their vision for change. Nevertheless, it is quite probable that some women are alive today because of activists' dedication to the belief that one day they would end violence against women. For these reasons, I dedicate this book to the women who organized these transition houses and services for battered women and their children.

1
Assisting Our Own: Beendigen, 1972-89

In 1978, Thunder Bay Anishinabequek,[1] a chapter of the Ontario Native Women's Association (ONWA), opened Beendigen, a shelter for Aboriginal women and children in crisis. Beendigen, Ojibwa for "welcome," offered emergency shelter and food for women who lived in or had just moved to Thunder Bay from their home reserves. Many of these women were fleeing violent relationships. Although there were other emergency shelters in Thunder Bay, organizers argued that this service was necessary to ensure that these families would not be further isolated in non-Aboriginal settings. Part of Beendigen's mandate was to assist women and children in adapting to living in the city by helping them cope with racism. Urban orientation was among their objectives, but Beendigen organizers developed programs that emphasized cultural retention. Thus, these programs contested the assumption that moving to the city indicated a decision to assimilate into Canadian society.[2] Beendigen organizers also insisted that women needed a service that would keep families together to assuage women's fears that their children would be taken from them if they entered into the social welfare system. Thus, Beendigen provided a necessary alternative to government programs that had adopted a policy of placing Aboriginal children from families in crisis in white homes.

Beendigen was one of many emergency shelters organized to address the growing number of homeless Aboriginal women in Canadian cities. In the late 1960s, non-Aboriginal activists initiated these programs with the goal of integrating people who had just moved from reserves into Canadian society. Aboriginal activists were critical of these services, and, in the early 1970s, they began to organize programs based on Aboriginal values. Anduhyaun, the first residence for Aboriginal women in Canada, opened in Toronto in 1968.[3] The YWCA and the Department of Indian Affairs initially sponsored the project to help young women recover from addictions. Even though the organizers sought advice from Aboriginal activists in Toronto, acculturation was the service's primary goal. Within Toronto's Aboriginal community, the shelter soon gained a reputation as a place that was trying to turn its residents into "nice little white girls."⁴ In 1972, a group of Aboriginal women took control of the operation of the home and created the first shelter for Aboriginal women that was managed by Aboriginal women. By the time ONWA chapters began to organize shelters for women in northwestern Ontario in the late 1970s, the Native rights movement had established the importance of Aboriginal-run services. ONWA members initially intended to organize these hostels for unwed mothers, students, women with addictions, and homeless women, but, by the 1980s, their key function had become providing emergency shelter for women and children fleeing violent families.

Anishinabequek was part of the Native women's movement that developed in conjunction with the Native rights movement and the women's movement in the 1970s. The most prominent issue of the Native women's movement was its challenge to the overt gender inequality in the Indian Act. Under section 12(1)(b) of the Indian Act, women who married non-Aboriginal men or non-status Indians lost their Indian status and were forced to leave their communities. When women began to draw attention to the gender inequalities that federal Indian policy had instigated within Aboriginal communities, many male leaders as well as women with Indian status criticized them. The predominantly male leadership of the Native rights movement maintained that fighting for the collective rights of all Aboriginal people was more important than addressing the specific inequalities of Aboriginal women. Leaders believed that since these problems were grounded in colonial relations, they would disappear once Aboriginal peoples had secured treaty rights and attained self-government.⁵ Women realized they would have to form their own organizations to prioritize Aboriginal women's needs.

Historians have studied the national and international campaigns Aboriginal women fought to change the Indian Act, but they have paid less attention to the political work that women did in their communities.⁶ This chapter contributes to the history of the Native women's movement by examining how women applied the analysis of Aboriginal women's oppression to the development of grassroots services. As was the case at the national level, prominent men in Thunder Bay's Aboriginal community tended to believe that feminist thought rather than Aboriginal values informed the

Native women's movement. Anishinabequek members insisted that their political work was inextricable from the goals of the Native rights movement. Women's understanding of their responsibilities to their nations and of their role in the Native rights movement shaped the development of Beendigen. Through service provision, Aboriginal women learned how federal Indian policy shaped their experiences of violence. This knowledge became the foundation of a theorization of family violence that explained that federal Indian policy had undermined the leadership roles Aboriginal women traditionally held in Aboriginal cultures. Activists argued that this general disrespect toward women in Aboriginal communities often manifested as violence against women.

Anishinabequek activists worked with feminists in Thunder Bay, but these movements were never formally integrated. Beendigen organizers supported groups in Thunder Bay that were also struggling to open transition houses for women. Likewise, the feminist community celebrated the opening of Beendigen in the *Northern Woman*, a feminist newspaper, and held a shower to supply the shelter with much-needed linens and supplies when it opened. Because Beendigen was the first grassroots shelter for abused women to open in the city, its founders could offer practical advice to feminists when they opened a transition house to serve women from across the region.[7] Even though there was mutual support between Aboriginal and non-Aboriginal women's groups, as well as a strong coalition among women's groups that were providing services for abused women, Beendigen organized independently from the other shelters in the region. Instead, Anishinabequek members allied themselves with the growing network of Aboriginal-run services in the city. The distinction between Beendigen and the other transition houses in the region became more clear in 1989, when ONWA published *Breaking Free*. This report was the first Canadian study of family violence in Aboriginal communities, and it laid the groundwork for subsequent theorization of family violence that connected it to colonization and the cultural genocide of indigenous peoples.

This chapter discusses the foundation of Beendigen and the development of an analysis of family violence based on gendered racial violence and colonialism. It discusses the intentions of the organizers but does not analyze how Beendigen operated or how its services changed as activists learned more about women's experiences of violence, as other chapters in this book do. I was unable to explore these themes because the board did not grant me access to the organization's records that pertain to this period.[8] Moreover, all of the elders whom I approached for an interview were unable to talk to me because of pressing family and community obligations. Understanding how and why Aboriginal women developed services for abused women and children based on a holistic approach to family violence is important because histories of the women's movement tend to depict Aboriginal women's organizing as a component of a feminist movement whose primary goal was to end sexism. Presenting the Native women's movement as evidence of "diversity" in the women's movement subsumes their activism in the more powerful narrative of the women's movement and shifts the emphasis away from Aboriginal women's opposition to the negative impact of colonization on their families and communities.[9]

Beendigen organizers developed their services in response to the specific social and economic circumstances of Aboriginal women in Thunder Bay and northwestern Ontario. Because Anishinabequek served Aboriginal women who lived off-reserve, it is necessary to understand responses to the increasing migration of Aboriginal peoples from reserves to cities. Thus this chapter begins with a discussion of how policy-makers linked urban migration to assimilation and of the corollary debates among Aboriginal leaders and federal and provincial governments about jurisdiction over social welfare for Aboriginal people. Because women's issues were generally ignored by the Native rights movement, gender was absent from these debates. These national debates influenced women's activism in Thunder Bay, shaped Beendigen policies and goals, and informed the explanation for the high rates of family violence in Aboriginal communities. The premise of Beendigen's services and of ONWA's analysis of family violence was that strengthening and restoring Aboriginal families as well as women's traditional leadership roles were integral to self-government and to attaining sovereignty.

URBAN MIGRATION, CITIZENS PLUS, CITIZENS MINUS

Urban migration occurred against the backdrop of a revived Native rights movement and the federal government's re-evaluation of its fiduciary responsibility to Aboriginal peoples. Native leaders insisted that the only solution to poverty in Aboriginal communities was the recognition of treaties and the inherent rights of status Indians. The federal government countered that this special status was responsible for the "Indian problem" and proposed solutions that would integrate Aboriginal peoples into Canadian society.[10] In their negotiations with the federal government, Native leaders ignored the particular circumstances of Aboriginal women whose status was forcibly removed under federal Indian legislation and who were consequently forced to leave the reserve. Aboriginal women organized autonomously to fight for their rights and found themselves in conflict with the male leadership of the Native rights movement.

In the late 1960s, increasing numbers of people migrated from the reserve to cities and towns. In 1966, 80 percent of the Aboriginal population still lived on-reserve, but migration increased steadily in subsequent years.[11] Migration patterns of women and men were different. In 1966, 16.4 percent of status women lived off-reserve compared with 15.4 percent of status men, a disparity that grew over time.[12] This difference may not seem to be significant, but it is probable that these statistics do not accurately measure the number of women who lived off-reserve. There was no accurate way to track the number of Aboriginal peoples living off-reserve because they were a transient group. Moreover, non-status Indians tended to be blended into poor populations in cities, and many women who lived off-reserve had lost their status when they married outside of their community.[13] Between 1958 and 1968, 4,605 women who had married men who did not have Indian status were removed from the Indian registry.[14] Although migration patterns of women and men were different, studies written in the 1960s and 1970s about Aboriginal peoples living in cities rarely discussed this issue.[15]

The increasing number of Aboriginal people living off-reserve complicated the debates between federal and provincial governments about which level of government should pay for the social programs that Aboriginal people used. Under the British North America Act, the federal government was responsible for services to status Indians. Improving the social and economic standards on reserves by providing individuals with training that would enable them to establish themselves in non-Aboriginal communities guided the objectives of federal Indian welfare policy in the early 1960s.[16] The Department of Indian Affairs designed social welfare programs for Aboriginal communities that were similar to those for non-Aboriginal people. According to Hugh Shewell, the branch opposed the development of parallel services for indigenous peoples in order "to help Indians join the broader society by erasing any perceived advantage to remaining in their own communities."[17] In short, the goal was to encourage the loss of Indian status and subsequently the number of people on federal Indian welfare rolls. This policy depended on the expansion of provincial programs to Aboriginal people.

Provincial governments resisted Ottawa's strategy, but they did accept limited responsibility for service provision to status Indians after 1965, when the federal government negotiated agreements with the provinces to extend services to reserves. Under this policy, the federal government provided funding to the provinces for welfare and specific social service programs for status Indians living on-reserve and for those who moved off-reserve for up to twelve months.[18] Provincial governments refused to accept further recommendations that they integrate status Indians into provincial welfare systems. Like the federal government, provinces maintained that rescinding the special status of indigenous peoples would improve service provision to Aboriginal people because it would streamline welfare bureaucracies.

Despite their reluctance to extend services to Aboriginal communities, provincial governments did take responsibility for child welfare services in the 1960s. When the federal government began to phase out residential schools, the Department of Indian Affairs gave provincial governments control over child welfare services for reserves. Provincial policies followed the federal goal of assimilating Aboriginal people. However, the provinces did not share the federal government's fiduciary obligation to Aboriginal peoples, and, consequently, provincial agencies were under no obligation to negotiate with Aboriginal leaders to develop programs specifically for Aboriginal people. This had a devastating impact on Aboriginal families and communities. White social workers almost always assumed that the best way to protect Aboriginal children was to remove them from their homes and make arrangements for white families to adopt them. The "sixties scoop" devastated communities and worsened addiction problems for women, who often did not know whether they would ever see their children again.[19] Fear that their children would be taken away made many women in violent families reluctant to leave their families and communities.

Aboriginal leaders opposed the transfer of services from the federal to the provincial government, arguing that it threatened their constitutional rights. They blamed federal neglect of reserves for the disproportionately high rates of welfare dependency in Aboriginal communities.[20] One federal report, *A Survey of the Contemporary Indians of Canada* (1966), supported them, stating that poor living conditions on reserves would not improve unless Aboriginal rights were respected. Commonly known as the Hawthorn report after its author, it coined the term "citizens plus" to describe the normal rights and duties of citizenship and the unique rights the British North America Act gave to the nation's first peoples. The report also advised that provincial governments should extend services to status Indians and that the jurisdictional disputes between Ottawa and the provinces had to be resolved quickly because the increased mobility of Aboriginal people was generating more demands for provincial social programs. Hawthorn predicted that the number of Aboriginal people living in cities would grow substantially because the reserves could not sustain the increasing population. Since past federal government policies had created unsustainable economies and unlivable conditions on the reserves, helping Aboriginal people adjust to urban life through special programs was a public responsibility. More importantly, the report concluded that Native organizations must have input in developing these programs.[21] The Native rights movement agreed with the latter recommendation and began to demand control over services for Aboriginal people.

Although the Hawthorn report supported Aboriginal demands, recognition of the special rights of Native people was incompatible with Trudeau's conception of a just society based on liberal conceptions of equality and individual rights. In 1969, the Liberal government released the *Statement of the Government on Indian Policy,* which became known as the White Paper. The policy rejected Aboriginal leaders' argument that dispossession of land, racial discrimination, and coercive tutelage were the root of "the Indian problem." Instead, the White Paper contended that poverty and social inequality in Aboriginal communities were the product of the special status of Aboriginal peoples in Canadian society, and it argued that the eradication of these rights would foster the improved social, economic, and political participation of Native people in Canadian society. The federal government announced that it planned to terminate the Indian Act and the Department of Indian Affairs and expected provincial welfare services to extend their services to all Aboriginal peoples.[22]

The White Paper's agenda for assimilation angered Aboriginal leaders, who had called for a stronger recognition of their inherent rights in the consultations that preceded the release of the policy.[23] Treaty Indians would not accept policy that undermined Aboriginal title because the well-being of future generations depended on control over their land. In their response to the White Paper, entitled *Citizens Plus,* the Indian Chiefs of Alberta argued that further erosion of Aboriginal land rights would condemn future generations to the "despair and ugly spectre of urban poverty in ghettos."[24] They defended the legal definition of registered Indians, adding that "if one of our brothers chooses, he may renounce his Indian status, become enfranchised, receive his share of the funds of the tribe, and seek admission to ordinary Canadian society. But most Indians prefer to remain Indians."[25] The chiefs also opposed the termination of the Indian Act, arguing that this would foster cultural annihilation by eroding peoples' connection to their territories.[26] These leaders believed that Aboriginal identity could not survive in urban environments. Resistance from the National Indian Brotherhood and provincial governments forced the government to retreat from this policy, and the federal government agreed that no part of the Indian Act would be amended without full consultation with Aboriginal leaders.

The absence of any discussion of women's loss of status if they married outside of their community illustrated the marginalization of non-status Native women in the movement. The defeat of the White Paper was a catalyst for the revival of activism in the 1970s, but Aboriginal leaders' defence of the Indian Act curtailed women's efforts to protect their rights. The central goal of the Native women's movement was the removal of section 12(1)(b) of the Indian Act, a clause that determined a woman's status by marriage, not by familial association or blood. In contrast, Aboriginal men could bestow status on white women they married. Thus, women's claim to treaty rights was weaker than men's. Instead of holding special status, Kathleen Jamieson asserted, the Indian Act constructed non-status Aboriginal women as "citizens minus."[27] Without status, women could not defend their right to live on-reserve and were vulnerable to band councils who tried to control women's actions with eviction notices and threats of violence.[28] Forceful removal from their ancestral territories mobilized women into political action. Between 1971 and 1981, individual women initiated national and international court actions to amend the Indian Act.[29] Indian Rights for Indian Women, which was founded in 1971, and ONWA mobilized support for these legal cases, which raised public awareness of Aboriginal women's issues. Nevertheless, there was no legal change until 1985, when the federal government passed Bill

C-31, legislation that removed section 12(1)(b) from the Indian Act and rein-stated women who had lost their status.[30]

The women's campaign to amend the Indian Act divided Aboriginal communities. Male leaders dismissed it as a feminist plot, arguing that a few women were putting their individual needs before the collective rights of Aboriginal people. Many women with Indian status agreed with them.[31] The support of the National Action Committee on the Status of Women created new political opportunities for Indian Rights for Indian Women, but the Native women's movement was based on an articulation of their identity and citizenship claims that was significantly different from the mainstream women's movement's focus on gender-based discrimination. Non-status women demanded improved rights based on the injustice they had suffered as Aboriginal people, and they struggled for women's rights to strengthen their role in the Native rights movement to restore the collective rights and pride of Aboriginal peoples.

These national political battles influenced Anishinabequek's organizing in Thunder Bay. At the local level, activists drew from the broader Native women's movement to help women understand the implications of federal legislation on their lives and to develop services that did not perpetuate the deep divisions created by the Indian Act. This was particularly important in urban contexts, where the indigenous population was made up of status and non-status Indians, Métis, and Aboriginal people who had never lived on-reserve. The development of services and programs for Native peoples based on Aboriginal traditions informed Anishinabequek's services, and Beendigen was a service that protected women from government agencies and social workers who were more concerned about children than they were about women.

THE NATIVE WOMEN'S MOVEMENT IN THUNDER BAY

Thunder Bay was the destination point for many Aboriginal people who left northern Ontario reserves hoping to find employment and better living conditions. Reflecting national trends, the Aboriginal population in Thunder Bay grew in the 1960s and 1970s. By 1978, an estimated 7,000 Native people lived in Thunder Bay, comprising 6.3 percent of the city's population; in 1979, 36.3 percent of Aboriginal people in the Lakehead District lived off-reserve.[32] In response to the increasing numbers of Aboriginal people living in the city, activists founded the Thunder Bay Indian Friendship Centre as an ad hoc organization in 1964. The organization incorporated in 1968 and acquired the resources to find a permanent home in 1972. The goals of the centre were to provide culturally sensitive services and help Aboriginal people retain their identity. Bernice Dubec, a founding member of ONWA and Beendigen whose political career began at the Thunder Bay Indian Friendship Centre, remembered that the most important programs they provided were advocacy to protect Aboriginal families from being exploited by landlords and aid to families recently arrived from the reserve in their adjustment to urban life. Dubec recalled that traditional teachings informed their work:

> I remember in the 1970s, largely through the friendship centre and different gatherings, they'd bring in elders to come and talk to the community ... It really hit me in my own spirit, in my own heart: This is the way we should be living. This is how we should be doing our services and our programs. We need to go back to the culture.[33]

Traditionalists proposed holistic approaches that addressed the colonizing practices perpetuating poverty and social problems.

In the 1970s, the Native rights movement embraced indigenous traditions in defiance of the Department of Indian Affairs' policy of assimilation. Aboriginal leaders emphasized preserving traditions that were being rapidly eroded. This was especially important in cities, where people were removed from elders and ceremonies. Aboriginal organizations sustained their cultures by organizing ceremonies, seeking out guidance from elders, and learning indigenous languages. Activists created services that followed indigenous knowledge and were critical of those charitable initiatives that cast white people as authorities on problems in Aboriginal communities.[34] Returning to traditional teachings afforded expertise to Aboriginal people.

Women played a vital role in the development of urban Aboriginal communities, first in their homes and later in formalized community centres and organizations.[35] Even though they were important figures in the community, women soon realized that Aboriginal organizations were not dealing with women's needs. Some women decided to organize separately from men because their voices were not respected by the male leadership. Audrey Gilbeau, who was raised in Longlac 15th First Nation, entered politics by volunteering at the Thunder Bay Friendship Centre, where "the ladies took [her] under their wings." She recalled how watching her elders struggle to be heard in meetings taught her that women needed to create autonomous organizations to develop a political voice. She explained,

> I can honestly say I had to be trained. And growing up in an environment that was very male dominated, I think you're somewhat conditioned that way as well ... So when I became involved with Anishinabequek and started to see, particularly the power of the women, and the strength of individual women ... And then listening and also observing the struggles they had in gaining that recognition ... You see things that you think are part of the natural order, and even though it doesn't feel right, you just assume that this is the way it's supposed to be done. It was a great deal of education that took place for me at the time.[36]

Gilbeau's comments demonstrate that men ignored women who challenged their authority and who demanded recognition as leaders.

The Native women's movement respected the traditional roles of women and men and agreed that it was important to reclaim customs, but ONWA members did not accept static gender roles. A cartoon by Alma Adams, in ONWA's 1977 Resource Manual, depicts a woman cooking over a campfire built in front of teepees. She is wearing a buckskin dress and a feather in her braided hair. The caption asks: "The O.N.W.A.?"[37] Gilbeau wryly criticized customs that defended male privilege, citing the tradition that women should walk behind men: "I think in the days when there were predators walking about it was appropriate."[38] These political activists acknowledged the particular roles of women and men in Aboriginal culture, but they challenged the use of customs that perpetuated inequalities between women and men.[39]

Women from across northwestern Ontario, who had been organizing independently from each other, met in Thunder Bay in May 1972 to found ONWA. The association served as a communication network for local chapters and encouraged women to support each other in their roles as leaders, homemakers, and craftspeople.[40] One of its goals was "to help women rediscover and develop [the] traditional skills which [were] unique to the Native culture."[41] ONWA activists reminded women that in traditional forms of indigenous governance, women were leaders because they were the mothers of the community; women had become less influential because the roles and responsibilities associated with motherhood had lost their value under colonial legislation that organized the family according to patriarchal structures. Encouraging women to be both homemakers and leaders was not a contradiction, according to Aboriginal values.[42]

From the outset, service provision that focused on children and families was an important part of ONWA's mandate. At their founding meeting, delegates agreed that opening hostels for girls was a priority. Developing alternatives to government-run programs that separated people from their families was another important goal. ONWA's program of action included establishing child welfare services that placed children in Aboriginal foster homes that would keep brothers and sisters together, homes for old people in or near their home territories, Aboriginal-run schools on reserves, boarding homes for students so that they could adjust from rural to urban living, and cultural centres.[43] Agendas were set locally, but all chapters agreed with the organization's principal tenet to "honour the belief of supporting the unity of all Native women, regardless of legal categories."[44] Respecting the heritage of status and non-status women was the foundation of promoting self-worth, and activists believed that this was essential to develop programs for all women claiming indigenous heritage. In their words, these services were "status-blind." Organizing effective services for women in Thunder Bay required an elucidation of the connections between women's experiences of urban migration and the impact of federal Indian policy on women's lives.

Aboriginal women's views of their responsibilities and their defence of women's rights were based on Aboriginal culture rather than on the liberal feminist demand for equality of opportunity.[45] An ONWA motto, which was based on the organization's acronym, stated the organization's priorities: "our home is first; Native women speak; working together; assisting our own."[46] The women's movement most likely influenced Aboriginal women's politics, yet the priorities and philosophies of the Native women's movement were distinct from those of the mainstream women's movement.[47] Maintaining these distinctions was difficult. In her study of the media representations of the Royal Commission on the Status of Women, Barbara Freeman argues that when Aboriginal women presented their case, the media and the women's movement transformed their arguments to comply with liberal models of equality so that they would be more comprehensible to non-Aboriginal people.[48] Most Aboriginal women, however, did not identify with the mainstream women's movement. Although feminist organizations supported the campaign against the Indian Act because it affected women, they were less interested in supporting issues that pertained to the entire Aboriginal community, such as land claims and the movement for self-government. Aboriginal women were also frustrated because they had to continually justify their alliances with men to white feminists who did not understand Aboriginal women's concerns about dividing their community.[49]

The conflation of the goals of the Native women's movement with those of the mainstream women's movement helps explain why most male leaders also misconstrued Native women's political objectives. They dismissed women's claims as feminist and believed that advocating for improved individual rights for women weakened the collective rights of Aboriginal peoples.[50] Dubec remembered defending the need for women's rights to men who were sceptical about women's autonomous organizing:

> They would kid you, saying you're just a bunch of women's libbers ... It was ribbing and that kind of thing. Or sometimes they would debate you. I didn't mind. I enjoyed it. I could debate with any of them ... But again we must have caused some fear, I guess ... because we were asking questions. Because we were able to debate and talk about our rights as Aboriginal people.[51]

Dubec clearly disagreed with the distinction between collective and individual rights. ONWA activists defended women's rights because they thought these were inextricable from their political work for Aboriginal people.

It is not surprising that women who took on leadership roles were confident that promoting women's rights would ultimately strengthen Aboriginal communities. Others were more wary. Dubec remembered that in some communities, many women told their husbands they were meeting women to do some sewing because they were afraid to tell them they were participating in women's organizing.[52] This resistance made cultural events important because they helped women develop social networks and promote ONWA's more explicitly political goals. For International Women's Year in 1975, Anishinabequek members organized a festival to give women the opportunity to "display their talents as homemakers and craft people" and to "get some new blood and new leadership for the local chapter."[53] Dubec remembered that social events were an effective way to draw women into the organization:

It was just an opportunity for us to meet together. And we'd do some fun things. We'd organize some different activities. Whether it was wrapping gifts for the children's Christmas party, having little socials and going out together. Just prior to that we had organized a daycare centre down at the friendship centre ... And the other program that was getting started ... was ... visitation [of] incarcerated people, older people in the nursing homes. I was involved with the resource centre. So those were some of the things that the Native women were doing, really concrete services in our community. Meeting unmet needs and addressing women's issues.[54]

The local's events appealed to many women: 175 of the 250 Aboriginal women living in Thunder Bay were members of Anishinabequek in 1975.[55] At these gatherings, organizers learned what issues women faced.

Family violence was among these issues. Gilbeau recalled that some women on reserves tried to organize safe home networks for abused women, but usually women who left abusive relationships could not remain in their communities because there were not enough services on reserves. Thunder Bay offered little more. The friendship centre referred people to the city's services, and the Native People of Thunder Bay Development Corporation was beginning to provide subsidized housing.[56] Activists knew that violence was a problem in Aboriginal families, but neither of these organizations had developed a policy for abused women. Gilbeau explained that apathy prevented action:

That issue was always there. People talked about it like that was just the way it was. "Violence, oh yeah, well, what about this? Women are getting beaten up. Oh well." There was no passion, no sympathy ... Not that people were oblivious to what was going on. It was just so prevalent. It was all around you, so people just chose not to get involved. I don't know how to explain it.[57]

Non-Aboriginal people shared the belief that violence had become an insurmountable problem in Aboriginal society. Sympathetic policy-makers may have attributed violence to poverty and discrimination, but underlying this analysis was the belief that Aboriginal communities had resigned themselves to a violent lifestyle.[58] The members of Anishinabequek did not share this general apathy toward family violence, and they decided to organize a shelter for Aboriginal women and children in crisis.

FOUNDING BEENDIGEN

Anishinabequek members founded Beendigen because the services available to women in Thunder Bay were not sensitive to the circumstances of those who had just left the reserve. Community Residences, a city-run shelter discussed in the next chapter, offered shelter to abused women, but few Aboriginal women stayed there. A study on the effectiveness of the service conducted by the Lakehead Social Planning Council in 1979 reported that Aboriginal women in the shelter were quiet and withdrawn.[59] In addition, Community Residences would only accept women who lived in Thunder Bay, leaving women who had just left the reserve with no place to stay. These women were less likely to have family and friends in the city to whom they could turn for help.[60] Isolation was not restricted to women who had recently arrived in the city. Dubec remembered that some women who lived in Thunder Bay moved away when they left violent spouses, but women who wanted to stay in town often did not know how to get out of their situation and needed some place to go.[61]

In February 1978, Anishinabequek received a Canada Works grant to develop a Native Women's Crisis Centre. They incorporated as Beendigen Inc. and organized a board of thirteen women.[62] The board worked with the Thunder Bay Native Development Corporation, which purchased a home to rent to Beendigen to use as a shelter and office. Because of zoning bylaws, the house was only allowed to accommodate one family at a time and did not meet the demand for the service. Staffing the shelter was difficult because the grant was designed to move people from welfare to work, and it stipulated that women could only be paid minimum-wage salaries. Because wages were low, the board could not retain staff to counsel women and to manage the home.[63] A substantially smaller grant from the secretary of state to pay for a fundraiser's salary supplemented the funding from Canada Works. This new fundraiser took on the responsibility of running the house when the Canada Works funds were exhausted and the board could no longer pay staff.[64] During its first year of operation, the shelter was in a funding crisis that threatened its future.

In their endeavour to stabilize funding, the women gained political experience. Dubec remembered that they lobbied many members of Parliament and government bureaucrats until they "finally hit the right one." The Department of Indian Affairs official in Thunder Bay was not receptive to the shelter, but an official who worked at the Ministry of Social Services, and who had worked closely with other Aboriginal-run programs, did support Beendigen's goals. He advised the board that if they reworked their proposal to emphasize how the shelter would prevent juvenile delinquency, then they would be eligible for funding through the Children's Services Department.[65]

The board submitted a proposal in 1978 that described the negative impact of urbanization and colonization on Aboriginal families, as the supportive government official had recommended. This emphasis on children also conformed to Aboriginal leaders' attempts to gain control over child protection and education, two issues that the Native rights movement had identified as crucial to self-determination in the 1970s.[66] The proposal included an extensive discussion about children, explaining that many Aboriginal children's problems were linked to the increasing pace of urban migration. Families who left the reserve looking for better opportunities often adjusted to urban life with difficulty, and lifestyle changes were exacerbated by economic hardships. Few Aboriginal people had adequate education or job training skills to find employment, and subsequently many lived in overcrowded housing. Poor living conditions and shattered expectations induced alcoholism, "leading to a general breakdown of family relations."[67] The authors of the proposal concluded that the loss of the support network that extended families had traditionally provided made it difficult for people to cope with their problems. For abused women, there were usually no family members to turn to when their relationships became violent.

The board had to defend Aboriginal-run services because the provincial government was reluctant to support services that targeted particular social groups.[68] Organizers insisted that Beendigen would not duplicate existing services because none of these was based on Aboriginal values. In addition, many women from remote reserves did not speak English. The board argued that their service would overcome this basic barrier because Beendigen employees would be able to provide counselling and advocacy in Cree or Ojibwa. Though often well intentioned, white people did not know how to serve Aboriginal women because they did not understand the culture. At Beendigen, counsellors understood the issues that Aboriginal women faced. Gilbeau explained,

You don't have to explain the challenges. You don't have to explain the geography. You don't have to explain the roles. You don't have to educate people as to what you're suffering. Often times, they've experienced it themselves. People give you that "poor dear." What are you going to do with that? But they don't know any better. They just don't know.[69]

For Aboriginal women, an advocate who understood their cultural background was important because they feared mainstream service intervention that tended to break up Aboriginal families.

Although the decision to emphasize the negative impact of child apprehension was strategic to some extent, it was also a response to the harmful impact of that practice on Aboriginal women and children. Dubec grew up as a ward of the crown, and she recalled how her family was treated unfairly:

The attitude then at Children's Aid was we couldn't see our mother. Our mother was alive, our father had passed away. But she was an alcoholic. And it was just the attitude then to protect the kids. So there were a few times when I saw her. We were just snatched away, taken away as if she was an axe murderer or something. She wasn't drinking. She was sober then. There was no reason why we shouldn't have been able to spend time with her, or she shouldn't have access to us. Eventually, she moved away. It must have been just heartbreaking for her to see her kids and not be able to interact with them. So that was the attitude in those days. The parents didn't have any rights – Aboriginal parents.[70]

To counter the destructive impact of child welfare services on Aboriginal peoples, keeping mothers and their children together was a cornerstone of Beendigen's programs.[71]

By providing shelter for single mothers who were having difficulty adapting to urban life, the organizers hoped to keep Aboriginal children out of the child welfare system and to protect women from the devastating impact of losing their children.[72] The proposal argued that Children's Aid policies for Aboriginal communities were the result of clashing world views that were based in different physical realities. The materialism of Canadian society conflicted with traditional Aboriginal values. Traditional lifestyles and social structures derived from the harsh realities of living in harmony with the land, and children, who were integral to the family, were expected to be independent. Where once Aboriginal people were the only people living in Canada, they now found themselves a minority group that was "trying to survive intact, preserving the values and traditions of their past."[73] What was most detrimental for children who were placed in white homes was their inability to develop pride in their ancestry because they lost their connection with their extended family and cultural education. The board acknowledged that alcoholism and violence were serious problems but added that breaking up families was just as harmful. The shelter, they argued, would "offer a kind of extended family situation, in keeping with Native culture."[74] The board proposed to provide counselling for the entire family in order to alleviate cultural dislocation and preserve Aboriginal children's sense of identity. The proposal was successful and provided core funding for three years.

The grant made it possible to move to a larger facility that could accommodate nine people. In 1982, the shelter operated close to full capacity throughout the year and provided services for 187 families.[75] Beendigen accommodated any Aboriginal woman and her children who were in a crisis, but abused women were given priority.[76] Its catchment area included all of northwestern Ontario because it was the only shelter in the region expressly for Aboriginal women. Gilbeau recalled stories of women from remote reserves who fled onto float planes at the last minute to escape abusers. Other shelters in the region accepted Aboriginal women, but many preferred to go to Beendigen, where they received cultural support as well as safety.[77]

Beendigen organizers continued to provide emergency services for abused women that were based on Aboriginal understandings of family violence. Not all initiatives for abused women established by Aboriginal women were able to maintain a holistic approach to family violence. In communities where Aboriginal and non-Aboriginal women collaborated to open a transition house, a feminist analysis of violence against women often replaced Aboriginal approaches to healing violent families.[78] Because almost all of the board members of Beendigen were Aboriginal women, they were not forced to concede to the feminist analysis that wife battering was fundamentally a manifestation of patriarchal relations.

DEVELOPING AN ABORIGINAL ANALYSIS OF FAMILY VIOLENCE
Despite their awareness of abuse in their communities, the few documents that pertain to the founding years of Beendigen were relatively silent on the issue of violence. Organizers mentioned family violence, but the primary rationale for the shelter was that women who moved to the city from reserves

needed services that would help them adapt to urban life while still maintaining their connections to the Aboriginal community. Both Dubec and
Gilbeau acknowledged that although they knew that abused women needed
help, they did not deem it to be a political issue at the time. The women's
movement had politicized violence against women, but Aboriginal activists
did not think that feminist theorization of spousal abuse that prioritized
gender over race captured the complexities of Aboriginal women's lives.
Studies on wife battering that included Aboriginal women grouped them
with other ethnic groups and did not analyze family violence within the context of colonial relations. In the late 1980s, when ONWA members conducted
research on family violence in Aboriginal communities in northwestern
Ontario, they learned that women could not separate the violence associated
with racism from their experiences of domestic abuse. This research was the
basis for ONWA's *Breaking Free*, which was published in 1989 and was the
first Canadian report to propose solutions for family violence that addressed
both gendered violence and the impact of colonization on Aboriginal families.

Breaking Free was also the first study to provide statistical evidence of the
high rate of violence in Aboriginal families, and the report's frequently cited
statistic that eight out of ten Aboriginal women had been abused at home or
assaulted by a stranger was shocking even to those who wrote the report.[79]
The authors of *Breaking Free* explained that family violence was "a reaction
against an entire system of domination, lack of respect, and bureaucratic
control"[80] over every aspect of Aboriginal life. In the preface of the report,
they stated that men lashed out at women and children because they were
growing increasingly frustrated with the federal government's refusal to
allow Aboriginal peoples to control their own lives.[81] Arguing that family violence was a consequence of colonization logically followed from Aboriginal
leaders' arguments for self-government. In the short term, the report called
for more Aboriginal-run shelters and second-stage housing for battered
women and children, as well as counselling services for abusive men. But the
authors concluded that family violence in Aboriginal families would not end
until Aboriginal peoples had attained self-government.

The report underscored the importance of restoring and strengthening
Aboriginal families. Protection for women and children was necessary, but it
had to be part of a broader program that did not "sacrifice" healing for abusive men. ONWA members insisted that men needed counselling because

many of them had experienced abuse in their families and had also been victims of abuse in residential schools. This connection between men's violence
and colonialism was a response to the assumption of many white people that
Aboriginal men were inherently more violent than non-Aboriginal men.[82]
Aboriginal activists accepted neither feminist explanations of violence against
women that blamed men nor the concomitant strategies to criminalize spousal
assault. While the authors of the report acknowledged that these solutions
might be effective for non-Aboriginal society, they questioned whether they
were appropriate for Aboriginal communities because of the uneasy relationship between the police and Aboriginal communities. Furthermore, putting
abusive men in prisons removed men from their families, which undermined
the holistic approach to ending family violence that the report insisted was
necessary.[83]

Instead of punitive solutions, ONWA members recommended an action
plan that would heal families and, as a result, communities. They called for a
grassroots approach, in which each community would define the problem
and create solutions, and they argued that these services would only be effective if organized according to traditional healing methods. Developing services on reserves was necessary because many people who stayed on the
reserve thought that leaving the community was tantamount to abandoning
one's family. When women returned, "they [were] outcasts."[84] In addition,
since so many women had no choice but to leave the reserve, the authors of
the report also recommended the creation of more culturally specific services
in urban areas and demanded that the provincial and federal governments
provide Aboriginal organizations with funds to organize healing lodges and
shelters.

The report compelled some Aboriginal leaders who had previously dismissed family violence as a women's issue to acknowledge that it was a problem that demanded immediate action. Reflecting on the impact that *Breaking
Free* had on Aboriginal leaders in Thunder Bay, Gilbeau recollected: "[The
report] was ... sent out to all of the people you worked with. It was very interesting to the Aboriginal leadership. It provided the forum in which to start
talking about ... violence."[85] The report also had an impact because it coin-
cided with the revelations of sexual abuse in residential schools. In a
thought-provoking analysis of residential school narratives, Dian Million
proposes that talking about abuse in institutional settings created a space for

conceptualizing family violence in Aboriginal communities as a political issue. Discussions of residential school abuse made it possible for the Native rights movement to acknowledge that family violence was a political issue because both women and men had suffered in the schools.[86] Subsequent analysis of violence in Aboriginal families would explain that the forceful removal of children from their families and the abuse in residential schools left an entire generation unprepared to raise families. Many men and women who had been physically or sexually assaulted in residential schools later abused their own children and often their parents, a pattern that Aboriginal activists have called intergenerational abuse. To counter the negative impact of government policy on families, Aboriginal services for abused women also included programs for all members of the family. In their analysis of family violence, Aboriginal women positioned themselves as the foundation of healthy families and, subsequently, their nations.[87]

Claude Denis argues that shelters were not initially a traditional Aboriginal resource because the mainstream women's movement opened the first transition houses. Nevertheless, Aboriginal-run shelters have become important because they are part of a larger project that is helping people escape from the impact of colonialism on their lives.[88] The political goals of the Native rights movement informed Aboriginal women's services for abused women and their children, as well as the analysis of family violence in Aboriginal communities. Beendigen organizers adopted a holistic approach to services for violent families that balanced indigenous traditions and knowledge with the new realities that Aboriginal women grappled with when they moved away from the reserve. ONWA insisted that Aboriginal organizations had a responsibility to protect abused women because families were the foundation of traditional forms of governance and strong First Nations. *Breaking Free* presented an analysis of family violence that resisted the argument that violence against women was an individual problem that must be secondary to the collective goal of self-government.[89] Despite increased attention to the problem of family violence, many women still struggle to convince their leaders that services for abused women must be central to the development and implementation of self-government.

The mainstream women's movement has also been reluctant to integrate Aboriginal women's theorization of family violence into programs, particularly those that are not specifically for Aboriginal women.[90] Support from non-Aboriginal feminist organizations was crucial to some of the successes of the Native women's movement in the 1970s and 1980s, but the mainstream women's movement also marginalized Aboriginal women's voices by insisting that gender be the central pillar of feminist analysis.[91] This has been particularly true in the anti-violence movement, which was especially resistant to analyses of male violence against women that stressed the intersection of race and gender in shaping women's experiences of wife battering and rape. Aboriginal women argued that solutions that did not consider how family violence affected men were inadequate because federal Indian policy that targeted Aboriginal families caused the high incidence of violence against women in their communities.[92] Bonita Lawrence explains that many feminists refused to accept analyses that did not focus on male violence against women because they were struggling with government and service agencies that de-emphasized the gendered nature of violence and promoted solutions that strengthened families.[93] The perception that it was necessary to present a unified argument to the government when lobbying for services helps explain the rift between activists in the battered women's shelter movement and women from marginalized communities. However, as Lawrence goes on to argue, feminists' insistence that all violence against women is grounded in patriarchal relations has occluded more nuanced analyses of gendered violence that consider how marginalized men are also victims of state-sanctioned violence.[94]

Feminist groups in Thunder Bay respected the distinctive analysis of family violence that supported those services organized by Aboriginal women's groups. In the next two chapters, we will see that feminists' respect for the need for independent Aboriginal women's organizations also meant that there was little exchange of ideas in the development of services. The organizers of Faye Peterson Transition House did not integrate Aboriginal women's theories of violence into their programs when the shelter opened, even though they did take in Aboriginal women when Beendigen was full. In Kenora, the women who tried to organize a transition house worked with Aboriginal women for a short period because they realized they needed their expertise to learn how to provide services for Aboriginal women. Although a significant number of women who accessed the services were Aboriginal women, activists in Kenora eventually adopted the feminist analysis of violence against women.

Maybe It Wasn't the Best Way to Do It, but It Got Done: Faye Peterson Transition House, 1972-85

Faye Peterson Transition House opened its doors in 1983 after a long struggle between Thunder Bay Social Services and the women's community over the quality and purpose of services for abused women and their children. Thunder Bay feminists planned initially to work with the city to open an emergency shelter for battered women. Community Residences was established in 1975 as a collaborative project organized by representatives from the women's centre and municipal social services. However, feminists withdrew their support for the project because they could not integrate a feminist model of service provision into the city's welfare practices, and they opened Faye Peterson Transition House as a woman-centred alternative to the city-run service.

Jurisdiction was one of the key debates between feminists and city officials. Like Beendigen, Faye Peterson Transition House sheltered abused women from the city as well as those who fled to Thunder Bay from the region. Women leaving abusive marriages often decided to move to Thunder Bay because there were more opportunities there and because the city offered them more anonymity than their home communities. In the remote communities in northwestern Ontario, women did not have access to basic social welfare programs because these municipalities did not have the resources to offer the range of services that larger centres provided. A feminist coalition of women's groups from communities in northwestern Ontario lobbied the city of Thunder Bay to support a regional shelter, but city council opposed the idea because they believed that these women would become dependent on city social services. Appealing to the province was as frustrating as working with the city because provincial funds were contingent on municipal endorsement of the shelter.

The relationship between the provincial government and its hinterlands also slowed down feminist plans for a regional shelter. Thunder Bay was the administrative hub of northwestern Ontario, but it was a hinterland community within the provincial bureaucracy. In the 1970s, the provincial government reorganized its services to provide better social and economic programs in the regions. New provincial-municipal fiscal relations gave the regions more control over the development and implementation of social services, but the province maintained ultimate authority over social and economic policy.[1] The Lakehead Social Planning Council criticized the restructuring because the provincial government did not invest sufficient resources in the infrastructures of hinterland communities; residents in resource towns had to accept minimum services or leave. For northern residents, this was a clear message that "the province's strategy for development in Northwestern Ontario [was] little more than a successive process of resource exploitation."[2] Northern critics of southern economic and social policies opposed the reforms because those policies reorganized the lives of northern residents according to southern economic agendas.

Northern alienation influenced feminist activism. Gert Beadle, known as the poet laureate of the regional women's movement, described their alienation in her poem "North Western Ont":

> Are we a different breed, has this
> abandoned bastard child of the pampered east
> seasoned us for the struggle of recognition
> conditioned us to rooting deeper
> in this stubborn soil of poverty and pot holes
> Having no need for servile gratitude
> Have we become more truly ourselves, with
> nothing to lose but the pretensions of rank
> and the lip service of delinquent politicians.[3]

Economic and social marginalization fostered a sense of independence that activists attributed to the physical geography and to having to do without.

This chapter examines how the Thunder Bay feminists who were involved in the campaign to open a regional transition house challenged patriarchal relations, municipal service provision, and provincial economic priorities. I begin with a discussion of the women's liberation movement in Thunder Bay and the founding of Community Residences. The women's community tried to change local practices in the margins of the city's bureaucracy but was unable to do so because welfare officials would not accept feminist demands for women-centred services. The next sections examine the founding of Faye Peterson Transition House and northern women's lobbying with the Ontario Association of Interval and Transition Houses (OAITH) to stabilize government funding of transition houses in the early 1980s. Negotiating with the provincial government made the women more aware of their marginalization from the main business of government not only as women but as northern citizens. In their negotiations with the provincial government, Thunder Bay feminists learned to use their marginal position as an effective political tool.

COMMUNITY RESIDENCES:
WORKING WITH THE CITY SOCIAL SERVICES

Feminists had been active in the Thunder Bay Women's Liberation Group since 1969, but their primary focus was not institution building. Joan Baril, a women's liberation activist, recalled, "I think what we saw as our main task was changing people's hearts and minds."[4] Women met in consciousness-raising groups and organized birth control services on campus in the late 1960s. Nancy Adamson argues that, as was the case in other cities, Thunder Bay women's liberation activity dropped in the early 1970s. It re-emerged more formally when feminists organized women's centres to give women a space to develop a new political agenda that broke down the traditional barrier between the personal and the political.[5] The Northern Women's Centre opened in 1974 to provide a space to mobilize women, facilitate feminist organizing, and educate women about their rights and the goals of the women's movement. At the women's centre, activists met women whose problems called for more than political awareness. Wife battering was one of the issues that made apparent the need for feminist alternatives that would challenge the patriarchal relations guiding municipal service provision.

The Northern Women's Centre offered services to attract women who did not identify with the women's liberation movement, but the organizers had not planned to concentrate on service provision. When they opened the centre, feminists had expected to refer women to the appropriate social services. Instead, community agencies sent women for whom they did not have programs to them. These services focused on issues that had been considered personal problems, such as rape and abuse, but that feminists were beginning to theorize as political issues. Because there were no government programs that addressed these problems, frontline service work became more important than organizers had anticipated. Julie Fels remembered the activities at the women's centre during its first year and the compromises the collective made:

> When the women's centre opened in '74 ... there was just a constant parade of women coming in – women on welfare, women who had been abused. No shortage of issues. I think the women's centre always wanted to be a political activist organization, not a service delivery, although it certainly has ended up being both. When I worked there, we had a lot of struggles. What do you do when a woman needed safety and there was nowhere for her to go? Well, obviously you're going to do that. You're not going to say, "Well, sorry, we only do the lobbying part."[6]

Rather than instilling a feminist perspective in government service provision through example, feminists found themselves doing the work that the city's social services did not want to do.[7]

Providing services was a controversial issue because the Northern Women's Centre, like most Canadian women's centres, relied on funding from federal citizen participation programs and job creation programs such as the Local Initiatives Project, Opportunities for Youth, and the Local Education Action Program. The mandate of these programs, which were established by the secretary of state and Manpower Canada, was to provide short-term funding to community development projects to mobilize citizenship participation. They did not fund projects that provided direct services. Women's centres often ignored these rules in practice because they realized that service provision was political work that was required to help some women become engaged in politics.[8] Not all women agreed that providing services would mobilize women into political action, and some members of the collective argued that the city was taking advantage of their decision to "never say no" to a woman in crisis. Still others felt obliged to provide services because they were funded by taxpayers' money, and they believed that this work would improve the credibility of the centre within the community.[9]

When feminists lobbied the city to change social welfare practices that treated women poorly, officials met with them to discuss the shortcomings of social services, but activists remembered that administrators were not receptive to their ideas. Fels acknowledged that there were moments of co-operation, but generally feminists "were just dismissed as a bunch of troublesome women."[10] The negative connotations associated with feminism prevented women from becoming influential in local politics, but the different opinions of feminists and bureaucrats were also gender- and class-based. Fiona Karlstedt, a former co-ordinator of the women's centre and member of the board of directors of the transition house, recalled:

> [We] faced ... decision-making bodies that were made up of men. And they just didn't get it. They came of age at a time when male and female roles were really quite clear ... Each time you went before city council, you were dealing with people who organized their lives differently. They were the haves. That was the biggest thing ... You always had to persuade them – never mind convince – just persuade them that what you were proposing had merit.[11]

The city was willing to assist women's charitable ventures, but it did not accept the feminist argument that women were entitled to state-supported social welfare programs.[12] The incompatibility of views between the city council and the women's centre became clear when they collaborated to open Community Residences.

The collective had anticipated that it would help abused women, but members were surprised by how many battered women came to the centre and how few options were available to them.[13] When a woman in crisis went to social services, the city paid hotel accommodation for one or two nights. If a woman went to the women's centre, workers and volunteers often took her home.[14] It did not take long to realize that battered women needed a place to go because the existing practices were not safe. A committee from the women's centre conducted a needs study and began to pressure city social services to open a shelter for battered women.

The committee proposed a plan to the city that would provide better services for abused women and satisfy parsimonious city counsellors. The city owned three houses that, once renovated, would be appropriate for a shelter. Council members agreed that this was a more cost-effective plan than the procedures that it had been using and approved the proposal.[15] The Northern Women's Centre expected to be an equal partner in the project because it was their idea and because they had money to contribute to the development of the shelter.[16] However, the partnership was never formalized because the two groups could not agree on how to renovate the homes and what services to provide for women and children. Feminists wanted a homey place where women would counsel each other, and they were disappointed that the city's primary concerns were cost and liability. The city's proposal for the renovations demonstrated that officials did not think that the comfort and security of the women were priorities. To reduce capital investment, city social services suggested that cast-offs from its other services should furnish the shelter; for example, it recommended that the city use old bedding from the retirement home "which has been worn in spots but which our home-making groups could make into crib sheets and blankets."[17] When it could not convince the city to make substantive changes to its plan, the women's centre withdrew its support for the project. It continued to monitor the shelter but was only able to convince the city to make minor improvements to the facility.[18]

Without feminist involvement, Community Residences did not instigate public education campaigns to change attitudes about wife battering as transition houses in other cities did. City social services did not even promote the service as a shelter for battered women because welfare officials thought that this would encourage women to leave their husbands and that they would become dependent on welfare.[19] Women found their way there despite the secrecy. During the first year of operation, 326 women and children stayed there.[20] This confirmed the need for crisis housing for women, but Community Residences remained a low priority and was further threatened by provincial cutbacks to social services. Community Residences was one of the services the city considered terminating to meet fiscal restraints in 1976.[21] Though dissatisfied with the service, feminists were more upset by the possibility of its closure and publicly criticized the city for saving money by ending services for a vulnerable group. In response to pressure to keep the service open, the city amalgamated Community Residences with a group home for young women, a plan that feminists opposed because it divided the few resources available to battered women between two groups with very different needs.[22] Nevertheless, when the city amalgamated the services, feminists conceded that it was necessary to keep the shelter open until they could secure funds to open their own service for abused women and their children.

Community Residences was an emergency shelter, not a transition house.

Its services were not based on a political analysis of wife battering, and there-fore its policies and programs did not address the structural barriers battered women faced. Indeed, Community Residence policies reproduced them and made it difficult for women to separate from their abusers. Women could not access social assistance until they had secured housing, even though most of them needed this money to rent an apartment. The city described its service as a "temporary homelike environment where clients can make future plans,"[23] but its rules and regulations created an institutional setting. It was common practice for feminist-run transition houses to have rules to prevent conflicts as well as guidelines for child care so that residents would not take advantage of volunteers and employees. Rules were minimal to protect the communal living in transition houses and to level unequal relationships between workers and residents. At Community Residences, regulations established a hierarchy between staff and clients. There were strict curfews, which were enforced by the threat of child apprehension. Transition house collectives expected resi-dents to participate in the daily maintenance of the house, but many also experimented with inviting residents to participate in its management. Com-munity Residences did not give clients a role in the governance of the home, and residents were required to "help out to the best of [their] ability, in areas of cleaning, preparing meals, etc., when called on by any staff member."[24] Some counselling was provided, but the staff's primary responsibly was to move women out of the shelter.[25] What most upset feminists was the prac-tice of discouraging women from counselling each other. A sign posted in the dining area notified residents that "This is not a meeting place, it is an eating place."[26]

The space itself exacerbated women's sense of helplessness. After a visit to Community Residences, feminists reported their dismay with the state of the homes in the *Northern Woman*, the regional feminist newspaper: "The rooms were spacious but furnished sparsely, often with only one or two sin-gle beds. Every room, including the kitchens in the two homes used for the residents, had beds. There were no curtains, the roll-down blinds were often torn and there was no other furniture, except for beds ... Pictures were non-existent."[27] The basements of the houses were the only common recreational space for families, but in the winter they were too cold and damp to use. In contrast, conditions in the city-run residence for girls adjacent to the women's shelter were "brighter, better decorated, and had a warmer more 'homey' atmosphere." This difference must have reinforced the prevailing view, internalized by most battered women, that they were to blame for their circumstances. Residents acknowledged that the poor condition of the buildings exacerbated their loneliness and depression. For women who had left middle-class homes, the shelter "gave them their first taste of what living on welfare might be like."[28] Even though their primary goal was to open a transition house, feminists continued to pressure the city to improve the shelter to make it more comfortable for women during the interim.

Community Residences improved, but in a piecemeal and sporadic manner. Although the homes were "cleaner and less depressing" after subsequent renovations, residents' assessments of the service were ambivalent. New counselling programs helped women cope with the dreary atmosphere. One resident described the staff as "friendly, cheerful, helpful; somewhat of a contradiction to the surroundings."[29] Those who had stayed in hotels thought that staying at the shelter with other women in similar circumstances was less depressing than being alone. For these women, the service was better than nothing.

Feminists were not sure that this was so. They questioned whether a service that reinforced hierarchical structures and provided a false sense of security was better than no service at all.[30] Doreen Boucher, a collective member who became the director of the Thunder Bay Sexual Assault Centre, remembered that Community Residences was not safe. But when she reflected on its shortcomings, she admitted that neither the city nor the feminist community knew how to help battered women. She recalled, "In all fairness, I don't think we realized what we were getting into. We had a lot of learning to do."[31] Leni Untinen was one of the founding members of Faye Peterson Transition House and the northwestern Ontario representative on OAITH. Her recollection of the transition house supported Boucher's assessment: "Even the first shelter we opened, I don't think, was the safest place in the world. Our first residents climbed out of the balcony on sheets and left us, so we weren't doing everything right."[32] The women would learn that the ideals they wanted to see in services were difficult to apply in practice.

Working with the city taught feminists how bureaucracies modified progressive ideas to conform to their own priorities. Margaret Phillips, founder of the *Northern Woman* and author of a report on services for battered women in the region, provided a blunt evaluation of their collaboration with the city: "We got shafted by city administration [and we knew] that Community Residences weren't going to be as useful a project as we wanted it to be."[33] Feminists realized that if they wanted a woman-centred shelter for battered women, they would have to do it themselves.

Women's groups across the region were learning this hard lesson. Activists in Atikokan, Fort Frances, Dryden, Kenora, and Geraldton were also trying to establish transition houses against varying degrees of resistance from their town councils.[34] These groups provided shelter for abused women in these communities, but in many cases women wanted to move to Thunder Bay because it was not safe for them to stay in their home communities once they had left an abusive husband. The city also offered better educational and employment opportunities than the small towns in the region. Activists organized ad hoc networks to help women move to Thunder Bay, but there were few services for these women once they arrived in the city. In exceptional cases, Community Residences would shelter them, but "transient families" were generally sent to the Salvation Army or to hotels.[35] With few options available to them, many women had "to accept a bus ticket back to the violence [they] left."[36] Northwestern Ontario feminists realized that to make sure all women were safe, they needed to organize a regional shelter in Thunder Bay.

FAYE PETERSON REGIONAL TRANSITION HOUSE

Thunder Bay's feminist community opened Faye Peterson Transition House, but its success depended on a strong regional women's movement. The ad hoc coalition among northern feminists was formalized at a planning conference held in 1976, where delegates founded two groups that would play a central role in the development of the transition house. The Northwestern Ontario Decade Council, commonly known as Decade Council, co-ordinated feminist lobbying and included representatives from all communities with feminist groups. Thunder Bay feminists who had lobbied for Community Residences incorporated as Crisis Homes Inc. and changed their mandate to investigate the need for a regional shelter rather than a shelter for women living in the city.

Between 1976 and 1983, Crisis Homes organized public education campaigns to generate community support, researched the problem, lobbied with OAITH, and organized fundraisers. The group was active but no closer to its goal of establishing a regional transition house because the municipality would not support the plan. City council opposed the shelter because it did not think that Thunder Bay taxpayers should be responsible for providing services for women and children who did not live there. It delayed the opening of the transition house by refusing to grant hostel status to the group's proposal, which would make the service eligible for per diem funding from the city.

While the city stalled, anti-violence lobbying and ad hoc service provision were exhausting the staff and the scarce resources of the Northern Women's Centre, and sheltering women in activists' homes was becoming too demanding. By 1982, Thunder Bay feminists were divided about whether the women's centre should continue to offer counselling and advocacy for battered women.[37] Those who questioned service provision argued that the collective needed to determine whether it wanted to provide services or be a women's centre based on political action and education.

Faye Peterson Transition House opened because of a unilateral decision by one woman who thought these ad hoc practices were no longer workable and who could no longer tolerate government excuses. In January 1983, Gert Beadle used her own savings to rent a house for the long-planned regional transition house. Beadle became a feminist in her retirement and was one of the founders of the Northern Women's Centre and a member of the committee that had lobbied for Community Residences. She also participated in a feminist theatre group and wrote poetry about feminist consciousness and activism in the region.[38] Fels remembered how Beadle informed the committee of her decision: "She said, 'Oh, I just rented the house because we need it. We can't keep doing this.' And she just moved in there and stayed there and it was a 'build it and they will come' kind of thing."[39] It was a bold move. The eight-month job creation grant was about to end, and the committee did not have enough money to staff and operate a transition house.[40]

Beadle's tactic flew in the face of the collective's consensus-based structure, but there is no evidence that the feminist community criticized her action. In local feminist lore, this story captured northern feminists' determination and ingenuity. It also revealed their disillusion with mainstream politics. Karlstedt remembered, "This group of women decided that they weren't going to wait any longer. Damn the zoning bylaw. Damn the fact that they didn't have any money ... It was just that this had to be done, and we'll worry about that stuff later."[41] Ignoring bureaucratic procedures did not improve their relationship with the city, but by this time feminists did not think they had to answer to city bureaucrats who had consistently thwarted their plans. Untinen explained, "It belonged not just to twelve women [who sat on the board]. It belonged to 100 or 150 women. I guess in a lot of ways, we felt accountable to those 150 women. It was a women's community place. It didn't belong to the community of Thunder Bay. They didn't want it."[42] Organizers felt accountable to the women because it was their money that made it possible for them keep the shelter open. One example of the support that Faye Peterson Transition House received from women was a shower that activists organized to furnish the shelter with basic necessities when it first opened: 120 women from Thunder Bay attended and donated linens and supplies.[43]

Feminists were determined that this shelter would belong to the women's community, not to the government. Naming the shelter in memory of a local activist affirmed this. When the shelter opened, feminists had recently mourned the death of Faye Peterson, a journalist and activist whose own experience as a battered woman made her aware of the need for a regional transition house. Fels shared the following memory:

> Faye Peterson was a woman from Atikokan who had been abused, had moved to Thunder Bay, been involved with the women's centre, single mom with a disabled kid. Had just been through a lot. Things were finally coming together for her and she was moving to southern Ontario. She and her daughter were in one car, and her son was in another [car with her partner]. And she [and her daughter were] killed in a car accident. It's in memory of her.[44]

The tribute honoured Peterson's confidence in women's ability to change the structures that prevented them from taking control of their own lives.[45]

The memorial was a testimonial both to Peterson's strength and to feminists' political struggle to open the shelter. Peterson became a touchstone for their activism. In a poem called "Report to Faye," Beadle wrote,

> With you in mind we dared to be
> an action in community.
> To take the step we lusted for
> and bring it to reality.

...

Your picture hangs upon the wall
we play no games with memory,
among the treasures that you left
we choose the word tenacity.[46]

Peterson had embodied what Beadle admired in the women's community: its daring and tenacity. Her picture would be a reminder of the women's movement's work so that the shelter would not stray from its founding principles.

At long last there was a place to go, but "worrying about that stuff later" had negative repercussions. The shoestring budget made the house less appealing than feminists had hoped it would be, and frontline work forced feminists to rethink their ideals. Organizers thought that co-operative living would relieve the discomfort caused by cramped quarters and the lack of privacy. They tried to give women a sense of ownership of the house in order to dissolve power relations among board members, staff, and residents. A non-hierarchical setting, they hoped, would encourage consciousness-raising and politicize the women who used the shelter. Some women who came to the shelter did become active in the battered women's shelter movement, but most were not ready to become involved politically. In retrospect, Fels recognized their expectations were based on an uninformed conception of the desperate situations of the women who would come to the transition house:

> Perhaps those of us who had this vision misjudged the intensity of the fear – and the neediness in some cases – of the women who used the services. That it was a major step for many women – to access shelters. It was pretty scary, and not knowing what's going to happen to me if I go to this place. So trying to reach out and incorporate the women and children using the shelter into the group, or the board or whatever the group became, I would say generally wasn't all that successful.[47]

One volunteer explained that she never agreed with the policy of combining frontline crisis counselling with political mobilization. She explained, "You knew [many] would end up going back to an abusive situation. All you could do is make them safe and comfortable while they were there."[48] In her assessment, urging residents and volunteers to embrace feminism was not a woman-centred practice because it did not allow women to define their circumstances on their own terms. Organizers may have been disappointed that most residents did not become political, but they did not question their choices. According to Brenda Cryderman, a former board member, "We didn't want to be like the batterer and tell her what to do. We didn't tell her she couldn't go back, even though it broke our hearts if she did. And I don't think you ever had the right to tell her she can't go back."[49] Accepting women's choices rested on the feminist belief that women were the experts of their own lives.

Between February and May, the shelter housed twenty-one battered women and twenty-three children and received fourteen crisis calls.[50] Opening with no guarantee of funding forced activists to focus on finding money to run the shelter rather than on improving counselling and advocacy programs. Its primary funding was municipal per diems, which the city would pay only for women from Thunder Bay. This did not come close to covering the shelter's operating costs. Churches and traditional women's groups supplied furnishings, linens, quilts, food, and money for rent, but community backing could not sustain the shelter.[51] Although requests for shelter continued, the collective decided to close for one month in August because members were worried that volunteers would become too exhausted.[52]

Faye Peterson House was not the only shelter whose funding was precarious; relying on per diem and short-term funding threatened all feminist shelters. What made their funding arrangements particularly difficult was the jurisdictional void created by local administrators. Thunder Bay Social Services conceded to paying per diems for women from the city but refused to pay per diems for women who came from other communities. The city expected feminists to negotiate support from the other municipalities in the region, but the women's home communities maintained they were no longer eligible for welfare assistance because they had moved away. These debates about jurisdictional responsibility delayed the application for provincial funds, but city council's refusal to grant hostel status to Faye Peterson Transition House remained the primary barrier. If the city granted hostel status to the transition house, then it would be eligible for the province's funding program for transition houses.[53] OAITH had lobbied the Ministry of Community and Social Services to reimburse 80 percent of the per diem costs to municipalities. The province accepted full responsibility for women from communities without municipal organizations and the federal government paid the per diems for Aboriginal women and their children.[54] City council stalled by demanding guarantees from the surrounding municipalities, and feminists were responsible for these negotiations.[55]

Municipal resistance and the lack of local resources made it clear to feminists that the only way to ensure that Faye Peterson House could stay open was stable funding from the provincial government. Representatives from Decade Council worked with OAITH to pressure the provincial government to provide core funding to shelters so that organizers could focus their work on helping battered women instead of raising money. The province turned down the appeal for funding from northwestern Ontario shelters, a decision that angered northern feminists. In their lobby against the decision, feminists used northern alienation to their advantage.

LOBBYING PROVINCIALLY FOR STABILIZED FUNDING

When Faye Peterson Transition House opened in 1983, wife battering was on the government agenda. In 1982, the federal Standing Committee on Health, Welfare, and Social Affairs tabled its *Report on Violence in the Family: Wife Battering*. The infamous incident when some members of Parliament laughed in the House of Commons in response to Margaret Mitchell's question concerning the incidence of wife battering gave lobbyists and politicians who supported the shelter movement some leverage to impel government action. Federal and provincial governments allocated more money to services for battered women, but their intervention undermined feminist contributions to discussions about strategies for change.[56] Decade Council members participated in the OAITH negotiations with the provincial government, and at the local level they resisted the modification of feminist analysis of abuse and women-centred services.

In July 1982, Ontario's Standing Committee on Social Development launched public hearings to investigate family violence. Feminist lobbying was instrumental in convincing the provincial government that wife battering was a serious social issue, but Gillian Walker's analysis of the hearings explains how the process ultimately marginalized feminist expertise. Rather than giving the shelter movement a leading role, the provincial government instituted control, regulation, and supervision of transition houses.[57] The province committed to raising awareness about family violence and to co-ordinating bureaucracies to improve services for women, but this did not alleviate the financial predicaments of shelters. OAITH lobbied the provincial government for both emergency funding to prevent shelters from closing and stabilized funding so that shelters could focus their efforts on serving women. In the fall of 1983, the provincial government allocated $1.4 million to cover the debts incurred by shelters and an additional $1.7 million to stabilize the shelters in the following fiscal year.[58] The decision was political. In June 1983, the provincial government had announced its plan to open Family Resource Centres in twelve northern communities, a program discussed in more detail in the next chapter. OAITH criticized the infusion of money into new shelters while the government ignored the dire financial circumstances of the existing transition houses.

The promise of stable funding was a victory for OAITH and shelters in southern Ontario. But when the government unveiled its funding allocations, neither of the northwestern shelters, Faye Peterson House and Atikokan Crisis Centre, was on the list for emergency funding. Untinen's account of the provincial government's announcement of emergency funds is worth quoting at length because it weaves together northern alienation, feminists' marginal position locally, and their frustration with politicians:

> I went down to a meeting in Toronto, representing the north. And they put up all these shelters on the wall, and how much money they were going to get. And neither Atikokan nor Faye Peterson were up there. Yet there were shelters up there that were getting $50,000. I was outraged. But the trick of the whole thing was that these shelters had submitted their deficit to the ministry ... And when they asked us, we didn't have a deficit. I always said because there wasn't a banker in the north crazy enough to let us have one. We barely had a bank account, never mind one with a deficit. People worked volunteer or on Canada Works. We did food drives. We did all sorts of fundraising things. We never had a deficit and so they weren't going to give us any money. Even though our whole operating budget for the year was $25,000 and there was a house in southern Ontario getting $50,000 deficit payment.[59]

The fact that some of the southern shelters were older than the northern shelters may account for the size of their deficits.

The provincial government gave feminists an effective mobilizing tool by turning down the northern shelters' requests for bail-out funds. Decade Council asked northwestern Ontario feminist organizations to send a telegram demanding emergency relief for the northern shelters to their own MPPs as well as to Leo Bernier, the minister of northern affairs. Crisis Homes sent a telegram to Bernier advising him that if Faye Peterson Transition House and Atikokan Crisis Centre were not added to the "bail-out" list "by 5:15 on Wednesday," the women would go to the press arguing that the government was ignoring women in the north. The lobby was successful. According to Untinen, Bernier called them at quarter to five to explain that there had been a clerical error and that Faye Peterson would receive $25,000 in emergency funds and Atikokan $15,000.[60] The aggressive tactic and quick strategic organizing demonstrated political savvy and regional unity.

In addition to the emergency funding, OAITH negotiated a stabilization formula with the Ministry of Community and Social Services.[61] However, funding for Faye Peterson House remained contingent on the organization's designation as a hostel. This time, the city argued that the shelter violated the city's zoning bylaws. Again, Beadle took matters into her own hands. Fels remembered:

> Gert [bought a] house in Fort William. It was not a collective decision. She found it and said, "I've bought it, or I've signed Crisis Homes to this mortgage, so we're gonna do it." And we did. Maybe it wasn't the best way to do it, but it got done.[62]

Organizers continued to get things done by ignoring red tape and taking risks. However, these decisions created more work for activists when they had to renovate homes to comply with city bylaws and persuade local administrators to support them after they had flouted their procedures and protocols. This group of women did not see a way to be politically engaged within municipal bureaucracies without compromising feminist principles.

Under the purview of the government, the shelter became more hierarchical, and those who had organized it struggled to maintain its founding feminist principles. One of the activists' proudest accomplishments was a new facility constructed under their direction. Battered women no longer stayed in old houses improved with haphazard renovations. A core group insisted that Faye Peterson Transition House remain identifiable as a feminist organization because they did not want it to become a government institution like

Community Residences. Maintaining the shelter as a feminist organization was challenging because new women who did not identify with the women's movement came to the shelter as workers and board members.[63] These women were not committed to feminist structures, such as collective organizing, and some did not accept the feminist analysis that wife battering was a manifestation of unequal patriarchal relations in the family. With government funding, it was difficult to insist that the facility belonged to the women's community and should be accountable to it. When the board adopted hierarchal management structures, the women who built it wondered whether they had been able to make significant changes in local service provision and governance. Community Residences changed, too. With more stable funding and new directors who believed that battered women were entitled to services that enabled them to leave abusive situations, it became a more comfortable and supportive service. Services for battered women improved, but not always in ways the women's community wanted or expected they would.

Organizing in isolated communities meant that feminists had to work together regionally to make change. Fels thought that collective action transformed their greatest obstacle into their principal strength. Baril agreed that isolation both inhibited and motivated their activism. She explained "Northern women have always just done it themselves. They might be isolated and cut off, but they figure it out somehow and they do it. I think that's what we did because we didn't have any information. We just went ahead and did our own thing."[64] Similarly, Boucher explained that fewer resources and less government support motivated them to be innovative:

> I think you have to be a pioneer. You have to be creative. You have to be persistent, to the point of stubbornness. You have to have a good sense of what your community is. And learning with experience and age, maybe, maybe not, knowing how far you can push the envelope. And know when not to push the envelope. You have to have a pretty thick skin. And you have to be willing to deal with, if you want to call it, the arrogance of males. I don't think they're enemies. I think some are. And you go without. It's a hard thing – to compromise.[65]

Effective activism incorporated a regional consciousness and an astute understanding of the community.

The women who founded Faye Peterson Transition House pushed the envelope far beyond what municipal administrators were willing to accept. Feminists demanded services that did not distinguish between deserving and undeserving as well as services that were responsive to women, to support them through transitional periods. Most important, feminists wanted services that encouraged women to be independent, a goal that was possible only if social service policy contested patriarchal family relations. The women's community urged municipal governments to put social justice before budgetary concerns in social planning. Municipal governments resisted these goals because they had neither the political will nor the financial resources to do so.

Women were unable to change the assumptions that informed municipal practices because they worked on the periphery of the city's bureaucracy. Yet their marginal position allowed them to be critical of social welfare policy. They were able to persuade the city to make superficial improvements but unable to build feminist practices into existing social services. Feminist alienation from the city's bureaucracy motivated women to forge ahead with their plans to open a regional shelter for battered women.

This strategy worked in Thunder Bay because the women had the resources within their community to take this risk. Kenora women were just as determined, but as we will see, they did not have adequate human and financial resources to open a shelter without stable funding. Provincial intervention pre-empted the possibility of a feminist shelter when it announced the Family Resource Centre Program. Feminists in Kenora pushed different envelopes. Tense relations between Aboriginal and non-Aboriginal people were more visible there than they were in Thunder Bay. Beendigen was far away, and helping women challenged intensely racist treatment of Aboriginal people as well as discrimination against women.

We're Here to Help: Kenora Women's Crisis Intervention Project, 1975-85

Kenora is a small community in Ontario's Lake of the Woods area near the Manitoba border. Because it is close to Manitoba, residents are oriented more toward Winnipeg than toward Thunder Bay or Toronto. The principal industry is logging; tourism is an important seasonal industry because fishing, water sports, and hunting make Kenora a popular vacation spot. North of the municipal area are unregulated territories, communities that are not incorporated as municipalities but are under provincial jurisdiction. The federal government is responsible for social welfare provision in the region's twelve reserves, which are organized under Grand Council Treaty No. 3. Most Aboriginal people living in the region are Ojibwa, but a significant proportion are Cree. The establishment of federal and provincial district or regional offices in Kenora in the 1950s made the community the centre for service provision and administration for the area, the population of which was 15,855 in 1978. Despite the area's small size, activists negotiated with a complicated municipal government structure. Until 1999, the community was divided into three municipalities, Kenora, Keewatin, and Jaffray-Melick, and each community had its own council.

The campaign to open a transition house in Kenora began with a rape crisis line. In 1976, a group of women met to plan a grassroots service to counsel women who had been sexually assaulted and to escort women to the police station and court. Within the first year, they expanded their mandate to include wife battering, because most of the women who called the crisis line wanted protection from violent husbands. For the next five years, the Kenora Women's Crisis Intervention Project (KWCIP) offered advocacy and shelter to women in crisis.

The women who founded the KWCIP did not identify with the women's movement. Their slogan, "We're here to help," captured the group's emphasis on caring. Some of the women became more critical of local welfare practices when they learned how these policies reproduced gender- and race-based discrimination, and the group became a feminist organization. City welfare officers were unsympathetic to battered women and belligerent toward the women who advocated on their behalf. According to the group's statistics, about half of the women who accessed the service were Aboriginal.[1] Advocating for them taught white women how poorly welfare officials treated Aboriginal women, and by organizing with Aboriginal women they learned how to provide culturally sensitive services.[2] The partnership between Aboriginal and white women did not last, but Aboriginal women continued to use the services, and the KWCIP members continued to challenge assumptions about indigenous women that were deeply ingrained in the local social and political culture.

The Fellowship Centre of the Presbyterian Church was another important service group in Kenora. It managed a detoxification centre and emergency shelter, a service that was a response to the growing number of homeless Aboriginal people in town.[3] Fellowship centre activists were important allies for the KWCIP. The Presbyterian service workers supported the women's bid to open a transition house and intervened on their behalf when the relationship between them and the municipality became unworkable. This co-operative relationship ended when both groups submitted proposals to manage the Family Resource Centre, a provincial response to wife abuse launched in 1983, and town officials awarded the contract to the Fellowship Board of the Presbyterian Church.

This chapter explains how municipal bureaucrats who were opposed to alternative models of service provision could prevent feminist groups from accessing federal policies that supported the development of transition houses. To establish local colonizing relations, I begin with a discussion of racism against Aboriginal people in Kenora. During this period of intense racism against Aboriginal people, Aboriginal and white women attempted to work together to end discrimination against Aboriginal women. This collaboration did not last, but a different group revived cross-cultural organizing when it organized services for abused women. This collaboration was also short-lived, and when it was over, feminists did not integrate Aboriginal theorization of family violence into their services, even though many Aboriginal women still accessed those services. I follow with an analysis of the evolution of anti-violence activism and municipal opposition to women's attempts to provide women-centred services that challenged the discriminatory gender and race relations embedded in local welfare practices. Although activists were unable to change these practices because of their marginal position in local politics, many of the women involved became feminists and continued to work to change the systemic causes of women's subordination in political and social life.

RACE RELATIONS AND WOMEN'S ACTIVISM IN KENORA

Collaboration between Aboriginal and white women for brief periods during the 1970s and early 1980s was a unique feature of women's activism in Kenora. With Beendigen and Faye Peterson Transition House, Aboriginal women and white women supported each other's projects but for the most part organized autonomously. In Kenora, however, women attempted to work across cultural differences, first to end racism and later to provide services for abused women and their children. The first project that brought Aboriginal women and white women together was a conference organized in 1975 to end discrimination against indigenous people and to learn about racism from Aboriginal women.

Anxieties about alcohol consumption informed race relations. Kenora had a reputation as a hard-drinking town. A 1977 study by the Addiction Research Foundation found that the Lake of the Woods area had the highest alcohol consumption per capita in Ontario, but studies focused on Aboriginal peoples' consumption of alcohol because of its growing visibility in town.[4] Although development and assimilationist policies were at the root of augmenting social problems in Ojibwa communities, most studies focused on individual responsibility rather than on the impact of colonization on Aboriginal peoples. In her study of the Grassy Narrows Reserve, Anastasia Shkilnyk argues that relations between indigenous communities and the town changed after the construction of the Jones logging road in the 1950s. The federal government moved the Big Island, Big Grassy, Sabaskong, Northeast Angle, and Grassy Narrows Reserves closer to the road to improve the communities' access to social services. The relocation dispossessed indigenous people from their traditional territories and destroyed traditional subsistence living and their independence. The communities reoriented southward, shopping for food rather than hunting, and frequenting the pubs for diversion. Bootlegging became a growing underground economy when white people began to sell alcohol on the reserves, and alcohol abuse on the reserves worsened.[5]

Unlivable conditions in the new reserves forced many Aboriginal people to move to town, where they were banned from certain establishments and were verbally and physically assaulted on the streets.[6] Homelessness and public drunkenness fostered discrimination against indigenous peoples from many white citizens, who argued that the increased "Indian presence" had undermined the community's respectability.[7] Racism in Kenora made national headlines in the summer of 1974, when the Ojibway Warriors Society staged an armed occupation of Anishinabe Park, an action that was a land claim as well as a protest against civil rights violations against Ojibwa people.[8] The protest angered non-Aboriginal residents, who were unsympathetic to the protestors' claims and who worried that it would have a negative impact on the summer tourist season. The most vitriolic attack on indigenous people was Eleanor Jacobson's pamphlet *Bended Elbow: Kenora Talks Back*, a discussion of alcoholism in Aboriginal communities based on the stereotype that Aboriginal people wasted taxpayers' money on alcohol.[9]

These events motivated a group of Aboriginal and non-Aboriginal women to organize the 1975 Women's Power Conference. The goal of the conference was to bring together women from Kenora and the surrounding reserves to "talk and learn from each other."[10] What made the Kenora conference different from other International Women's Year conferences was its focus on improving race relations and the women's concerted effort to address inequities among women. To foster unity among women, Ojibwa women on the committee insisted that women from the reserves "should not be treated differently or separately."[11] Each workshop was facilitated by an Aboriginal woman and a white woman, a formal device intended to "break the ice" so that women could work together to "replace present attitudes of bigotry with understanding."[12] This attention to race is noteworthy because it precedes the debates of the 1980s that created an explicit anti-racist agenda in the women's movement.[13] Given the immediacy of racial tensions in Kenora, it is not surprising that the organizers attempted to integrate cross-cultural co-operation into their agenda. This group did not organize any programs after the conference, but similar cross-cultural organizing, when Aboriginal women were involved, would distinguish the KWCIP from other feminist projects in the region.

THE KENORA RAPE AND SEXUAL ASSAULT GROUP

A personal experience instigated women's political organizing against violence against women in Kenora. A woman who had been sexually assaulted told a nurse who was counselling her how poorly social services and the police had treated her, and the nurse suggested that the woman organize a crisis line. The woman who had been assaulted followed this advice, and in 1976 she brought together a small group who named themselves the Rape and Sexual Assault Group. Their beginning was modest; the crisis line was basically an answering service run out of the founder's home, and volunteers carried pagers when they were on duty.[14]

Although feminists elsewhere had theorized rape as a political issue, this group did not engage with those discussions, nor were they interested in the women's movement. Marilyn Fortier recalled that she did not consider her involvement with the group to be political:

> I came in there with the idea of wanting to be active working with women who had been sexually abused. And I wasn't interested in the political part of it back then. For me it was just I felt that maybe I was just a caregiver, and that was just part of it. I was a mom. I was married young, too. I had this need to do something more than just my everyday routine kind of thing.[15]

Dianne Singbeil joined the group because the organizer was her friend and she wanted to support her. She explained,

> [She] was the person we were focusing on at that time. Of course knowing that it had happened to her. And you get talking to your friends or other women ... and even though a women had been raped there was no help for her. She wasn't necessarily believed. She wasn't protected or supported. And it just made me aware of the fact that such a thing existed.[16]

Over time, frontline work changed Singbeil's analysis of rape. These women realized they were bringing forward issues that were taboo, and to counter the shame and blame experienced by women who had been sexually assaulted, they criticized the criminal justice system for its poor treatment of women. They did not, however, connect this to patriarchal relations or to the need for a strong women's movement to change systemic discrimination against women.[17]

The improvement of local practices and, to some extent, self-fulfilment motivated them, but their activism did not focus on ending women's inequality.

By defining their work as caregiving, members of the Rape and Sexual Assault Group identified with accepted gender roles rather than with politics. Focusing on caregiving was a way to talk about changing patriarchal structures without becoming associated with feminism, a political stance that most Kenora residents opposed. They were not prepared for the town's resistance to talking about rape and, later, wife battering, nor were they prepared for the personal attacks against them when they raised these issues. The community expressed its opposition to the politicization of family life by targeting activists' femininity and respectability as defined by normative heterosexuality. Opponents tried to undermine their credibility by spreading rumours that the women were lesbians; the rumours persisted even though most of the women were in heterosexual relationships.[18] Those who opposed the group labelled them radical feminists, "man-haters," and "ball-breakers."[19] The assumption that they must be radical feminists because they advocated for women-centred services was common. As Barbara Freeman argues in her analysis of the media coverage of the Royal Commission on the Status of Women, many women who participated in the struggle for women's equality in the early 1970s did not affiliate themselves with feminism. Nevertheless, the media tended to label them as radicals because woman-centred analysis and the discussion of the personal as political were revolutionary at the time.[20]

Although the service was advertised as a rape crisis line, most of the women who called were trying to leave abusive husbands. To help these women, the group expanded its mandate and started to shelter women in 1977. The first strategy was to accommodate women in hotels, but this was too costly since the group's only revenue source was community donations. The group acquired a single furnished room with an affordable rent, an arrangement that was more secure and cost-effective, but only one family could be sheltered at a time. Because it was a volunteer group, women and children were left alone, and counselling services were limited to immediate needs.

Because these arrangements were not providing adequate protection and counselling for women, securing municipal funding to establish a crisis centre became a priority. Improving the service was difficult because the work was already demanding for volunteers, particularly since most of the women also worked full-time. Moreover, the women were supplementing donations from church groups, individuals, and service clubs themselves. The financial burden must have been significant, given that there were few employment opportunities for women in Kenora, and those positions tended to be in the low-paid service sector. In April 1978, the Rape and Sexual Assault Group attended a Kenora town council meeting seeking financial assistance. Even though by this time the group helped abused women primarily, their proposal to town council focused on sexual assault. They requested that council temporarily fund a volunteer organization, which could include men, that would focus on public education, legal and medical advocacy for victims, and continued counselling.[21]

The meeting was a jarring lesson in politics. Marilyn Fortier and Joanne Frost remembered council's reaction: "They basically just laughed us out of there. And it was like these women have been raped. That's what the name connoted."[22] Soon after the meeting, they changed the group's name to the Kenora Women's Crisis Intervention Project because town gossip undermined the women's credibility.[23] None of the women was prepared for this kind of resistance, and they realized that involvement with this project would require more than a desire to help women. To become more politically effective, they invited women who were knowledgeable about service provision, counselling, and local politics to join them. These women did not identify themselves as feminist either, but they were experienced community-based social workers who believed that women were entitled to social welfare services. More importantly, they recognized that since many of the women who called the crisis line were Aboriginal, it was necessary to have Aboriginal women in the organization.[24] When the group incorporated in 1978, the women decided that a minimum of one-third of the board members should be Aboriginal women.[25] With a $28,000 Canada Works grant, the group rented an office and hired three staff to maintain the crisis line, conduct a needs study for a crisis centre that would serve abused women and their children, and counsel victims of sexual assault.[26]

Aboriginal women held influential positions in the organization and taught white women how to best serve Aboriginal women. Rosalind Copenace, an Ojibwa woman and political leader in her community, was the project's first co-ordinator. Her political connections garnered support for the proposed crisis centre from band councils and the Kenora Native Women's Association.[27] She was an important member of the group because she trained activists how to counsel Aboriginal women in crisis. Charlotte Holm, one of the women recruited to join the group in 1978, remembered,

> Rosalind was a very important person in the organization ... I think that actually the crisis centre was maybe one of the first opportunities for Native and non-Native women to work together ... And I think also that Rosalind being involved was quite likely able to give us a much better perspective than we might otherwise have had around ... responding to Native women on the crisis line.[28]

The number of Aboriginal women who used the service suggests that the organization was known to be culturally sensitive. The KWCIP did not specify the cultural background of the women who accessed the service in its first year of operation, but its applications for funding and statistics from 1979 to 1980 indicate that many of its clients were Aboriginal women.[29] In 1977, the group provided shelter for 175 people.[30]

In the autumn of 1977, before the group incorporated, the women had conducted a needs study to support their proposal for a transition house. The most supportive responses were from women who had left abusive marriages. One woman, whose friend had helped her leave a violent marriage, explained, "Friends can only do so much and an official organization would be better equipped to offer help and counselling to women who finally find themselves 'alone.'"[31] Other women who had been abused added that it was difficult for women to face social services and police by themselves and that women needed informed advocates to access the services they needed.

People who worked in the social services that served Aboriginal communities were also enthusiastic about the project. The survey found that half of the people who used the various service organizations were Aboriginal. Those who responded to the survey acknowledged that family violence was a problem, but none of these services had instigated programs for battered women. The community health nurse who worked in the White Dog Reserve reported that most abused women did not ask for help: "It seems the women come forward only when beaten next to death's door. At that time they can't avoid the nurse."[32] Although she did not acknowledge it in her report, it is clear that women living on-reserve were reluctant to ask for help from non-Aboriginal service providers because they distrusted state intervention.[33]

Isolation made them more vulnerable because the distance from town made police protection unreliable, and police would escort a woman from the community only if she pressed charges.

Many employees of service agencies that responded to the survey were wary of the proposal for a transition house because it would not focus on keeping families together. They agreed that a crisis centre for abused women was a good idea, but some advised the group to remember that the children and men also needed assistance. One respondent suggested that counsellors should focus on "get[ting] couples on the road to recovery" and remember that men also suffer because of physical and emotional abuse.[34] The mayor of Keewatin supported the shelter at his first meeting with the group, but the women reported that in a subsequent meeting they had to reassure him that they hoped to strengthen rather than break up families. Only the Knights of Columbus opposed the project outright, arguing that the KWCIP was encouraging women to find problems in their marriages.[35]

Welfare administrators questioned whether municipal budgets would be able to sustain an overnight service. They also argued that another hostel would duplicate services provided by the Presbyterian Church, which operated a detoxification centre for women, and suggested that battered women might be sheltered there. Although the manager of the Kenora Detox Centre disagreed with the welfare administrators, he offered to allow battered women to stay at the centre until the women were able to open their own shelter.[36] Despite the community support for the transition house, welfare officers and the municipal governments continued to oppose the project and blocked women's attempts to provide services for abused women.

During the period when KWCIP members were negotiating with the municipal councils of Kenora, Keewatin, and Jaffray-Melick for support for a transition house and submitting applications for funding to buy a house, the group continued to shelter battered women in apartments. Between April 1979 and March 1981, they provided emergency refuge for eighty-eight women and their children.[37] The first shelter was in the Knights of Columbus building. Holm remembered that the apartment "was terrible. It was two flights of very steep stairs up so we had women with babies and carriages trying to negotiate this incredibly steep high staircase."[38] Battered women had a place to go, but one shelter worker described an environment that was busy and crowded: "There was a crisis line set up and we answered the telephone

... There were two workers there twenty-four hours a day ... There were two bunk beds and I think there were mattresses ... probably up to three women with their children could crowd in. It was very small."[39] A year later, the Knights of Columbus, who thought that the service threatened the stability of the family, terminated the lease on the pretext that they were planning to do renovations. Holm remembered that the renovations were never completed, and she insisted that "they just wanted to get rid of us." The shelter's next location above a drugstore was not much better.

The activists realized that the poor conditions probably exacerbated women's isolation and shame, but they argued that it was necessary until enough money could be raised to buy a house, which would be more comfortable. When they applied for hostel status so that they would be eligible for per diems, council rejected their application, arguing that the shelter duplicated services and that the organization had not firmly established the need for a crisis centre for abused women.[40] The service the town provided was accommodation at a cheap and disreputable hotel, as was the case in many other communities. In the end, council argued that the centre violated zoning and fire regulation infractions and forced the KWCIP to close its temporary crisis shelter in March 1981.[41] Activists changed the name of the organization to Women's Place Kenora because it could only claim to be a women's resource centre. However, the group did not have enough money to rent an office, and once again, the women operated the crisis line and counselling and advocacy services from their homes while lobbying for a shelter.[42]

WOMEN'S PLACE KENORA

The closure of the crisis centre obliged feminists to work with the city to help women who needed emergency shelter access the hotel room. Relations between Women's Place Kenora and municipal officials worsened as the women developed an oppositional feminist position that was critical of the town for its welfare practices, which they argued endangered women and children. Council's continual refusal to support their proposal for a transition house and the stress of advocacy work had a negative impact on the relationships among the women in the group, and as a result of the internal tensions, Aboriginal women left the organization. Nevertheless, Aboriginal women still called the crisis line, and advocates continued to demand that the municipality had an obligation to support battered women when they left violent relationships.

Acting as an advocate for battered women at the welfare office was the most difficult responsibility for activists, and it was necessary to go to the office if a battered woman needed a voucher for a hotel room. Both advocate and client braced themselves for belligerent treatment. Holm described one welfare administrator as "extremely abusive toward the women. There was a certain nasty tone. He was just a mean man."[43] Advocates coached clients before they met with him and informed them that provincial policy obliged the local office to approve battered women's requests for welfare assistance. It was harder for Aboriginal women to obtain social assistance because welfare officials assumed that the federal government was responsible for providing social services to them. Singbeil explained that the welfare office believed that "her place was to go back to the reserve and to stay on the reserve and to keep her business there and that it had nothing to do with people in town. Even if they were on the street, you know. It was hard."[44] Racist stereotypes and the local presumption that alcoholism and homelessness among Aboriginal people were moral flaws and signs of racial inferiority must have influenced these attitudes.

Political experience and support from Presbyterian activists helped the group work around welfare officials' opposition, and over time, activists learned who their allies were within the town's bureaucracy. Singbeil explained, "After a while you found out if you go to the police there is a certain cop, if you can talk to him, he'd be better. Don't talk to so-and-so ... You don't go into the welfare when [the man] was in, you went when the lady was in. You just kind of learned the game."[45] Another strategy was simply to avoid the welfare office, particularly when a woman needed accommodation. When the office was closed, police gave women vouchers for the hotel room, and some officers tended to be more co-operative than welfare administrators. Even though Women's Place Kenora activists had support from the local police chief, some police officers continued to refuse assistance to battered women. The Presbyterians intervened to help activists get battered women to safety, and in 1982, the minister of the church became the after-hours liaison who approved women's requests to stay in the hotel.[46]

Anti-violence work was taking its toll on women who had not anticipated becoming political. Some women became angry with officials who refused to support battered women and became more outspoken critics of municipal bureaucrats; others were uncomfortable with this assertive stance.[47]

This, in turn, created tension within the group. One consequence of the internal divisions was that Aboriginal women began to leave the organization. There is no evidence in the documents to explain why this happened. It is possible that women moved on to other projects and therefore had less time to dedicate to the shelter.[48] But Holm explained that cultural differences and the political relationships among white women made Aboriginal board members uncomfortable. She recalled asking a former board member why Aboriginal women were no longer interested in working with the crisis line. The woman's terse, yet revealing, response was that white women talked too much.[49] In her analysis of the marginalization of women's voices in the battered women's shelter movement, Bonita Lawrence argues that "it does not require individual racism or elitism to effect the silencing of marginalized voices."[50] She explains that the feminist emphasis on a universal experience of violence has made it difficult to find a space to talk about race within the movement. Aboriginal women may well have left Women's Place Kenora because they could not influence the direction of the organization. Once the group adopted a violence-against-women framework, Aboriginal women may have had difficulty integrating the impact of colonization on their communities into the group's discussions of family violence.

As their volunteer pool decreased, the board observed that those who were left had to maintain "a strong nucleus of women that are going to commit their time and energy toward providing increased awareness programs."[51] Opposition from municipal service administrators undermined the group's credibility within the community and with many traditional service groups. Holm explained that this had a detrimental impact on volunteers' self-esteem and belief in their political effectiveness. According to her assessment, the community thought that

> If this group was any good they would be getting money. They would be getting support ... It had a really debilitating effect on us, on the organization and on the women who really wanted to support it but just couldn't handle that kind of pressure ... Besides the physical kinds of demands that we were putting on women, and then the emotional and psychological effects of the crap that we were taking from the community. It's hard for women to take.[52]

The frustrations ensuing from the lack of co-operation between the various levels of government on the development of family violence policy must have been hard to take, too. As was the case in Thunder Bay, every time the women tried to overcome municipal barriers by appealing to senior levels of government for money, they learned that funding was contingent on local endorsement of the transition house.[53] New federal and provincial initiatives changed their strategy, and Women's Place Kenora activists concentrated on obtaining federal funds allocated for transition houses. The 1982 *Report on Violence in the Family: Wife Battering* recommended that the federal government provide initial capital to cover the costs for new emergency shelters.[54] To implement this recommendation, the federal government authorized the Canadian Mortgage and Housing Corporation (CMHC) to provide low-interest mortgages to registered non-profit organizations serving battered women. Women's Place Kenora submitted two proposals. The CMHC declined the first proposal because the money designated to northwestern Ontario for non-profit housing had been allocated to other communities.[55] The announcement of the Family Resource Centre Program stopped their second bid.

THE FAMILY RESOURCE CENTRE

When Frank Drea, the minister of community and social services, announced that a Family Resource Centre would be built in Kenora, he created an unexpected obstacle for the feminist campaign at a point when the local press and the community seemed more supportive of a transition house. In response to increasing pressure for services for abused women, the province planned to build eight centres in northern municipalities and four on reserves. The government was trying to appease two constituencies: feminists and northerners who needed jobs.[56] The program would not be too costly for the provincial government since federal money from the BUILD job creation program provided capital for the construction of new buildings. Municipalities were expected to comply with the per diem rates outlined in the General Welfare Act and would be eligible for provincial payback schemes that the Ontario Association of Interval and Transition Houses (OAITH) had negotiated with the provincial government.[57] In 1983, town council debated two proposals, one for a now explicitly feminist transition house and the other for the Family Resource Centre, which was based on a charitable model of service provision. Municipal opposition to feminist input into the development of services for battered women validated women's increasing awareness of their political marginalization.

The Family Resource Centre Program is a good illustration of Gillian Walker's argument that the state modified initiatives to end wife battering proposed by the women's movement and marginalized grassroots expertise. Walker argues that even though the women's movement had some influence on programs for abused women that were not organized by feminists, when the Ontario government took up the issue in the mid-1980s, it did not promote services that sought to end systemic inequalities that prevented women from leaving violent relationships.[58] The province did not consult frontline workers in transition houses when it developed the Family Resource Centre Program, and the program's sweeping mandate demonstrated that the planners knew little about the dynamics of woman abuse. In the initial plan, the centres would accommodate battered women, single mothers, homeless women, elderly women, and Aboriginal women in crisis situations. Feminist groups were not identified as the most suitable candidates for the management of these provincial shelters. The proposal recommended that "serious consideration should be given to approaching the Church as a potential provider since their stable organization structure and their given interest in social services would link itself well to this type of program."[59] The report suggested that if a church group could not manage the service, then women's groups and other charitable organizations might be appropriate. When the province released the budget for the program, it proposed that workers be paid the minimum wage. The director, who would presumably be male, would be paid more. Untinen, who was the spokesperson for Decade Council, remembered her opposition to the recommendation that men would manage the centres: "*He* would get more, because *he* would be in charge of protecting everybody inside. We had to say, 'No, *he* is not even going to be there.'"[60] The Family Resource Centre Program expected volunteers to supplement a minimal staff, which Kenora activists questioned because they doubted people would volunteer to work in a government facility.[61]

Initially Decade Council organized to prevent the implementation of the provincial program, but when it became clear that the province would go forward with it, a coalition of local feminists, Decade Council, and OAITH quickly organized to modify the plan. The coalition used the prospective clientele to reveal the province's ignorance about wife battering. Feminists argued that battered women required confidentiality and security; elderly women, on the other hand, would want the centre to be open to their visitors.

Feminists insisted that the proposed centres would not protect battered women if their location was known and if access was not restricted.[62] In addition, homeless women could bring addiction problems to the centres. Most transition houses in Ontario refused services to women using drugs or alcohol because it intensified an already volatile environment.[63]

Because of the program's shortcomings, Women's Place Kenora continued to lobby for a transition house and criticized the provincial government for funding an ill-conceived plan instead of their proposal.[64] The municipal government was as persistent in denying the need for a transition house as feminists were insistent that the transition house would better serve battered women. Municipal opposition was the only impediment to the transition house, since the CMHC had approved funding in 1983. Council refused the feminist proposal and opted for the provincial plan instead. Feminists believed that they would still be able to open a transition house until January 1984, when the CMHC notified Women's Place Kenora that it could no longer hold the funding it had set aside for them.[65]

Those who had been advocating for a transition house decided that their best plan of action was to work with the town to improve the Family Resource Centre Program.[66] Despite their outspoken criticism of the program, feminists secured a seat on a steering committee that was struck to modify the proposal to suit the complicated municipal governing structure and to develop operational policies. They convinced the steering committee that the centre should serve only battered women, an agreement that the municipal welfare office eventually accepted. The decision to limit the service to battered women ended feminists' misgivings about applying to operate the centre, and in addition, Decade Council persuaded Kenora feminists they should apply for the contract to ensure that the service would be woman-centred.[67] However, the city did not award it to feminists and instead chose the board of the Presbyterian Church Fellowship Centre. The choice of a church, a traditional philanthropic service provider, confirmed that the town did not want feminist analysis to influence social welfare practices and ensured that feminists would not have a direct impact on local policy. It also ended a long relationship of co-operation between these two organizations.

Competition between feminist and non-feminist groups caused tension between the Family Resource Centres and the women's movement locally and regionally. Publicly, Women's Place Kenora members congratulated the fellowship centre.[68] But privately, they were angry that their proposal had been rejected, and they declined an offer to sit on an advisory committee, regardless of the years of collaboration between the organizations. In retrospect, Holm regretted that they were not more willing to share their expertise with the new directors.[69] Untinen also acknowledged that an unproductive and competitive relationship developed between feminist transition houses and the Family Resource Centres. She explained that OAITH's decision to deny membership to the Family Resource Centres exacerbated tensions between feminist and non-feminist advocates for battered women. Yet she insisted that they were not motivated by selfish aims: "We were only fighting for the best deal. We weren't just fighting against Family Resource Centre people because they got nice new houses. We were just trying to get the best deal for everybody. And you know the government uses those little rifts and manipulates them, too."[70] Competition for scant resources and political influence further entrenched their positions, making co-operation impossible among those groups who were vying to be the expert on the issue and to influence how services would be provided to battered women.[71]

What became of Women's Place Kenora? In December 1986, the Ministry of Northern Development and Mines announced that it would spend $100,000 to combat family violence in northwestern Ontario. At a Decade Council meeting, a representative from the ministry outlined its plan to divide the money equally among women's groups; Women's Place Kenora, however, was not eligible for funding because it did not provide frontline services to battered women. Decade Council stood in solidarity. All of the member organizations refused to accept any money unless Kenora was funded. Impressed with this show of solidarity, the ministry found $100,000 for the group. The women bought a house with the money, and after eleven years of activism, Women's Place Kenora finally had a place.[72]

For a short time, Aboriginal women and white women worked together to develop services for battered women. This co-operation did not last, but by working with Aboriginal women, white women learned how deeply embedded racism was in local social welfare practice. Negative stereotypes about Aboriginal peoples restricted indigenous women's access to the social services they needed when they left abusive relationships and unlivable conditions on reserves. Through advocacy, it became clear to white women that

Aboriginal women were denied basic social rights. Aboriginal women taught white women how to help women in a culturally sensitive manner, but cross-cultural activism could not be sustained without a critical anti-racist framework. The feminist framework of violence against women, which emphasized common experiences among women, dominated the organization's politics after Aboriginal women left the group.

Those who initiated anti-violence activism in Kenora did not anticipate such strong resistance to their work. Over time, they learned that the values that made it difficult for women to leave abusive relationships were embedded in social welfare policies and practices. The experience of the Kenora women demonstrates how local administrations could subvert federal policies designed to give voice to alternative service provision. Scrambling for funds and recognition diverted attention away from more important questions about how to improve services for abused women. At best, the women could only provide ad hoc services that met women's immediate needs. Feminists were also marginalized in local decision-making processes and thus were not able to challenge the gender and race relations that influenced how battered women were treated. What did change was the consciousness of the women who sheltered women.

Competition for recognition as the experts about wife battering and for influence in the management of services for battered women was less prominent in Nelson than in northwestern Ontario. Collaboration between feminists and non-feminist community services was possible because feminists did not want to provide services. The next chapter discusses the debates about service provision among Nelson feminists, as well as the contributions that people who were not affiliated with the women's movement made to the battered women's shelter movement.

4
It's a Band-Aid Service, and It's a Damn Needed One: The Nelson Safe Home Program, 1973-89

In the 1970s, Nelson residents witnessed many changes in the political and cultural character of their town when the Slocan Valley became a destination point for "urban refugees" and draft resisters who were part of the back-to-the-land movement. These new residents introduced New Left politics to the community, and their alternative lifestyles defied staid town dwellers' expectations of respectability. The women who joined this migration were feminists, many of whom had developed their political analysis of women's oppression in student politics and rejected women's traditional benevolent and supportive roles.[1] They opened a women's centre in 1973, the first in British Columbia outside of the Lower Mainland.

Some dismissed the newcomers' new approach to politics and community development and believed that "Americans" and "hippies" should not influence local politics. But it was not only the back-to-the-landers who wanted to develop community-based, democratic politics. In 1972, representatives from Canada Manpower, the Ministerial Association of Nelson, and the Selkirk Mental Health Unit opened the Nelson Community Services Centre, a lay counselling centre and crisis line. The centre was based on contemporary theories that argued that the best services were grounded in local expertise and that volunteer participation promoted community cohesiveness.[2]

This chapter compares how these groups responded to violence against women and discusses why they were able to work together, even though their analyses of wife battering contradicted each other. The women's centre and the community services centre organized services for battered women from different political perspectives. Nelson feminists counselled women in the hope of empowering them and ultimately women as a group, and they based their advocacy for battered women and public awareness campaigns on a critical analysis of the family. In contrast, the community services centre did not incorporate gender analysis into its programs. Advocacy was premised on the conviction that people were entitled to social services, but counsellors focused on individual rather than structural change. The Nelson Community Services Centre organized the Nelson Safe Home Program in 1980. This service combined family reconciliation with emergency shelter for women and their children. The safe home program attracted volunteers who wanted to help but were not necessarily aware of how patriarchal relations operated in the family and how this prevented women from leaving abusive homes. Hence, in its early years, the safe home program reproduced many of the social structures that made women feel ashamed and powerless. Rather than criticizing the safe home organizers, the women's centre worked with the program, offered training to safe home operators, and supplemented the individual counselling programs at the community services centre with battered women's support groups and woman-centred advocacy.

In general, the women's movement did not endorse safe homes as alternatives to transition houses. Feminists in northwestern Ontario opposed the Ontario government's proposal for safe homes in rural areas because it ignored feminist expertise and kept wife battering hidden in private homes.[3] Nelson feminists and the community services centre agreed that a transition house would serve abused women better than safe homes. Nevertheless, in the political and economic climate of British Columbia in the late 1970s and 1980s, Nelson community groups could not obtain provincial funding for a transition house. After the Social Credit Party, led by Bill Bennett, won the election in 1975, fiscal accountability replaced local control as the guiding principle of social planning. The government cut provincial funding to feminist services, and there was no money for new initiatives after the 1982 budget.

We have seen that competition over meagre resources and debates about which analysis of woman abuse should guide services for battered women estranged community groups from each other in northwestern Ontario communities.[4] This did not happen in Nelson. There are two reasons that Nelson feminists did not oppose the safe home program of the community services centre, even though its practices did not accord with feminist goals. First, the women's centre collective did not want to become primarily a service provider. Many Nelson feminists thought services were "band-aid" measures. While they recognized that services were a necessary component of a broader critique of women's social and economic oppression, a majority of the collective's members believed services diverted energy from political work that would bring about more fundamental social change. Second, the Social Credit fiscal policies hurt all community services, especially those in rural areas. This strengthened political alliances among community groups that were trying to help people cope with the ramifications of the government's repressive economic policies. The government's decision to fund voluntary agencies that served families instead of groups that were interested in advancing women's equality was an appropriation of feminist goals. At the same time, Nelson feminists' refusal to organize a shelter without sufficient funding was a strategic decision not to volunteer to do work that they believed the state should be funding. This position was based on their political identity as feminists, not benevolent caregivers.

THE NELSON AND DISTRICT WOMEN'S CENTRE

In the mid-1970s, federal and provincial funding cuts instigated a re-evaluation of the role of services in the women's movement. Feminist collectives were forced to make difficult decisions about whether to focus their scarce resources on desperately needed services or on political lobbying and educational programs. In discussions, many women expressed frustration about the increased emphasis on services in feminist organizations. Some who opposed the shift from direct action to service provision believed that services weakened the women's movement's radical challenge to patriarchy and were reluctant to work with women whose analysis of patriarchal relations was less complex than their own. While the debate was common in women's collectives, the division of service provision and politics was never as clear in practice as it was in theory. At the Nelson and District Women's Centre, the false dichotomy between service provision and politics did not describe what feminists were doing and caused divisions within the women's centre collective that at times diminished its effectiveness as a resource centre.

Nelson feminists introduced a critical analysis of women's oppression in the family and interrogated how social expectations about women's respectability limited women's potential. The influx of back-to-the-landers who held radical political views reversed typical urban-rural dynamics. It was the city dwellers in the area who were labelled conservative. Sam Simpson, who moved to the area to join the Slocan Valley back-to-the-land movement, explained that most Nelson residents considered the women's centre out of place:

I think we were just generally seen as another part of the weird phenomenon which had hit the area. We were dressed in jeans and boots and plaid shirts, which was interesting because sometimes urban women would come to visit and they'd think that all of the women's community were lesbians because they all looked so butch. Mostly it was more a reflection of coming in off rural properties. We didn't necessarily change to go into town. We just wore the same kind of clothing that farm women wore ... To some extent we were seen as an aberration or something ... Within the Slocan Valley ... community of hippies, feminism was considered to be the prevalent thinking among the women.[5]

These women deliberately defied expectations about appropriate self-presentation to expose how everyday life reinforced oppressive gender relations. As newcomers, they were less constrained by the strictures that community and family surveillance imposed on people. Though comprising a small group, the women who congregated in Nelson did not feel isolated as a radical fringe because the local counterculture supported them.

The women's centre founders did not want it to be exclusive to their own circles. They hoped to raise the awareness of both women and men about the problems women faced in order to politicize them and work for change.[6] The women's centre was primarily a political action centre, but it was also a comfortable place for women to rest or breastfeed while doing errands in town. Bonnie Baker, who was raised in New York and became active in the women's liberation movement in Montreal, remembered how they recruited women: "It was welcoming. And we got her there, and she's comfortable, she's drinking coffee, and we'd give her the literature. Read this. Isn't this interesting? Hey, would you like to work here?"[7] It was more important to create a welcoming environment for women who came to the centre seeking counselling and advocacy. Although they tried to assuage visitors' misgivings about feminism, many women were uncomfortable with the politics of the women's centre, especially with the radical feminist stance that developed alongside the centre's educational mandate. Nelson feminists believed that it was important for women to organize independently from men because men prioritized other forms of social oppression over sexism. To protect the women's centre as a place where women could meet freely, the collective posted a notice on the door asking men to knock before entering the centre.[8] Feminists explained that a women-only space was necessary because many women who had been battered or sexually assaulted did not feel comfortable around men.

The collective's conception of a "safe space" followed the assumption held by many feminists that women in crisis were more comfortable in women-only places. However, this policy fed rumours about the sexual orientation of collective members as well as the perception that the centre was "full of strident feminists who hate men and who want to break up your family."[9] For this reason, many women were apprehensive about being seen there. Bette Bateman, a former co-ordinator of the centre, remembered that she had to convince women to come to the centre for counselling. She explained,

> At the time, it was very hard to get [the local women] to come into the women's centre because they saw it as something totally foreign. They saw us as some kind of kooky women. They thought we were all Americans, because there were a number of American women. And some of them that finally came would walk over and there was a long ramp into the women's centre, and they were too frightened to walk along the ramp to come in because they'd heard such negative things. And they also thought all the women in the women's centre were lesbians. That was frightening for them. But that was the rumour mill out in the community.[10]

Fear of lesbianism was a common issue for feminists in smaller communities. The Nelson Women's Centre was different from those in many other small communities because it confronted the community's homophobia. Nelson had a visible lesbian community who ran a drop-in at the centre, and the centre's promotional material opposed stereotypes about lesbians.[11]

Although some women who needed help were afraid to go to the centre, enough went there for activists to realize that wife battering existed in their community and that the available services did not help women. Through advocacy, feminists learned that abused women in rural communities faced different obstacles than women in cities. Women lacked anonymity in small towns. It was common that the officials dealing with a battered woman knew her husband, and in these instances she was less likely to receive fair treatment. Diane Luchton, one of the founders of the women's centre, explained that wife battering was slow to develop as an issue in Nelson because women were worried that they would become the subject of local gossip, and hence they were apprehensive to talk about their abuse. She remembered how she became aware of the importance of confidentiality: "A woman I went with [to the family court] opened my eyes so much. When she left and she went to family court, the judge – it's a small town – knew her husband ... and he said 'What!? Nice Tom, he couldn't do that.'"[12] While doubting battered women was not unique to rural communities, in small towns a woman's husband was more likely to be known in the community's social circles and her credibility was more likely to be questioned.[13]

The rural idyll was a barrier for political initiatives against family violence. Many refused to acknowledge that family violence happened in small towns. Feminists refuted the myth of rural tranquility, pointing out that the rural solitude that most cherished as a sanctuary from urban bustle was a trap for battered women. In an edition on violence in the local feminist newspaper, *Images*, one woman explained, "Rural women are more unprotected than city women ... There's a book out called *Scream Quietly or the Neighbours Will Hear*. Well, for many rural women, there are no neighbours who could hear."[14] Officials dismissed activists who insisted that Nelson needed a transition house. Carol Ross, who co-ordinated the women's centre in the early 1980s, remembered that the "local bigwigs" quite openly denied that wife battering was a significant problem in their community.[15]

The women's centre was a new option for battered women because it offered a woman-centred alternative to charities and government services.[16] Although the collective took on advocacy work, members were reluctant to call their frontline work service provision. Luchton explained, "At least half of our group at any one time felt that it wasn't so much trying to ... provide services. It was trying to make what services that were there woman-friendly."[17] Baker explained why working for political change took priority over service provision: "We saw this as politics. It wasn't to set up services. It was to change the world so that women wouldn't be vulnerable in this world."[18] However, feminists learned that some women had reasons for being more concerned with their own immediate needs than with long-term social change. Consciousness-raising was enough for most women who came to the centre, but some needed more help than others. These women needed a place to which they could go to become self-reliant.[19] There were discussions about opening a transition house in 1976, but the collective decided not to "waste energy" writing a grant proposal since the Social Credit government planned to phase out transition houses. Moreover, it was clear that this government would not fund grassroots feminist initiatives.[20] The decision not to open a transition house was pragmatic, but it also demonstrated that most West

Kootenay feminists preferred practising a form of feminism that was not defined by service provision. Their subsequent programs that addressed violence against women concentrated on advocacy and education.[21]

Without consensus within the collective and resources, the centre could only offer loosely organized ad hoc programs for women. In 1979, the women's centre organized a rape and sexual abuse crisis line. Most women who called were battered women who needed emergency shelter. Bateman, who inaugurated the service, took many of the women and their children home. At the time, she was the only collective member who had the resources and time to shelter battered women. Many Nelson activists learned about battered women's desperate situations after they became involved in the women's movement, but Bateman came to the women's movement with this knowledge. She explained that she knew many women who were in abusive relationships "and I just could not believe that society was going to go on this way. When I discovered the women's movement, it was an answer for me to try to solve this."[22] Eventually taking care of abused women became too demanding for her. She explained, "I just got completely burnt out. I just got exhausted because I was dealing with these women in trauma constantly. And I was so angry about what was happening to them that I began to lose perspective on everything. I just got so focused on rape and violence that I began to not be able to see anything pleasant in the world."[23] Contrary to government policy, relying on volunteers to fill in the gaps in social services was not an effective alternative to state-funded social programs.

The crisis line was disconnected within months of Bateman's departure. The Nelson Community Service Centre incorporated the rape crisis line into a service it had been offering since 1972, but the line was no longer a gender-specific service. Crisis line volunteers counselled both women and men, and women were not guaranteed a female counsellor when they called.

The projects at the women's centre continued to prioritize violence against women, a decision that divided the collective. Some members insisted that the focus on violence compromised the centre's role as a radical political institution. In the summer of 1983, members of the co-ordinating collective had intense discussions about the relationship between service provision and politics. During the re-evaluation, women were asked to consider whether "feminism is revolutionary or reformist? ... Can the Women's Centre be for all women as well as politically active?"[24] The latter question assumed that a strong political stand and serving needs identified by women were contradictory goals, and it echoed debate that was becoming more important within the women's movement. Those who defended services insisted that they were political and that feminists could not expect women who needed help to have a complex analytical framework to understand their oppression. Neglecting women who were not at the same level of analysis as those who were active in the women's movement did more harm than good.[25] Conceptualizing services and politics as opposing praxes contradicted the feminist belief that useful analysis of women's oppression had to be grounded in women's experiences. Reflecting on this debate, Sally Alexander explained why service provision was important for the movement:

> There was always a conflict. We were funded to promote feminism, do the lobbying, do the educational work. But that couldn't happen without the direct service stuff because that was where women came in the door, where you got a chance to talk to them, where you got a chance to find out what was going on around this particular issue in the community.[26]

Alexander's reflections reinforce the fact that the division between service provision and lobbying was not as clearly demarcated in practice as it was in theory.

The debates in the 1980s clarified the mandate of the Nelson Women's Centre but likewise weakened unity among feminists and, consequently, the effectiveness of the centre's programs. Ross recalled that the organization was not healthy at that time because the debate about services had become so divisive that it was impossible for these two forms of feminist praxis to co-exist. Those who wanted to concentrate on helping women decided that their work would be more effective if they left the women's centre and set up their own advocacy centre. She explained, "In the evolution of groups there is a self-destructive phase. And the Women's Centre was in one of those phases ... You needed to be more removed ... to practice a particular kind of feminism."[27] The women's centre continued to provide advocacy, refer women to appropriate services, and lobby for a shelter, but its activist corps became smaller.

NELSON COMMUNITY SERVICES CENTRE SAFE HOME SYSTEM
By the end of the decade, there were more options for battered women in the Kootenays. In 1979, the Women in Need Society opened a transition house in

Trail, which is 69 kilometres from Nelson. Before its founding, the closest transition houses for women living in the West Kootenays had been in Leth-bridge, Alberta, and Penticton, British Columbia. Women from Nelson stayed at the Trail shelter, but for most it was not an appealing option. Going to Trail put distance between women and their abusers, but moving away from Nelson disrupted their children's day-to-day patterns too much. Battered women needed shelter closer to home. In 1980, the Nelson Community Services Centre submitted a successful proposal for a safe home program to the Ministry of Human Resources. From the outset, the safe home program was intended to be a temporary measure until the community had the resources to open a transition house.

The community services centre attracted people with various political and ideological perspectives. Records indicate that most volunteers were not interested in the systemic underpinnings of wife battering. The safe home program was a family service, not a woman-centred service. Its guiding phi-losophy was that "inter-spousal violence [was] a *family* problem in which both spouses require[d] assistance in order to make the decisions necessary to continue together or apart."[28] Women's centre activists did not agree with this analysis of wife abuse, but the different philosophies did not cause ani-mosity between the organizations. Feminists realized that the safe home pro-gram was necessary until the government lifted cuts to new services.[29]

The drastic budget cuts and fiscal restraint of the Bennett government delayed their plans. In 1982, Grace McCarthy, the minister of social services, froze spending on new social services. The cuts were deep in rural commu-nities, where Ministry of Human Resources staff was reduced by 50 percent.[30] The government argued that the impact would not be serious because churches and voluntary organizations would take over these services. Existing feminist services lost much of their funding, and the government introduced more stringent reporting mechanisms that increased the workloads of underpaid employees in grassroots organizations. Feminists argued that these new mea-sures were attempts to undermine women's demands for political and social equality. Their protests were apt, but they did not alter the government's agenda to privatize feminist services.[31] Even community-based services whose goals shared the Social Credit government's family-centred ideology had dif-ficulty expanding and improving. These cutbacks galvanized grassroots activ-ists, unions, and community groups against the government. The solidarity movement in 1983 formalized the coalition among Nelson's service groups, which were all struggling to maintain a satisfactory level of services during a period of provincial fiscal restraint.

Safe home programs fit into the Social Credit's ideological and economic agendas better than transition houses because the government promoted service provision based on good will. More importantly, safe homes reconciled with the policy of fiscal restraint. Providing emergency shelter for battered women relieved the ministry of investment in the long-term maintenance of a facility and salaries for employees. Volunteers received a small per diem when they had families in their homes.

In this political climate, the Nelson Community Services Centre was a better candidate than the women's centre for provincial funds to run a program for battered women because its politics were not confrontational and political agitation was not part of its mandate. Its organizers believed that individual problems were linked to broader social relations, but self-help philosophy was the foundation of its programs.[32] Rather than advocating for structural change, the centre concentrated on helping clients understand their situations so they could develop strategies to cope with personal problems. Despite the centre's apolitical stance, the safe home program was not entirely removed from feminist analysis because it was part of a network of services in the West Kootenays that offered support for battered women. The safe home program was part of a coalition that included the Nelson and District Women's Centre, the transition house in Trail, and the Nakusp District Homemaker services. The coalition promoted a feminist analysis of spousal assault, advising women that they had the right to freedom from physical and mental abuse and that men had to take responsibility for their violence.[33] Women's centre activists led training workshops for safe home operators, so volunteers were exposed to feminist analysis of spousal assault. Nevertheless, the community services centre's training material for the safe home program did not connect women's individual circumstances to patriarchal relations.

How effective were safe homes for women? The program was an alternative to institutional settings, such as the Salvation Army. Alexander and Bateman remembered that abused women sometimes stayed in the psychiatric unit at the Kootenay Lake District Hospital.[34] Safe homes sheltered women without the stigmatizing effect of being labelled "crazy." Yet there were philosophical and structural differences between the safe home program and transition houses that made the former a less useful option for women who wanted to live independent, violence-free lives. One of the program's most significant shortcomings was its assumption that staying with middle-class nuclear families would console battered women. Clients tended to be from poor families, while safe home operators were usually middle-class families,[35] and some women were grateful that there was any place to go, but the class differences between them and their hosts upset some women. Ross explained, "It was hard to be in a 'nice home.' It was very hard to be in a middle-class home when yours wasn't. Some women were uncomfortable with a male presence."[36] Staying with a stable family could exacerbate women's feelings of shame and failure that they had not been able to make their family conform to social expectations.

The community services centre maintained that a strong home environment would help women. Training material for volunteers advised them not to change their daily schedule because "the role modelling of a functioning, active family or individual can be invaluable. Often the safe home environment is the first outside of their own situation that a battered woman has experienced."[37] Those operating safe homes varied in their understanding of the dynamics of family violence. A few volunteers indicated that they had lived in violent homes, and these families may have been more sensitive to their guests' discomfort. Others suggested that the strength of their families would comfort the women and children who stayed with them.[38] Since there were no client files or reports from the women who stayed in the homes, it is difficult to know how they felt. Many safe home operators reported that women made alternate arrangements after their first night, which is a good indication that feminists' perceptions about clients' discomfort were accurate.[39]

Safe homes were lonely places for many women not only because of their discomfort but because they were usually left alone during the day. Women did not have the immediate access to counselling they would have had in a transition house and were unlikely to meet other women who were trying to leave abusive partners and working through the bureaucracies of the social welfare and criminal justice systems.[40] Former women's centre co-ordinators remembered that when feminists were on staff, and if women were able to choose their counsellors, these counselling services could be helpful for battered women.[41] According to the crisis intervention protocol, women who stayed in safe homes were supposed to have a counselling session with one of the crisis centre counsellors as soon as was possible. However, the centre did not have adequate resources to provide ongoing counselling, and women were therefore referred to the battered women's support groups organized at the women's centre.

More significant than the lack of adequate counselling was the fact that women who called the crisis line were not guaranteed shelter. It was difficult to recruit volunteers, and the community services centre could not maintain a consistent level of services because the organizers had to accommodate the needs of the volunteer families. Usually, the program consisted of fewer than five homes and a few people who drove women to the safe homes or the transition house in Trail.[42] In 1983, there were only four safe homes, one of which would not take in children. One family stopped providing services because they decided to take in a foster child.[43] A motel provided accommodation when the homes were full or when operators were not able to take in a family, and the centre expected crisis line workers to maintain contact with these placements to relieve their loneliness. If clients staying in a hotel had no money for food, the centre would pay their restaurant cheques, but volunteers were supposed to advise clients "that food costs should be kept to a minimum (no steak and lobster)."[44] The centre operated on a tight budget, but this expressed restriction must have made battered women feel like they were accepting charity.

Volunteers did not intend to make women feel ashamed, but the weaknesses of the program were structural. They tried to provide comfort to abused women and to alleviate their loneliness by listening. Nevertheless, offering consistent services to battered women was impossible because the program depended on what volunteers were able and willing to offer. The cases below illustrate the limitations of the safe home system.

The program made extraordinary demands on volunteers and could not guarantee safety for women. Ideally, the homes had an extra bedroom, so that a woman could have some privacy and enough beds for her children. This was not always the case. One safe home operator submitted the following report:

12 noon, Friday 12: [Woman] came to the centre on my instructions following a phone call to me. She was extremely upset and feeling very ill. (She is 8 weeks pregnant) having severe abdominal cramps. Following a brief chat I took her to

my home and got her settled on the couch. She did not want to see a doctor. She and I talked that evening. She was afraid more of a miscarriage than the stress of her home life. [It] was more than she could cope with.[45]

Not only was there no privacy for the client, but the possibility of a miscarriage must have been stressful for both the client and the volunteer. On Sunday, the client returned to her husband "for one final try" but called the centre on Monday afternoon "frantic to be out of the house." Because the safe home operator was not able to take her in that day, the client found alternate accommodations for the evening, and a counsellor at the centre made arrangements for her to go to the Trail transition house on Tuesday morning. Late Tuesday evening, the client phoned from Trail expressing uncertainty about the transition house but agreed to "give it a try." This case became more complex for the volunteer after the abusive husband called the volunteer when he discovered a note that his wife had left for him. The volunteer met with him, and he reluctantly accepted the volunteer's suggestion that he needed counselling to save his marriage. It is unclear whether he contacted the crisis centre and by chance found the same volunteer or called the volunteer's residence. If the latter situation was the case, then the confidentiality of the safe home was compromised in this instance.

Confidentiality and secrecy were critical for maintaining the program and for protecting both the volunteers and the clients. This was particularly important in a small town where it was difficult to hide from volatile and abusive spouses. The following case illustrates that both clients and operators were at risk:

16:04 Picked up [woman] at MHR back door. She and kids looking tired, faces were dirty, clothes were ragged. She was scared to death but kept up her outlook. She refused food, but the kids ate. She talked very open and free.
19:00 Left for bus depot – she's going to Vancouver. I got her a ticket and saw her to the bus. The police were there and followed the bus.[46]

The woman's fear and the fact that the police escorted the bus suggest that she was fleeing from a very dangerous man. The crisis centre had arrangements with the Nelson police and the RCMP, who would pick up a woman at her home if she called when her husband was there and was under threat.[47] I found no protocols indicating that police offered extra protection to families who were sheltering women. The clandestine measures taken in this case must have fostered feelings of shame. The volunteer's compulsion to note their "dirty faces" and "ragged" clothes suggest that there was some judgment on the part of this safe home operator.

Counselling programs for children were less well developed. This was not an oversight, because there were scarcely sufficient resources to organize the safe home system. Even though the Nelson Community Services Centre reported a 50 percent increase in demand for its services in 1984, the government did not grant more funding for the hire of more counsellors.[48] If children were physically or sexually abused, volunteers and counsellors were legally obligated to refer them to the Ministry of Human Resources, which was responsible for child welfare services at the time. A crisis line manual instructed volunteers that witnessing abuse had a long-term impact on children and that abusers often used them as pawns. While acknowledging that living in a violent family was often confusing for children, the training manuals did not offer safe home operators advice about counselling them.[49] One safe home operator reported her perceptions about how the children staying with her were coping with their family's breakdown. She was concerned that the mother was trying too hard to be strong for her daughters, and she noted tension between the client and the client's eldest daughter but was not sure whether to intervene. She explained how she handled the situation:

> At one point I mentioned to [the mother] ... that [her daughter] seemed to keep a lot of things hidden inside and this caused a reaction in [her] where I thought she was going to break down but she regained control quickly (a very strong lady). This whole incident was very hard for me to deal with. I felt as though I should intervene between mother and daughter but also didn't think I had that right. I also told [her] how I dealt with my own tension and tried to get across that we don't always need to be strong and everyone has to have some sort of release.[50]

That the family stayed in the safe home for over a week, an unusually long time, suggests that there was a rapport between this woman and the client. Nevertheless, the safe home operator did not think she was trained adequately to counsel women in crisis.

The safe home program helped many women during a period when the provincial government had suspended funding to organizations thought to pose a threat to the stability of the family. Notwithstanding the flaws in the system, feminists admitted that it was an important stop-gap until resources for a more permanent service were available. The provincial government's endorsement of the safe home program over transition houses ignored local assessments about what battered women in Nelson needed. A 1989 study concluded that existing services for battered women were inefficient because none of Nelson's community service organizations had enough money or staff to co-ordinate them, and that without a transition house, none of those services was very useful to abused women.[51] In the 1980s, the women's centre submitted many proposals for a transition house to federal funding agencies but did not follow through because without provincial funds, the shelter would rely on volunteer work. Both the women's centre and the community services centre wanted a transition house, but neither would endorse a service that the government would not fund because they knew from experience that services for battered women that relied on volunteers were inconsistent and could only address women's immediate needs. Their goal was not achieved until 1995, when, under the NDP government, the BC Ministry of Women's Equality funded the Nelson Community Services Centre to establish the Aimee Beaulieu Transition House.[52]

Accepting the inadequacies of the safe home program until the government funded a transition house was a strategic choice. Commenting on the various lobbies to open a transition house, Baker, who had been active in the women's centre since the 1970s, explained that she supported those who pressed for a shelter in Nelson but did not want to do frontline work: "I didn't want to set it up because I thought setting it up was a band-aid service. But I'm glad that the women who didn't see it that way did set it up, because I think that it's a band-aid service and it's a damn needed one."[53] The decision of women's centre members not to bid for the contract to operate the shelter was consistent with the group's history of choosing to focus as much as possible on political lobbying and organizing the local women's movement.[54] Unlike northwestern Ontario activists, these feminists were not adamant that the shelter had to belong to the women's movement to provide good services. By the time Aimee Beaulieu Transition House opened, there were other agencies in the community with strong feminist leaders; the Nelson Community Services Centre was one of them.

Fiscal restraint certainly influenced the women's centre's decision not to organize a shelter. However, the political culture that developed in the West Kootenay women's movement was also an important factor. The Nelson and District Women's Centre saw itself as a political action group and defined politics as lobbying and direct action. A few members of the collective thought that service provision was political work, but most opposed straying from the centre's original mandate to politicize women by educating them about patriarchal relations. While feminists understood that politics and advocacy were integral to each other, enough members disagreed on which aspect of feminist organizing was more important to cause divisions within the collective.

The organizers of the Nelson Community Services Centre co-ordinated service agencies and recruited volunteers who did not share a political ideology. Although it followed democratic principles of local control and encouraged its clients to acknowledge their entitlement to social assistance, the centre did not actively pursue a political agenda. Its safe home program did not incorporate feminist criticisms about the family and was not woman-centred. Despite the different analyses of wife battering, an amicable working relationship allowed the women's centre and community services centre to work together to help battered women. The budget cuts introduced by the Social Credit government restricted programs for both organizations, and the coalition to oppose the government's cutbacks improved their alliance.

These two community-based groups held divergent views of volunteerism. The Nelson Community Services Centre believed that mobilizing volunteers was essential to democratic governance. The women's centre opposed volunteerism in service provision because it perpetuated the undervaluation of women's work. Nelson feminists thought that their counselling and advocacy work was politics, not volunteer work. Many women's groups debated how much work volunteers should do but relied on them to keep their underfunded services open and were obliged to pay low salaries to the few staff they could hire. The next chapter examines how feminists in Moncton struggled to balance the need to keep their transition house open with their goal of paying a living wage to the women who worked there.

It Was Never about the Money: Crossroads for Women/Carrefour pour femmes, 1979-87

Crossroads for Women/Carrefour pour femmes was one of three transition houses that opened in New Brunswick in the early 1980s. Like other transition houses in Canada, it relied on short-term government grants and per diem funding, and this piecemeal funding did not cover expenses. In the early years of operation, there were times when there not enough money for payroll, and consequently staff members were often unsure whether they would be paid. Crossroads/Carrefour was not alone in this quandary. Relying on women who were willing to work for little or no remuneration was a controversial issue in feminist services because it conflicted with the emerging critical analysis of the undervaluation of women's work.

Crossroads/Carrefour organizers were more critical of the unjust treatment of shelter workers than the staff themselves were. In press releases and public speaking engagements, the organizers criticized the government for discriminating against women, stating that "Crossroads has two groups of abused women: its clients and its staff."[1] Organizers recalled that securing funding to pay decent wages was a priority for them; staff, however, insisted that working at the shelter was "never about the money."[2] Political commitment to ending violence against women motivated them to continue to work at the shelter despite personal economic insecurity.

This chapter explores how Crossroads/Carrefour organizers negotiated the contradiction between their political work for women's equality and paying women low wages for valuable work. I begin with a discussion of the political context for women's organizing in New Brunswick and the founding of Crossroads for Women/Carrefour pour femmes. Acadian women played an important role in the organization of the provincial women's movement and in the first bilingual shelter in the province. An examination of the collective structure follows. The organizers adopted this structure to share power with the employees and to set an example for the women staying in the shelter. This strengthened the staff's dedication to the survival of the shelter. I conclude by examining negotiations with the provincial government for funding. The organizers effectively mobilized support for the shelter and changed the view that family violence was a private matter. But in their negotiations with the government, they could not change opinions about the value of women's caring work.

ORGANIZING CROSSROADS/CARREFOUR

Acadian women organized the first feminist groups in Moncton and were able to draw on the political networks already established by the Acadian movement.[3] Women had always been active in the movement for Acadian rights, and with the revival of the women's movement they began both to demand recognition for their crucial role in maintaining Acadian culture and to lobby for women's equality.[4] La Fédération des dames d'Acadie, which was founded in 1968, initially organized to address women's issues in the Acadian community and later launched the early provincial feminist campaigns.[5] A university course taught by Corinne Gallant, a philosophy professor at the Université de Moncton, was another catalyst for formal feminist organizing in the city. Gallant recalled,

> I started an evening class ... There were eighty women coming to talk about [women's issues]. It was consciousness-raising ... At the end of that session, women came to me and said, "We're not going to stop meeting on Tuesday nights. We're going to continue meeting." So this was the first feminist group here. We continued meeting and we organized big meetings where we invited all of the women in New Brunswick. It was mainly French-speaking. There were English women who were interested, but we proceeded mainly in French.[6]

The consciousness-raising groups were formalized in 1973 when women founded LES FAM, an acronym for Liberté, Égalité, Sororité – Femmes Acadiennes de Moncton. The organization's goal was to implement the recommendations of the Royal Commission on the Status of Women, in particular its call for the creation of provincial advisory councils on the status of women.[7]

The provincial campaign to lobby for an advisory council started a year later at a conference held in Memramcook. Delegates agreed that a council affiliated with the government would be in a stronger political position to lobby for women's issues than grassroots groups. Gallant supported the foundation of a provincial organization because she believed it would hasten the achievement of feminist goals. She recalled arguing that "in 1970 we were asking for daycare, and ... in 1975 [we were] asking for the same things. It [was] time to organize something official so that somebody [could] take care of it and solve all of the problems."[8] In the early years of the women's liberation movement, many feminists shared Gallant's optimism that women's problems would disappear once people recognized the systemic underpinnings of women's oppression. The Progressive Conservative government passed legislation to create a council in 1975 but did not appoint the first council until two years later. Madeleine Delaney-LeBlanc was its chair, and its first office was in Moncton.[9] Creating the New Brunswick Advisory Council on the Status of Women (NBACSW) did not solve all of the problems women faced, but the council was an effective lobbying group and encouraged local initiatives to address women's issues.[10] Domestic violence soon became one of those issues.

The NBACSW organized public meetings to discuss wife battering and encouraged women's groups to develop services for abused women. In conjunction with Public Legal Information Services, a non-profit organization dedicated to educating people about their legal rights, the council produced a resource book entitled *Battue/Battered* that advised women in abusive relationships about their legal rights and the options available to them. Published in 1979, it was the first of its kind in Canada.[11] The booklet recommended solutions for wife battering that shifted the blame from women to men. The authors argued that it was "unjust ... that many women are forced to leave their homes, taking their children with them, while the man, who is the cause of the crisis, remains in possession of the home."[12] In addition to short-term measures to protect women, such as the establishment of transition houses throughout the province, the council demanded improved legal aid services and long-term counselling for both women and abusive men.[13] When the booklet was published, the only shelters for abused women in New Brunswick were in northern Acadian communities. The Religieuses Hospitalières de Saint-Joseph had established emergency shelters in St. Basile (Centr'aide LeRoyer) and Bathurst (Vallée Lourdes) in 1978 and at Tracadie (Accueil Sainte-Famille) in 1979. Women from the religious orders would continue to play an important role in the New Brunswick battered women's shelter movement, and Sister Cécile Renault would be the first president of the New Brunswick Association of Transition Houses.[14] Research conducted by the advisory council three years later stressed the urgent need for more shelters because the domestic murder rate in New Brunswick was higher than the national rate. In its submission to the 1982 federal Standing Committee on Health, Welfare, and Social Affairs on Wife Abuse, the NBACSW reported that in 1978, 59 percent of homicides in New Brunswick were domestic murders, compared with 36 percent in Canada.[15]

To encourage the establishment of services for abused women, the NBACSW showed the film *Alice, Who Did That to Your Face?* to women's groups across the province. The movie was shocking to those who were unaware of the severity of the violence many women faced in their homes. Huberte Gautreau, a professor at the Université de Moncton and one of the founders of Crossroads/Carrefour, remembered the impact of the film on her: "I couldn't accept that women couldn't have control, that men were at times violent ... I hadn't even thought about it before ... I had the impression that homes were not violent. I was kind of surprised when all of a sudden I was faced with that kind of reality."[16] In discussion groups after the film, women's groups decided to investigate the incidence of wife battering in their communities with the goal of establishing a transition house. Fredericton Transition House organized in January 1980, and Saint John women established Hestia House in 1981, the same year that Crossroads/Carrefour opened.[17] Although these shelters began providing services within the same year, the organizers did not form a coalition to lobby the provincial government until 1987.

In Moncton, Delaney-LeBlanc organized the first meeting to discuss the establishment of a transition house that would serve women living in southeastern New Brunswick. Women in abusive relationships often called the NBACSW office for help, but because of the shame associated with domestic violence, many of these women claimed that they needed the information for a friend. When Delaney-LeBlanc suspected that they were themselves battered women and asked them if this were so, women generally admitted they were.[18] Delaney-LeBlanc invited activists from women's groups to a meeting in September 1979 to convince them to organize a transition house, and this group agreed that Moncton needed a centre that would compensate for the lack of services for women in the city and the surrounding area. Their initial goals were ambitious. They proposed to open a women's resource centre that would include a transition house. To generate interest for a women's centre, organizers held monthly information sessions and discussed a variety of issues, including domestic violence, women and health, women in fiction, and women and art.[19] They surveyed women to rank the need for a shelter as well as to gauge interest in a resource centre that would provide information about family planning, legal rights, budgeting, sexual assault, and spiritual and mental health; 84 percent of the women who responded ranked services for abused women as the highest priority.[20]

Canvassing local legal and medical authorities to determine the most urgent shortcomings in the existing social service network produced similar results. In discussions with doctors, social workers, family court workers, and police officers, organizers learned that eighty-nine women who had been physically or mentally abused had sought help from local services in March 1980. Some of these women had stayed at the Fredericton Transition House, which was 182 kilometres away.[21] The group also sought advice from organizers of established transition houses in other provinces. These activists explained that dealing exclusively with abused women was an overwhelming task and recommended that they limit their mandate to opening a transition house.[22] Moncton activists listened to this advice and abandoned their plans for a women's resource centre.

The group incorporated as Crossroads for Women/Carrefour pour femmmes and organized a board of nine women from various backgrounds, including two university professors, a doctor, a lawyer, a housewife, and an artist. The board held weekly meetings to expedite the opening of the shelter and met with local women's clubs to solicit financial and political support. Federal grants from the secretary of state and the Department of Employment and Immigration job creation programs covered operational expenses, salaries, and renovations.[23]

Crossroads/Carrefours, the first bilingual shelter in New Brunswick, opened its doors on 28 June 1981. The first home of the shelter was a dilapidated four-bedroom house that the City of Moncton rented to the board for a nominal fee of $100 per month.[24] The collective invested $25,000 of its federal operational grant to do extensive repairs and hired construction workers under the project name "Project Alice" to maintain the secrecy of the location of the transition house.[25] Even after the renovations were completed, the house was dreary. Community volunteers and staff did what they could to make the house livable. Women's groups provided linens and food, while men's groups fixed the windows and maintained the grounds. Later, former clients donated their time and skills to make the home cheerier. Rina Arseneault, who worked as a crisis intervener and eventually became the principal spokesperson for the shelter, listed some their donations:

> We had an artist who came there who did some wonderful work. One woman painted our logo on the wall. It was gorgeous. She did a wonderful job. And one woman gave us a wonderful pamphlet ... And that was another strength. All these women came [to Crossroads] with a lot of skills. And they were quite willing to help. We had one woman who, for at least six Christmases, made dinner for Crossroads ... For her it was important that she pay back. And that was her way. Others paid back in different ways. There was a lot of that happening at that time also. Women wanted to pay back for all of the support.[26]

Supporting the shelter offered women a way to contribute to the battered women's shelter movement.[27] The community support for the shelter indicated that it was more than a service.

Organizers soon realized that the little house that they had rented from the city was not large enough to accommodate all of the women who needed emergency shelter. There were no residents at the transition house during its first week of operation, but this was the only time that it was empty. Even though the maximum capacity for the shelter was twelve residents, there were days when up to twenty people were packed into the house. When the beds were full, families slept on the couches in the living room, which left no common area to relax and talk to other women. During the first three months of operation, the shelter housed fifty-four women and sixty-five children.[28] In March 1982, the collective made the difficult decision not to admit more than twelve people at one time and to turn women away when the shelter was operating at capacity.[29] According to 1982 statistics, staff refused accommodation for thirteen women and children one day and were forced to turn away five people another day.[30] By the end of the first year, 178 women and 208 children had stayed there.[31]

In addition to overcrowding, the board faced a funding crisis from the very beginning. The federal government provided start-up funds but expected the provincial government and community groups to sustain the service. The Canada Community Development Program granted the transition house $73,097.60, enough to cover salaries at minimum wage for the first year of operation. Federal funding was substantially smaller in the next two years and covered only 66 percent of the wages in the second year of operation and 33 percent the next year.[32] The provincial government was not willing to replace the federal money, and the diminishing funds made it impossible for the organizers to fulfill their commitment to offer employees good salaries.

Donations from community organizations became crucial to keeping the shelter open. Women's church groups made important contributions to the transition house during the years that the organizers were negotiating with the provincial government for permanent funding. Arseneault remembered,

> I've seen more basements of churches across New Brunswick than you'd ever imagine. I got served more teas. I knew where the best scotch cookies were. There's a lot of networking in the churches. And that has helped many transition houses, but also many women. We need to realize that ... The women's movement inside the church ... did all of the organizing. [The women] and the leaders seemed to be two different things altogether. And I'm sure some of the women never told their pastor or their priest that they were in some ways networking and helping [the transition houses].[33]

Before the transition house opened, Les Sœurs de Notre-Dame du Sacré-Cœur gave $5,000 to Crossroads/Carrefour, the largest donation the shelter received, and women's church auxiliaries organized fundraising campaigns to furnish the house.[34]

Raising awareness about wife battering was supposed to be the reason for public education, but it became an important fundraiser. Arseneault was torn about this:

> I used to hate it because I thought I was selling [the issue] ... I wanted people to have knowledge about this. But then they would send their cheques. And the better you get [at selling the issue], the more money you'd get, but then you'd have to sell this ... I remember feeling that struggle inside of me.[35]

Although Crossroads/Carrefour wanted the public to share their political analysis of woman abuse, it was often more effective to present it as a charitable issue. Helene Robb, a former board member, recalled that men's groups tended to be moved by the poor conditions for children who stayed at the shelter: "You get more money from people who have pity than you should. It's awful to just use pity and parade the poor little children, but that still works to get money, unfortunately."[36] Eliciting sympathy was an effective strategy: the Lions Club built a playroom for the shelter when Robb informed them that children did not have room to play in the transition house or to run outside.

Reliance on community donations made Crossroads/Carrefour organizers reticent to identify as feminist because they did not want to alienate people who held negative opinions about the women's movement. Yolande Saulnier, one of the original crisis interveners, described the political position of the shelter as "not feminist. We wanted our rights. We still had husbands and children and families ... We just wanted women to be able to cope with their lives without leaning on someone or needing somebody to help her."[37] Arseneault explained that even though many women were committed to feminist goals, they did not call themselves feminists:

> People were not ready, and they did not want to be called feminist ... They were humanist or they were peer supporters, but they were not feminists. They gave care ... You had to demystify feminism. "It's okay. We're not going to burn our bras. We're talking the same language." I don't know what they were so scared of, but there was a lot of fear.[38]

Distancing themselves from the negative stereotypes associated with the women's movement was necessary to ensure long-term community support for the transition house and to recruit volunteers for the service. Organizers focused on raising awareness about wife abuse, not the women's movement.

Despite its public facade, the shelter operated according to feminist principles. Soon after it opened, the shelter reorganized as a collective to provide a living space and work environment where women could share power. The collective structure was effective in that it helped some of the women who worked at Crossroads/Carrefour to become more confident in their abilities, but it also created tensions between the shelter organizers and government bureaucrats who opposed the introduction of alternative structures and practices.

WORKING WITHOUT A BOSS: COLLECTIVE ORGANIZING

After six months of operating as a board and a staff, the board of Crossroads/ Carrefour decided to adopt a collective structure.[39] This decision reflected the board's commitment to creating a service that would promote women's independence. To prevent a hierarchal relationship from developing, members of the board of directors were called volunteer collective members. These women managed the transition house, applied for funding, lobbied government for support, and accepted the legal responsibilities of a board. Staff members were responsible for the day-to-day operation of the transition house and for counselling, but they also played an important role in the governance of the organization.[40] Gautreau proposed the collective model and recalled that she had to convince new staff and volunteers that organizing as a collective was feasible and necessary because abused women needed new models for family life:

> It was a concept that was not accepted by most of the new volunteers and staff. We always had to have training for that. Sometimes we had workshops on the collective. We were always trying to sell the idea of the collective ... We wanted to create a new model ... We wanted to show [the women who were battered] that this house could be an environment without a boss so that they could do the same thing at home. Why would you need a man to bring you down?[41]

Some women became frustrated by working in a collective and left the organization. But those who accepted the structure became adamant supporters because they believed that collective organizing showed abused women that there were alternatives to patriarchal family relations and that women could form co-operative relationships. An advertisement announcing the opening of the transition house in the Acadian newspaper *L'Évangéline* asserted that battered women and their children had a right to refuge. It went on to propose peer counselling among women as an effective way to help women leave violent relationships, stating that "une femme en état de crise a le droit de choisir les moyens qui pourront le mieux lui permettre de réévaluer ses relations avec les hommes et les femmes."[42] Bringing battered women together would foster mutually supportive relationships.

Collective organizing presented residents with alternatives and also helped staff to become more confident. Saulnier explained:

It gave us more power, more independence. I came here to work and I had to take charge of the house. Also for the clients that were here. She would come here and there was no boss. She had had to live with a boss all her life. "You do this. You do that. Don't do this." But here the collective was more like a group. I wasn't here to be a boss. I was just here to make sure that the house would function.[43]

Because ideally work was shared equally in collectives, women were obliged to perform tasks that made them nervous. For example, all staff members were expected to accept public speaking engagements to promote the transition house. Initially this was daunting for some, but with experience they overcame their anxieties.[44]

Although it was a common practice for feminist services to operate as collectives, Crossroads/Carrefour was the only New Brunswick transition house that did so.[45] The staff's commitment to its collective structure was one of the factors that prevented the first attempt to organize a provincial coalition of transition houses. In October 1982, shelter workers met at a conference on violence against women held in Fredericton with the goal of founding a provincial coalition. A survey of transition house workers conducted just before the conference found that staff from all of the New Brunswick shelters preferred structures that gave them more input in the management of the transition house. Comparing abusive homes with hierarchical relationships, those who reported on the survey insisted that the government fund shelters without forcing them to give up their autonomy because "[like] the battered woman, the transition house needs to be autonomous."[46] On the basis of the survey results, shelter workers proposed that the coalition adopt a collective structure, a recommendation that the boards of the other transition houses rejected. This was one of the reasons Crossroads/Carrefour staff members were ambivalent about the proposed coalition. Moreover, although they recognized that the coalition would be in a better position to bargain for standard wages and benefits for workers, they were also concerned that the specific needs of each shelter would not receive adequate attention if the shelters were members of a coalition.[47] Transition houses continued to negotiate individually with the government until the foundation of the New Brunswick Association of Transition Houses in 1987.

Even though the shelters did not belong to a formal organization, organizers co-operated when lobbying the provincial government. An important disagreement between transition house organizers and government officials revolved around how long women could stay at transition houses. Transition houses allowed women to stay for up to eight weeks, but they would not force a woman to leave if she was not ready to live on her own. In August 1983, the Department of Social Services announced that it would only pay per diems for each woman for a maximum of thirty-one days. At a meeting held in September, the organizers of the transition houses decided to work together to fight this decision.[48] The next month, representatives from Crossroads/Carrefour made a presentation to the New Brunswick Working Group on the Problem of Wife Battering, and their primary demand was full funding with the guarantee that each shelter would have control over policies and programs.[49] Officials at first insisted that if the government supported the shelters, then they should comply with government standards and regulations, but by working together, the shelters eventually convinced the government to reverse this decision.[50]

This incident demonstrated the effectiveness of unified action, but, as was not the case with the transition houses in Ontario, each board developed an independent relationship with the government, a practice that established disparities among the shelters. The shelters had different pay scales, policies, and pro-cedures. In the absence of a coalition, local groups and the municipal government supported Crossroads/Carrefour in its long struggle for adequate funding from the provincial government.

NEGOTIATING THE VALUE OF WOMEN'S WORK

Improving staff salaries was an important issue at Crossroads/Carrefour because organizers did not want to create a service that reproduced women's oppression. The guidelines of the federal job creation programs that funded the shelter made it difficult to achieve this goal because the programs provided only temporary employment, to encourage people to move from social assistance programs into the permanent workforce. Designers of the job creation programs were concerned that employees would become dependent on the government, and so they stipulated that employees work at the minimum wage.[51] The organizers of Crossroads/Carrefour opposed this condition. Beth McLaughlin, one of the original board members, explained:

[The salaries] were roughly $8,000 per person ... And we all said women cannot live on that. It was just recreating exactly what we were trying to get people out of. So we committed to raising $12,000 [to increase the wages]. Still it wasn't a huge amount of money, but we reckoned that they could at least live on that. It wasn't poverty wages. And I think that was ... the way we dealt with what was going on ... We looked at it through the same lens ... Is this abuse or is this enhancing or empowering women? So I think that was a very strong part of our mandate.[52]

Not every transition house shared Crossroads/Carrefour organizers' commitment to trying to pay staff good wages. As Maureen MacDonald's examination of Byrony House in Halifax demonstrates, some boards of feminist services insisted that staff accept the fact that neo-conservative fiscal agendas made it impossible to pay good wages. Moreover, some volunteer board members believed that since they were working hard to keep the doors open, workers should also consent to lower wages for the cause.[53]

Keeping women's wages above the poverty line meant that the salaries had to be adjusted yearly according to increases in the cost of living. To meet the collective's commitment to increase wages by 13 percent to improve the original salaries, and then to offer yearly raises to keep up with inflation, collective members, including the employees, organized fundraising events to supplement insufficient government grants.[54] They took advantage of community events and did traditional woman's work to raise money. The women sold chicken fricot at Acadian celebrations, fudge at the mall for International Women's Day, and organized dances, auctions, and car washes. Local television and radio stations donated their facilities to host a variety show and telethon. Perhaps the most creative event to raise funds for Crossroads/Carrefour was a "cyclethon" by two professors from Moncton to Miscou Island, an event that raised $700 for the shelter.[55] These projects were creative and fun but also tiring and time-consuming. Fundraising produced minimal returns. In the first five years of operation, these events garnered a total of $119,963, but this covered only one-quarter of the annual operating costs each year.[56] Although finding money to pay wages was an important motive for organizing fundraising events, the collective did not make this known. According to Arseneault, the collective thought that people who supported the transition house did not want to donate money for wages.[57]

Staff knew that their personal survival depended on the success of fund-raising campaigns. Arseneault recalled:

> We're saying we're here to help women, but how can we help each other? The money was terrible. But there was always a sense that we could get more money. So we'd work for our salary. It was important to sell the fudge and the blankets and the tickets. It was as much for the house, the food, the electricity, and all of that, as it was for our own food and electricity. There was always that dichotomy of trying to stay alive and believing in the issue. How do you do that?[58]

The collective experimented with ways to incorporate perks into the job to help women make ends meet. For example, since the collective could not compensate workers for daycare expenses, staff could bring their children to work.[59] Many could not deal with the economic instability and demands of the job, and counselling abused clients was too difficult for some. One employee, who was trained in social work, resigned within the first year of operation because the work was too stressful and unpredictable; another woman reported that she cried every day after work.[60] After a few months of operations, the collective was also worried about burnout: none of the staff had taken time off because there were not enough workers to cover vacations.[61]

The financial situation became so serious that the collective discussed closing the shelter because it did not have enough money to meet payroll and operating costs. Workers refused this option. Saulnier remembered, "We said no. We will find some money. No one is going to close this house. It's needed." Arseneault explained that they were willing to make personal sacrifices because they were committed to helping abused women: "There were three months when there was no money for salaries at all. There was nothing. We were just trying to keep the doors open ... There was a buy-in that had to happen. You needed to believe in the issue. It was not work. We believed in the issue and that's why we worked there."[62] Once the collective acquired money from the provincial government, it compensated the staff for some of their back wages but was unable to pay the full amount.

The provincial government refused to provide core funding for the shelter. The Department of Health and Community Services paid only a $70 comfort allowance for each resident and a per diem of $10 per resident for the shelter. As the federal money was depleted, organizers became more vocal in their criticism of the provincial government's refusal to replace the federal funds. At lobbies with the government and in press releases, they admonished the provincial government for ignoring abused women and for discriminating against women. Tension between the collective and the provincial government made matters worse, and the organizers began to wonder whether they would be able to keep the shelter open. One month after the federal funding had ended, when "panic was at its height,"[63] a representative from the Department of Social Services, with the assistance of the NBACSW, conducted a fact-finding study to determine how much support the department would give to the shelter. The report found inefficiencies in the operation of the service that it connected to the collective structure of the organization. Nevertheless, it recommended that the department continue to purchase services from Crossroads/Carrefour and that the government either increase the per diem rate or give the shelter an operating grant. To improve the relationship between the collective and the government, the study also advised the department to assign a liaison who was knowledgeable about family violence.[64]

The Department of Social Services implemented the recommendations of the report, but this did not end financial crisis at the shelter. The provincial government committed itself to covering 80 percent of the operating costs for transition houses, but it based its funding on a figure that was smaller than the actual budget of Crossroads/Carrefour. According to the collective's calculations, the province actually paid only 60 percent of its budget. The government also agreed to pay a per diem for ten residents even when fewer people were staying at the shelter, and it raised the per diem rates by 90 cents to $16.90. The collective was not satisfied with this small increase and argued that it discriminated against women because it was far less than the $35 per diem the John Howard Society had negotiated with the province for its halfway house.[65]

The new arrangement with the Department of Social Services worsened working conditions at the transition house. The government provided only enough money to pay salaries for four full-time and one part-time staff members, which forced the collective to reduce staff to one person per shift. The level of service consequently declined. With only one person staffing the house, workers could not escort women to court or to the hospital during emergencies and were unable to counsel women in the shelter while they answered the crisis line. The collective asked for additional money to hire a staff member to answer the telephone in August 1984.[66] The Department of Social Services did not respond to this request until January 1985, when the director of Adult Residential Services visited the shelter and agreed that it was important to have more than one person working during the day. It was not until March 1985 that Crossroads/Carrefour received a $7,000 grant to hire a person to work on the crisis line.[67] The numerous delays in government responses to the collective's requests for money further aggravated the relationship. To make matters worse, government payments were often late, which put pressure on employees and board members, who were never sure that they would be able to cover the payroll.[68]

Wages remained low. The starting salary for a full-time worker was $13,156 for a work week of thirty-seven and a half hours. The most experienced staff members earned $16,000 per year, less than their counterparts in other provinces. There had been no cost of living adjustment since June 1984.[69] Activists argued that the government's treatment of the workers was abusive: "As well as being overworked, the Crossroads staff is grossly underpaid. This is another reason for high staff turnover. It is not easy to recruit persons with the necessary qualifications to work for substandard wages and no pension or medical plans."[70] The organizers' rationale for increased salaries did not move provincial bureaucrats. Robb recalled her frustration with the government excuses:

> It was a struggle, a constant struggle. [Wife battering] wasn't really recognized as a problem ... So we were sort of militant around that issue. I remember going up to the premier of the province and almost grabbing him by the lapels of his suit and saying, "I'm doing this because I feel this has to be done. I don't get paid for it. I'm a volunteer. It has to be done. I'm not doing this for self-interest. It's for everybody in the province. Why don't you pay a decent amount of money to transition houses? They're not even getting by."[71]

The government was committed to reducing debt and spending, not investing in new services. McLaughlin thought that in the mid-1980s politicians believed that it would not reflect badly on them if they ignored services for battered women.

Politicians may have believed that family violence was an issue they could dismiss, but the editors of New Brunswick newspapers were very critical of the parsimonious funding of Crossroads/Carrefour. Even though the editors of the newspaper generally supported the government's fiscal policy, a 1986 editorial in the *Moncton Times-Transcript* argued that "there is a difference between being careful with the taxpayers' monies and being so close with the purse-strings that the taxpayers' nose is cut off to spite his/her face." The accompanying cartoon showed a drunk man in the background. In the foreground a badly beaten woman on the telephone explained to a friend, "He didn't seem to want to wait until Crossroads got its government funding. He decided to beat me anyway."[72] Donations from the community were the lifeline for the shelter. The *Saint John Telegraph-Journal* reported that Moncton citizens contributed more money per capita to Crossroads/Carrefour than the residents of Fredericton and Saint John did to their transition houses.[73]

In 1986 the collective negotiated an additional $30,000 from the provincial government, but the home remained on the verge of bankruptcy.[74] The collective needed more money because it realized that it could no longer function in the little house, which at the time was the smallest transition house in the province. The occupancy rate in May 1986 was 106 percent, and staff were forced to turn eight women and twelve children away. When the collective heard that Premier Hatfield had dismissed the need for a larger shelter because he thought that Crossroads/Carrefour was underused, they quickly corrected his misperception. In a letter to the minister of health and community services, they explained that women and children had slept on the floor that week, but, despite the overcrowded conditions, an RCMP officer had insisted that the collective admit another woman and her children because their lives were in danger and "Crossroads was the only safe place."[75] By the end of 1987, activists finally persuaded the provincial government to cover 80 percent of the actual budget, and the United Way agreed to pay the remainder.[76] In December of that year, the collective closed on a new house that would accommodate eighteen people, using a $5,000 grant from the city. They moved into the new location in February 1988.[77]

The new location alleviated the overcrowded conditions in the shelter, but the government still refused to increase staff salaries. Contemplating the opposition to paying the crisis interveners good wages, McLaughlin stated that most people did not acknowledge the experience and skills of frontline workers. The commonly held view was that "these women weren't very well-educated.

They were working in a transition house. It was kind of that mainstream attitude that this was a poor person's issue. Let the poor look after them."[78] The
collective had changed attitudes about wife abuse but was less successful in
changing attitudes about the value of women's work.

Many women were unable to make ends meet on the low wages and moved
on when better employment opportunities arose. The women who continued to work at the transition house throughout the numerous funding crises
explained that the opportunity to work in an environment that allowed them
to improve women's lives outweighed their personal financial circumstances.
Before taking a position at the transition house, Arseneault had worked in a
psychiatric ward, an experience that made her wonder "why it was so easy to
keep women out of society when they didn't fit the mould that they were
supposed to fit into." She wanted to work at Crossroads/Carrefour because
she thought that it would help women before they lost control of their lives.[79]
Saulnier started working there two years after she left an abusive relationship.
Before leaving her husband for good, she had returned to him many times
because there had been no social support for her. This experience sustained
her dedication to keeping the Crossroads/Carrefour open. Saulnier described
her political commitment to the transition house as traditional caring work:
"To me it was never like a job. It was more like helping people ... To me it's
almost like a second home. It's a part of my life."[80] Collective members' reflections on the struggle with the government echoed these activists' commitment to helping abused women. Doreen Gallagher, one of the early volunteer
collective members, explained in an interview with the local newspaper,
"We've no way of knowing how many lives we've saved, but if only one life
was saved it has been worth the effort."[81] The little house that was the first
location of Crossroads/Carrefour certainly made a difference in many lives.
Between 1981 and 1987, it was a refuge for 833 women and 1,042 children.[82]

In her study of family violence and the women's movement, Gillian Walker
recalled a discussion with an anti-violence activist who "wondered whether
[the battered women's shelter movement] had achieved anything beyond creating a lot of (poorly paid) jobs for feminists in transition houses."[83]
Women's groups that opened shelters accomplished much more than this.
Yet this pessimistic assessment of the movement's accomplishments conveys
a central paradox that feminist services faced. Activists in the battered women's

shelter movement argued that women leaving abusive relationships needed jobs with good salaries and benefits so that they could live independently, but they realized that transition houses reproduced the very working conditions that needed to change.

Against opposition from the provincial government, the organizers of Crossroads/Carrefour attempted to create a work environment that met their political goals. Organizers chose to operate as a collective to provide an alternative to the unequal relationships that women who stayed in the shelter had just left. They also thought that this structure would help employees become confident enough to accept responsibility and leadership. By doing so, they valued the experience that women brought to their jobs as crisis interveners and the skills that frontline workers developed in counselling battered women. When they lobbied the government for stable funding for the transition house, the collective insisted that the government acknowledge that expertise with good salaries. In retrospect, crisis interveners who stayed at the shelter throughout the funding crisis were less concerned about the low wages and economic instability than organizers were. Belonging to a movement dedicated to improving women's lives was more significant to them than ending the undervaluation of women's caring work. The organizers of Crossroads/ Carrefour were as dedicated to improving the lives of the staff as they were to helping abused women and their children. They convinced the community that abused women and their children deserved government support, but in the end they were less successful in their campaign for the rights of the women who worked in the shelter.

Conclusion

In the 1970s, feminists hoped that making the connections between wife battering and unequal patriarchal relations would end violence against women. Aboriginal women argued that this was not enough and called for services that addressed the interconnectedness of the negative impact of colonization on families and the high rate of violence in Aboriginal communities. When activists began to organize transition houses and services for abused women, they soon learned that convincing governments to base services on women's needs would be more difficult than they had anticipated. They faced vehement opposition from government officials, who thought that transition houses would break up families. Parsimony also guided government responses to feminist demands for women-centred services, and conflicting agendas for women's equality at different levels of government complicated negotiations for stable funding for transition houses.

This book has documented women's campaigns to establish transition houses in four communities, and it has shown that strategies for change were grounded in local politics. In previous analyses of women's organizing in smaller communities, it was assumed that the muted feminist goals of these women were a product of the inherent conservatism of small towns.[1] Conceptualizing urban women's movements as more radical than rural, small-town feminist groups does not capture the complexity of the local politics that informed activists' decisions. Women's struggles with local bureaucracies, community ambivalence, and municipal and provincial governments varied from place to place. Consequently, women developed tactics to change people's attitudes about wife battering and to convince their communities to support their projects. To gain community support, some women's groups decided not to publicize their feminist politics.

The groups discussed in this book raised awareness about violence against women in various ways. The members of Thunder Bay Anishinabequek and the Ontario Native Women's Association (ONWA) promoted women's rights by linking them with the goal of advancing self-government for Aboriginal peoples and by explaining how colonialism had undermined women's traditional leadership roles. This analysis informed the programs that Beendigen offered for abused women and their children. Feminist groups in Thunder Bay and Kenora developed a political stance that was critical of local welfare practices, and they insisted that feminists must have control over services for battered women if those services were to be effective. In Nelson, many feminists resisted becoming involved in service provision because they thought this would diminish the radical potential of feminist politics. Crossroads/ Carrefour organizers did not distinguish between political work and service provision. They operated as a feminist collective but did not always identify themselves as such in the community. Muting the political goals of the transition house was sometimes a strategic decision to solicit support from groups that held negative views of the women's movement and to encourage women who did not identify as feminist to work with the activists. For many women, organizing services was an entry point into the women's movement. Recognition of their political marginalization stimulated a feminist consciousness in many of those who initially believed that they were merely providing care when they became involved in the battered women's shelter movement.

Even if feminists in small towns held diverse political views, they were usually obliged to work with each other because there were fewer political activists in their communities than in larger cities. Women were able to bridge some ideological differences, but in the communities discussed in this book there was no long-term collaboration between Aboriginal women and white women because non-Aboriginal groups did not integrate the impact of colonization into their analysis of violence against women. Improving women's status in Aboriginal communities was the priority of Thunder Bay Anishinabequek and of ONWA. The Aboriginal women's groups collaborated with feminist groups to make their issues known. Even though white feminists supported the Native women's movement, the feminist focus on gender oppression made Aboriginal women's connection to the women's movement tenuous. Although Aboriginal women believed that their work accorded with the goals of the Native rights movement, women had to organize autonomously from men, who argued that women were putting their own needs before the collective goals of indigenous peoples. Alliances with the mainstream women's movement helped Aboriginal women achieve some of their goals, but the Native women's movement did not accept feminist political analyses and strategies that would result in their having to choose between fighting for their rights as women and fighting for their rights as Aboriginal people. Aboriginal women based their activism on their responsibilities to their communities and to their families, and thus they developed strategies to end family violence that healed men as well as women and children.

This book demonstrates that race, class, colonization, and gender relations intertwined in unique ways at the local level, and these intertwinings, in turn, informed local strategies to establish services for abused women. There is still much more to know about the history of the battered women's shelter movement. Following the literature on the women's movement, I began my research at women's centres, assuming them to be the most logical starting places since feminists were the first to politicize wife battering. However, future histories should look beyond feminist groups, too. When Aboriginal community health representatives reported incidents of family violence on reserves, Department of Indian Affairs officials told them not to intervene to help these families because it was not a health issue.[2] In the communities discussed in this book, Aboriginal people were the most significant racialized group, but this is not the case for all rural areas. Examinations of the strategies of women from racialized communities in both urban and rural contexts are needed. It is important to acknowledge that other motivations, such as religion, informed advocacy for battered women; for many, religion and feminism were not incompatible. Finally, more research on the debates within transition houses and on union movements within feminist services will advance the historiography by analyzing how feminists balanced commitment to the movement with their obligations to their employees.

Today, battered women and their children have many places to which they can go. Transition houses offer protection from abusive spouses, programs to help women begin independent lives, and programs for their children. Second-stage housing provides extended counselling and accommodation for women who need longer periods to recover from abuse. Perhaps the greatest accomplishment of the battered women's shelter movement has been the broader acceptance of abuse as a political issue. Although they are proud that they changed attitudes about violence against women, many of the activists whom I interviewed also regretted that the transition houses they established were no longer the feminist services initially envisioned. Rather than emphasizing women's political agency within a comprehensive, equality-based agenda, government discourses on violence portray a fearful victim and promote the criminalization of spousal assault.[3] Provincial and federal governments acknowledge that family violence is an urgent issue, but despite the number of government reports that identify violence against women as a barrier to women's equality, funding for transition houses remains precarious.

In response to the shift toward gender-neutral analysis of family violence, anti-violence activists have adamantly defended analyses of domestic violence that argue that it is fundamentally caused by male domination over women. This has deepened divisions in the battered women's shelter movement. Many activists have not accepted the Aboriginal holistic approach to family violence because they fear it will weaken feminist strategies. Shortly after the completion of the research for *Breaking Free,* Patricia Monture-Angus spoke at a conference on the women's movement in May 1989. She refused to talk exclusively on "violence against women," explaining to the audience of predominantly white women that it forced her to "jump into that 'little box' you created to deal with my life in a way which you defined because you found it convenient."[4] She called this silencing a form of violence. A more recent example demonstrates that it is still difficult for Aboriginal women to speak about family violence at feminist meetings. In 1996, the year of the NAC/CLC Women's March against Poverty, I attended the NAC Annual General Meeting. During the discussion of a resolution demanding that the federal government allocate more resources to end male violence against women, a representative from the Aboriginal women's caucus asked to amend the resolution. The caucus wanted to replace "male violence against women" with "family violence," explaining that it would be easier to mobilize Aboriginal peoples against family violence because naming men created divisions within their communities. Many delegates shouted their disapproval. Silenced, the Aboriginal woman quickly returned to her seat. Struggles with police, politicians, and policy-makers who discredited gender analysis of woman abuse probably informed some advocates' opposition to amending the resolution. Nevertheless, silencing this Aboriginal woman was an assault, too.

Insisting that the women's movement present a more unified voice and an uncomplicated analysis of family violence to governments will not result in policies that redress the multiple and interlocking oppressions reproduced in state practices.[5] This strategy inevitably has pitted women against women, each group vying to have their analysis of violence against women heard so that their services will be funded. Andrea Smith, a co-founder of INCITE! Women of Color Against Violence, argues that the feminist campaign to end violence against women has not recognized that all women will benefit from the adoption of an analysis of violence based on theories of intersectionality, which stress the historical and contemporary differences among women in order to understand how all forms of oppression are interconnected. The mainstream women's movement has accepted that minority groups may need distinctive programs to address their specific needs; however, activists have not given enough consideration to how prioritizing solutions that focus on ending gender oppression ultimately increases inequalities among women. Smith argues that until feminists accept strategies for change based on an analysis of the connections between interpersonal violence and state violence, the dominant feminist analysis of violence against women will continue to ignore the needs of Aboriginal women as well as those of women from other minority groups.[6]

Strategies to end domestic violence will be successful only if they are based on a political praxis that does not posit one claim as more legitimate than another because it might benefit the majority of women. Such a praxis requires constant critical self-reflection to ensure that the analysis integrates various theoretical perspectives on how social inequalities shape women's experiences of violence. Recognizing how feminist services exclude the most marginalized groups of women has been difficult because many activists have taken personally the criticism of systemic inequalities within feminist organizations. Acknowledging the shortcomings of the battered women's shelter movement does not discredit the hard-won achievements of the women who opened the first transition houses. Indeed, their passion and determination should inspire activists who are working to develop inclusive services that will help women and their children live violence-free lives.

Appendix: Interviews

The informed consent forms indicated that if interviewees did not request confidentiality, I would identify them by name in the text of publications. I followed a list of questions, asking activists about how they became involved in the women's movement, their perceptions about violence against women, the services available to women, how they understood feminist service provision, their relationship with local and provincial governments, and their perceptions about volunteer work and government funding. I also asked them to expand on specificities about their community, which I had discovered in my research. The interviews were taped and transcribed and are in the possession of the author.

Alexander, Sally. Interviewed in Crescent Beach, BC, 17 May 2000. Born and raised in West Kootenays. Collective member of *Images*, NDP activist, and co-ordinator of Nelson and District Women's Centre in late 1980s.

Arseneault, Rina. Interviewed in Fredericton, NB, 3 March 2004. Worked in a psychiatric hospital before she left to work as a crisis intervener and public educator at Crossroads for Women/Carrefour pour femmes. Associate director of the Muriel McQueen Fergusson Centre for Family Violence Research.

Baker, Bonnie. Interviewed in Winlaw, BC, 19 May 2000. Born New York City. Active in Montreal Women's Liberation and Vancouver Status of Women. Moved to Nelson in 1974. Active in Nelson and District Women's Centre and collective member of *Images*.

Baril, Joan. Interviewed in Thunder Bay, ON, 11 October 1999. Born Thunder Bay. Founder Thunder Bay Women's Liberation, Northern Women's Centre. Taught women's studies at Confederation College.

Bateman, Bette. Interviewed in Creston, BC, 20 May 2000. Born Vancouver. Lived in Nelson 1976-81. Co-ordinator of Nelson and District Women's Centre, 1977. Organized Rape Crisis Line; ad hoc safe home operator.

Member of British Columbia Federation of Women anti-violence committee.

Boucher, Doreen. Interviewed in Thunder Bay, ON, 3 August 2000. Born Thunder Bay. Became active in women's movement through pro-choice activism in 1969. Active in Northern Women's Centre, Crisis Homes, Inc. Founder of Thunder Bay Sexual Assault Centre, now its executive director.

Cryderman, Brenda. Interviewed in Thunder Bay, ON, 25 July 2000. Born in Thunder Bay. Her first political act was organizing a walk-out in high school. Her first feminist act was delivering a speech at age fifteen about the sexual double standard. Active in Northern Women's Centre and board member of Faye Peterson Transition House.

Dubec, Bernice. Interviewed in Thunder Bay, ON, 26 July 2000. Born in Thunder Bay. Political activism began at Thunder Bay Native Friendship Centre. Active in Thunder Bay Anishinabequek, Ontario Native Women's Association, and Beendigen. Currently executive director of Anishnawbe Mushkiki, Thunder Bay Aboriginal Community Health Centre.

Fels, Julie. Interviewed in Thunder Bay, ON, 22 July 2000. Moved from US to Thunder Bay in 1973. Active in women's movement and civil rights movement in US. In Thunder Bay joined welfare rights organization. Active in Women's Centre, Crisis Homes, Inc. and board member of Faye Peterson Transition House.

Fortier, Marilyn. Interviewed with Joanne Frost in Kenora, ON, 29 October 1999. Born Kenora. Became interested in women's issues in college and was influenced by her sister, who was very political. Original member of Women's Crisis Intervention Project.

Frost, Joanne. Interviewed with Marilyn Fortier in Kenora, ON, 29 October 1999. Born Kenora. Original member of Kenora Women's Crisis Intervention Project. Learned about project through work at Information Referral Centre.

Gallant, Corinne. Interviewed in Moncton, NB, 29 March 2003. Active in Acadian rights movement and women's movement. Professor of philosophy at the Université de Moncton, where she taught the first course on feminism. Helped organize New Brunswick Advisory Council on the Status of Women.

Gautreau, Huberte. Interviewed with Beth McLaughlin, Moncton, NB, 27 March 2003. Worked on women's issues in Africa in the 1970s. Founder of Crossroads for Women/Carrefour pour femmes. Organizer of New Brunswick Committee of the World March of Women against Poverty and Violence (2000) and founder of New Brunswick Coalition for Pay Equity. Recipient of the Governor General's Award in commemoration of the Person's Case 2004.

Gilbeau, Audrey. Interviewed in Thunder Bay, ON, 28 June 2000. Born Longlac, 15th First Nation. Became active in Native women's movement when she was thirteen as a volunteer at the Thunder Bay Native Friendship Centre. Member Thunder Bay Anishinabequek. Former employee at Beendigen.

Holm, Charlotte. Interviewed in Kenora, ON, 22 October 1999. Born Kenora. Joined Kenora Women's Crisis Intervention Project in 1977. Crisis line worker and board member. Member of Decade Council.

Karlstedt, Fiona. Interviewed in Thunder Bay, ON, 26 July 2000. Raised in Thunder Bay. Active in student politics at Lakehead University in the late 1960s. Joined Thunder Bay Women's Liberation. Co-ordinator of Northern Women's Centre in 1980s. Board member of Faye Peterson Transition House.

Luchton, Diane. Interviewed in Nelson, BC, 18 May 2000. Born West Kootenays, but raised in Michigan. Heard about the "woman question" when she was fourteen years of age and started to read Emma Goldman, Simone de Beauvoir, and Betty Friedan. Active in civil rights movement and student movement in the US. Returned to Nelson area in 1969. Joined consciousness-raising groups, founder and former co-ordinator of Nelson and District Women's Centre, and daycare activist.

McLaughlin, Beth. Interviewed with Huberte Gautreau, Moncton, NB, 27 March 2003. Became active in the women's movement while in university. Founder and collective member of Crossroads for Women/Carrefour pour femmes. Environmental activist.

Phillips, Margaret. Interviewed in Thunder Bay, ON, 10 November 1999. Became politically active when she was fifteen, opposing Ottawa's encroachment on rural communities. Moved from Billings Bridge to Kenora in 1960, where she worked as the director of recreation. Moved to Thunder Bay. Founder of Northern Women's Centre, Northern Woman, and the Northern Women's Book Store. Active with the Lakehead Social Planning Council.

Robb, Helene. Interviewed in Moncton, NB, 28 March 2003. Teacher. Collective member of Crossroads for Women/Carrefour pour femmes. Became involved in women's movement while working at the transition house.

Ross, Carol. Interviewed in Nelson, BC, 10 May 2000. Social worker in northern Ontario in 1970s; worked on crisis line, where she became aware that spousal assault and sexual abuse of children were issues that needed more analysis. Moved to Nelson in 1980. Co-ordinator of Nelson and District Women's Centre early 1980s. Founder of the Advocacy Centre.

Saulnier, Yolande. Interviewed in Moncton, NB, 28 March 2003. One of the original crisis interveners at Crossroads for women/Carrefour pour femmes. Has worked there for twenty-three years.

Simpson, Sam. Interviewed in Winlaw, BC, 19 May 2000. Educated at University of Winnipeg, 1965-69. Became active in women's issues in Halifax, 1969-70. Moved from Vancouver to Slocan Valley in 1974 to live rurally. Active in countercultural politics, organizing community centre and alternative school in Winlaw. Collective member of *Images*. Co-ordinator of Nelson and District Women's Centre in late 1980s.

Singbeil, Dianne. Interviewed in Kenora, ON, 4 November 1999. Original member of the Kenora Women's Crisis Intervention Project. Crisis line volunteer and advocate.

Untinen, Leni. Interviewed in Thunder Bay, ON, 13 November 1999. Born Thunder Bay. Became active in feminist politics when she was hired to do needs study for Crisis Homes, Inc. Founder of Faye Peterson Transition House, lobbyist for Decade Council. Awarded honourary doctorate from Lakehead University for her activism against violence against women and her community work.

Worden, Doreen. Interviewed in Kenora, ON, 29 October 1999. Moved to Kenora in 1962, lived in Winnipeg 1976-78. Active in the Winnipeg Lesbian Society. Published *Voices: A Survival Manual for Women* with her partner 1980-86. Active in the Kenora Sexual Assault Centre, where she organized a lesbian support line.

Interview with Shelter Worker. Interviewed in Kenora, ON, 1 November 1999. Interview with Faye Peterson Transition House volunteer. Interviewed in Thunder Bay, ON, 24 July 2000.

Notes

INTRODUCTION

1 In this book, the term "Aboriginal" refers to all people of indigenous ancestry. It is important to acknowledge that the imposed legal distinctions (status Indian and non-status Indian) created tensions among Aboriginal peoples. However, the Native women's groups examined here refused to acknowledge the legal identities and accepted all women with indigenous backgrounds.

2 Moreover, some scholars have argued that the expansion of the battered women's shelter movement into smaller communities made the movement more conservative. For example, Leslie Kenny and Warren Magnusson argue that "as the transition house movement spread from the cities to the suburbs and the outlying towns, its radicalism was muted." Leslie Kenny and Warren Magnusson, "In Transition: The Women's House Saving Action," *Canadian Review of Sociology and Anthropology* 30, 3 (1993): 363. Mariana Valverde argues that the battered women's shelter movement was primarily an urban movement. Mariana Valverde, "A Post-Colonial Women's Law? Domestic Violence and the Ontario Liquor Board's 'Indian List,' 1950-1990," *Feminist Studies* 30, 3 (2004): 566-88.

3 The belief that family violence is primarily a city problem is relatively recent. Joan Sangster argues that in the early twentieth century, social reformers blamed the immoral conditions in the rural "badlands" for the incidence of incest. Joan Sangster, "Masking and Unmasking the Sexual Abuse of Children: Perceptions of Violence against Children in 'the Badlands' of Ontario, 1916-1930," *Journal of Family History* 25, 4 (2000): 504-26.

4 For international perspectives on the battered women's shelter movement, see R. Emerson Dobash and Russell. P. Dobash, *Women, Violence, and Social Change* (London and New York: Routledge, 1992); Martha Albertson Fineman and Roxanne Mykitiuk, ed., *The Public Nature of Private Violence: The Discovery of Domestic Abuse* (London and New York: Routledge, 1994); Susan Schecter, *Women and Male Violence: The Visions and Struggles of the Battered Women's Movement* (Boston: South End Press, 1982).

5 Ruth Roach Pierson, "The Politics of the Body," in *Canadian Women's Issues,* vol. 1: *Strong Voices: Twenty-Five Years of Activism in English Canada,* ed. Ruth Roach Pierson et al. (Toronto: James Lorimer, 1993), 98-122.

6 Feminist newspapers demonstrated a similar focus. I have read *Kinesis* (Vancouver), *Northern Woman* (Thunder Bay), *Images* (Nelson), and *Upstream* (Ottawa). For early feminist discussions of rape, see Noreen Connell and Cassandra Wilson, ed., *Rape: The First Sourcebook for Women by New York Radical Feminists* (New York: Plume, 1974); Susan Brownmiller, *Against Our Will: Men, Women, and Rape* (New York: Simon and Schuster, 1975); Lorenne Clark and Debra Lewis, *Rape: The Price of Coercive Sexuality* (Toronto: Women's Press, 1977).

7 Nancy Adamson, Linda Briskin, and Margaret McPhail, *Feminist Organizing for Change: The Contemporary Women's Movement in Canada* (Toronto: Oxford University Press, 1988).

8   Joan Baril, interview by author, 11 October 1999, Thunder Bay, ON, tape recording.
9   Barbara Freeman, *The Satellite Sex: The Media and Women's Issues in English Canada,
    1966-1971* (Waterloo: Wilfrid Laurier University Press, 2001), 128-30.
10 "But Why Doesn't She Just Leave Him?" *Kinesis* 6, 3 (1977): 1, 3.
11 Linda MacLeod, "Appendix A, Transition Houses by Province across Canada," in *Wife
    Battering in Canada: The Vicious Circle* (Ottawa: Canadian Advisory Council on the Sta-
    tus of Women, 1980), 68.
12 Debra J. Lewis, *A Brief on Wife Battering with Proposals for Federal Action* (Ottawa: Cana-
    dian Advisory Committee on the Status of Women, January 1982), 7.
13 Linda MacLeod, *Battered, but Not Beaten: Preventing Wife Battering in Canada* (Ottawa:
    Canadian Advisory Council on the Status of Women, 1987), 3.
14 Pierson, "The Politics of the Body," 111; House of Commons, *Debates*, 12 May 1982, 17334.
15 In her study of the Toronto campaign for child care in the 1970s and 1980s, Rianne Mahon
    examines the inter-scalar arrangements embedded in social welfare policy. She argues that
    although municipalities were excluded from provincial-federal agreements, Toronto day-
    care activists were able to "jump scales" and organize alternatives to provincial daycare
    schemes based on a liberal residualist model of the social welfare state. Rianne Mahon,
    "Child Care as Citizenship Right? Toronto in the 1970s and 1980s," *Canadian Historical
    Review* 86, 2 (2005): 285-315.
16 Gillian Walker, *Family Violence and the Women's Movement: The Conceptual Politics of
    Struggle* (Toronto: University of Toronto Press, 1990); Sue Findlay, "Facing the State: The
    Politics of the Women's Movement Reconsidered," in *Feminism and Political Economy:
    Women's Work, Women's Struggles*, ed. Heather Jon Maroney and Meg Luxton (Toronto:
    Methuen, 1987), 31-50; Jane Ursel, "Considering the Impact of the Battered Women's
    Movement on the State: The Example of Manitoba," in *The Social Basis of Law: Critical
    Readings in the Sociology of Law*, 2nd ed., ed. Elizabeth Comack and Shelley Brickey (Hal-
    ifax: Garamond, 1991), 261-88; Jan Barnsley, *Feminist Action, Institutional Reaction:
    Responses to Wife Assault* (Vancouver: Women's Research Centre, 1985); Leslie Timmins,
    ed., *Listening to the Thunder: Advocates Talk about the Battered Women's Movement* (Van-
    couver: Women's Research Centre, 1995); Lise Gotell, "A Critical Look at State Discourse
    on 'Violence against Women': Some Implications for Feminist Politics and Women's Cit-
    izenship," in *Women and Political Representation in Canada*, ed. Carol Andrews and
    Manon Tremblay (Ottawa: University of Ottawa Press, 1998), 39-72; Karlene Faith, "State
    Appropriation of Feminist Initiative: Transition House, Vancouver, 1973-1986," in *Seeking
    Shelter: A State of Battered Women*, ed. Karlene Faith and Dawn H. Currie (Vancouver:
    Collective Press, 1993).
17 For an overview of the early literature on family violence, see Wini Breines and Linda
    Gordon, "The New Scholarship on Family Violence," *Signs: Journal of Women in Culture
    and Society* 8, 3 (1983): 490-531.
18 For a discussion of how violence against women is treated in the mainstream media, see
    Sharon D. Stone, "Getting the Message Out: Feminists, the Press and Violence against
    Women," *Canadian Review of Sociology and Anthropology* 30, 3 (1993): 377-400.
19 National Film Board, *Loved, Honoured, and Abused*, 1980; National Film Board, *A Safe
    Distance*, 1986; National Film Board, *The Next Step*, 1986; Sylvia Hamilton, *No More
    Secrets: A Two Part Series on Violence against Black Women*, Maroon Films, 1999.

20 Timmins, *Listening to the Thunder*; Fern Martin, *A Narrow Doorway: Women's Stories of Escape from Abuse* (Burnston, ON: General Store Publishing House, 1996); Mary Lou Stirling et al., *Understanding Abuse: Partnering for Change* (Toronto: University of Toronto Press, 2004). The Alliance of Research Centres on Family Violence have also produced important participatory action studies that highlight the regional variations in services and women's and girls experiences of violence. The five centres are FREDA Centre for Research on Violence against Women and Children (BC and Yukon), http://www.harbour.sfu.ca/freda/; RESOLVE Research (Prairie region), http://www.umanitoba.ca/resolve/; London Centre for Research on Violence against Women and Children (Ontario), http://www.crvawc.ca/; Le Centre de recherche interdisciplinaire sur la violence familiale et la violence faite aux femmes (Quebec), http://www.criviff.qc.ca/; and the Muriel McQueen Fergusson Centre for Family Violence Research (Atlantic Canada), http://www.unbf.ca/arts/CFVR/.

21 Linda Gordon, *Heroes of Their Own Lives: The Politics and History of Family Violence, Boston 1880-1960* (New York: Penguin Books, 1989), 3.

22 Constance Backhouse, *Petticoats and Prejudice: Women and the Law in Nineteenth-Century Canada* (Toronto: The Women's Press, 1991); Elizabeth Pleck, *Domestic Tyranny: The Making of Social Policy against Family Violence from Colonial Times to the Present* (New York: Oxford University Press, 1987); David Peterson del Mar, *What Trouble I've Seen: A History of Violence against Wives* (Cambridge: Harvard University Press, 1996); Karen Dubinsky, *Improper Advances: Rape and Heterosexual Conflict in Ontario, 1880-1929* (Chicago: University of Chicago Press, 1993); Joan Sangster, *Regulating Girls and Women: Sexuality, Family, and the Law in Ontario, 1920-1960* (Toronto: Oxford University Press, 2001).

23 Erin Pizzey, *Scream Quietly or the Neighbours Will Hear* (Harmondsworth, Middlesex: Penguin Books, 1974). Pizzey was not a feminist, but her book was influential. Elizabeth Pleck argues that her marriage to a prominent BBC reporter gave her access to the media. Pleck, *Domestic Tyranny*, 188. Pizzey's opposition to feminist analysis in Women's Aid created a rift in the National Women's Aid Federation. See National Women's Aid Federation, *Battered Women: Refuges and Women's Aid* (London: The Federation, 1977).

24 Nancy Adamson, "Feminists, Libbers, and Radicals: The Emergence of the Women's Liberation Movement," in *A Diversity of Women: Ontario 1945-1980*, ed. Joy Parr (Toronto: University of Toronto Press, 1995), 252-80; Pierson et al., *Canadian Women's Issues*; Adamson, Briskin, and McPhail, *Feminist Organizing for Change*.

25 Findlay, "Facing the State"; Alicia Schreader, "The State Funded Women's Movement: A Case of Two Political Agendas," in *Community Organization and the Canadian State*, ed. Roxana Ng, Gillian Walker, and Jacob Muller (Toronto: Garamond Press, 1990), 184-99.

26 Walker, *Family Violence and the Women's Movement*. See also Barnsley, *Feminist Action, Institutional Reaction*; Marina Helen Morrow, "Feminist Anti-Violence Activism: Organizing for Change," in *Reclaiming the Future: Women's Strategies for the 21st Century*, ed. Somer Brodrib (Charlottetown: Gynergy Books, 1999), 237-58. For the American case, see Schecter, *Women and Male Violence*.

27 Cindy Katz, foreword to *RePlacing Citizenship: AIDS Activism and Radical Democracy*, by Michael P. Brown (New York: Guilford Press, 1997), x.

28 Cited in Walker, *Family Violence and the Women's Movement*, 65. For other discussions of the term "family violence" see Barnsley, *Feminist Action, Institutional Reaction*, and Jan Forde, "True North, True Solutions?" in *Listening to the Thunder*, 93-108.

29 For an analysis of how the adversarial debates between "violence against women" advocates and "family violence" advocates played out in one community, see Ruth M. Mann, *Who Owns Domestic Abuse? The Local Politics of a Social Problem* (Toronto: University of Toronto Press, 2000).

30 For a critique of strategic investments in maintaining established theories and truths about violence against women, see Janice L. Ristock, *No More Secrets: Violence in Lesbian Relationships* (New York: Routledge, 2002).

31 Patricia A. Monture-Okanee, "The Violence We Women Do: A First Nations View," in *Challenging Times: The Women's Movement in Canada and the United States*, ed. Constance Backhouse and David H. Flaherty (Montreal and Kingston: McGill-Queen's University Press, 1992), 193-200; Caroline Lachapelle, "Beyond Barriers: Native Women and the Women's Movement," in *Still Ain't Satisfied: Canadian Feminism Today*, ed. Maureen Fitzgerald, Connie Guberman, and Margie Wolfe (Toronto: Women's Press, 1982), 257-64.

32 Lee Maracle, *I Am Woman: A Native Perspective on Sociology and Feminism* (Vancouver: Press Gang Publishers, 1996), 18.

33 Sarita Srivastava, "'Immigrant Women' Meet 'Canadian' Feminism: Transnational Encounters Multiculturalism" (paper presented at Rethinking Women and Gender Studies: Transnational Conditions and Possibilities, a Colloqium at the University of Toronto, Toronto, ON, 28-30 September 2006).

34 I have followed Jo-Anne Fiske's criteria for assessing scholarship on Aboriginal women: whether scholarly agendas have paid attention to Aboriginal women's self-definitions and agendas; how these agendas have been presented in scholarly studies; how non-Aboriginal scholars have responded to Aboriginal women's critiques of feminist discourses and political agendas; and how Aboriginal women have adopted or resisted feminism. Jo-Anne Fiske, "By, For, or About? Shifting Directions in the Representations of Aboriginal Women," *Atlantis* 25, 1 (2000): 12.

35 Benita Roth, *Separate Roads to Feminism: Black, Chicana, and White Feminist Movements in America's Second Wave* (Cambridge: Cambridge University Press, 2004), 3.

36 Suzanne Morton argues that studying women's understanding of regional disparity and community will help us move beyond the underdevelopment model that has dominated Canadian regional history. Suzanne Morton, "Gender, Place, and Region: Thoughts on the State of Women in Atlantic Canadian History," *Atlantis* 25, 1 (2000): 119-28. For a discussion of the impact of the metropolis-hinterland thesis on Canadian sociological discussions of social movements, see William K. Carroll, "Social Movements and Counterhegemony: Canadian Contexts and Social Theories," in *Organizing Dissent: Contemporary Social Movements in Theory and Practice*, 2nd ed., ed. William Carroll (Toronto: Garamond Press, 1997), 3-38.

37 Christopher Walmsley, *Protecting Aboriginal Children* (Vancouver: UBC Press, 2005), 14.

38 Patricia Monture-Angus, "A Vicious Circle: Child Welfare and the First Nations," *Canadian Journal of Women and the Law* 3, 1 (1989): 1-17.

39 ONWA, *Breaking Free: A Proposal for Change to Aboriginal Family Violence* (Thunder Bay: The Association, 1989). For an overview of the historical context that informs the theorization of family violence in Aboriginal communities, see Anne McGillivray and Brenda Comaskey, *Black Eyes All of the Time: Intimate Violence, Aboriginal Women, and the Justice System* (Toronto: University of Toronto Press, 1999), 22-52.

40 For Aboriginal women's concerns about the criminal justice system, see McGillivray and Comaskey, *Black Eyes All of the Time*. For critiques of feminist strategies for ending

woman abuse that explain why they do not work in minority communities and immigrant communities, see Himani Bannerji, "A Question of Silence: Reflections on Violence against Women in Communities of Colour," in *Scratching the Surface: Canadian Anti-Racist Feminist Thought*, ed. Enakshi Dua and Angela Robertson (Toronto: Women's Press, 1999), 261-77; Sherene Razack, "Domestic Violence as Gender Persecution: Policing the Borders of the Nation, Race, and Gender," *Canadian Journal of Women and the Law* 8, 1 (1995): 45-88; Dianne L. Martin and Janet E. Mosher, "Unkept Promises: Experiences of Immigrant Women with the Neo-Criminalization of Wife Abuse," *Canadian Journal of Women and the Law* 8, 1 (1995): 3-44; Karen Flynn and Charmine Crawford, "Committing 'Race Treason': Battered Women and Mandatory Arrest in Toronto's Caribbean Community," in *Unsettling Truths: Battered Women, Policy, Politics, and Contemporary Research in Canada*, ed. Kevin D. Bonnycastle and George S. Rigakos (Vancouver: Collective Press, 1998), 91-102. On racism in the shelters, see Vijay Agnew, *In Search of a Safe Place: Abused Women and Culturally Sensitive Services* (Toronto: University of Toronto Press, 1998).

41 Bonnie Murray and Cathy Welch, "Attending to Lavender Bruises: A Dialogue on Violence in Lesbian Relationships," in *Listening to the Thunder*, 113.

42 Ristock, *No More Secrets*, x.

43 Becki L. Ross, *The House That Jill Built: A Lesbian Nation in Formation* (Toronto: University of Toronto Press, 1995).

44 M. Julia Creet, "A Test of Unity: Lesbian Visibility in the British Columbia Federation of Women," in *Lesbians in Canada*, ed. Sharon Dale Stone (Toronto: Between the Lines, 1990), 183-97.

45 Some issues from 1981 are in the Vancouver Status of Women Collection at the University of British Columbia Library, Rare Books and Special Collections, Vancouver Status of Women Papers, Box 33, File 40.

46 Doreen Worden, interview by author, 29 October 1999, Kenora, ON, tape recording.

47 The heated debates about June Callwood's resignation from the board of Nellie's in 1990 after staff members raised the issue of racism in the shelter brought this issue to the foreground. For a discussion of this incident, see Sarita Srivistava, "'You're Calling Me a Racist?' The Moral and Emotional Regulation of Antiracism and Feminism," *Signs: Journal of Women in Culture and Society* 31, 1 (2005): 37-38.

48 For example, see the analysis of the contentious labour relations at Byrony House in Halifax in Maureen MacDonald, "Chalk One up for Sisterhood," *New Maritimes: A Regional Magazine of Culture and Politics* 13, 6 (1995): 4-14, 17.

49 Meg Luxton, "Feminism as a Class Act: Working-Class Feminism and the Women's Movement," *Labour/Le Travail* 48 (2001): 64.

50 In 1985 and 1986, the organizers listed the occupations of the clients and abusers, but they did not provide a statistical breakdown. Crossroads for Women/Carrefour pour femmes Records, Filing Cabinet, "Statistics" File.

51 Marjorie Griffin Cohen, "The Canadian Women's Movement," in *Canadian Women's Issues*, 3.

52 Ibid.

53 The literature on the ethical responsibilities of oral historians and the critical analysis of the nature of the evidence gleaned from interviews guides my interpretation of the oral histories. See Joan Sangster, "Telling Our Stories: Feminist Debates and the Use of Oral History," *Women's History Review* 3, 1 (1994): 5-28; Robert Perks and Alistair Thompson,

ed., *The Oral History Reader* (New York: Routledge, 1998); Julie Cruikshank, "Oral Tradition and Oral History: Reviewing Some Issues," *Canadian Historical Review* 75, 3 (1994): 403-18.

54 This observation is based on a question Katherine McKenna asked me when I presented my research at the 82nd Annual Meeting of the Canadian Historical Association, Halifax, May 2003.

55 Informants decided whether or not they wanted anonymity. Most activists wanted to be named in the text.

56 Adamson et al., *Feminist Organizing for Change*, 256-62; Judy Rebick, *Ten Thousand Roses: The Making of a Feminist Revolution* (Toronto: Penguin, 2005): 116-24.

57 Angela Davis, "Women, Punishment and Globalization," Vancouver, BC, 12 February 2000. The Vancouver Status of Women organized the lecture. Davis made this comment in response to a question from a person in the audience.

58 Ruth Lister, *Citizenship: Feminist Perspectives* (London: Macmillan Publishers, 1997), 39.

CHAPTER 1: BEENDIGEN, 1972-89

Parts of this chapter were previously published in *American Indian Quarterly* 27, 3/4 (2003): 548-65.

1 "Anishinabequek" means "woman" in Ojibwa and was a common name for ONWA locals.

2 For a discussion of women's resistance to the commonly held view that Aboriginal identity could not exist in cities, see Evelyn J. Peters, "Subversive Spaces: First Nations Women and the City," *Environment and Planning D: Society and Space* 16, 6 (1998): 665-85.

3 "Anduhyaun" means "our home." The shelter still operates in its original location and is one of the oldest shelters in Canada.

4 Catherine Jan Freedman, "Anduhyaun: A Toronto Residence for Canadian Indian Girls Migrating to the City for Retraining" (master's thesis, York University, 1974), 51. Freedman criticizes Aboriginal activists because they accepted money but refused "valuable cooperation from interested members of the White community." Freedman, "Anduhyaun," 51.

5 This continues to be a divisive debate in Aboriginal communities. On the tension between collective and individual rights, see Sharon Donna McIvor, "Self-Government and Aboriginal Women," in *Scratching the Surface: Canadian Anti-Racist Feminist Thought*, ed. Enakshi Dua and Angela Robertson (Toronto: Women's Press, 1999), 167-86; Val Napoleon, "Aboriginal Self-Determination: Individual Self and Collective Selves," *Atlantis* 29, 2 (2005): 31-45.

6 For discussions of the history of the campaign to change the Indian Act, see Janet Silman, *Enough Is Enough: Aboriginal Women Speak Out* (Toronto: Women's Press, 1987); Sally Weaver, "First Nations Women and Government Policy, 1970-1992: Discrimination and Conflict," in *Changing Patterns: Women in Canada*, ed. Sandra Burt, Lorraine Code, and Lindsay Dorney (Toronto: McClelland and Stewart, 1993). There is a growing literature on contemporary Aboriginal women's community activism. See Kim Anderson and Bonita Lawrence, *Strong Women Stories: Native Vision and Community Survival* (Toronto: Sumach Press, 2003); Bonita Lawrence and Kim Anderson, ed., Special issue: "Indigenous Women: The State of Our Nations," *Atlantis* 29, 2 (2005).

7 Dori Pelletier, one of the founders of Beendigen, met with the organizers of Faye Peterson Transition House in 1979 to give them advice about the transition house that they

were planning. Faye Peterson Transition House (FPTH), "Back Logs and Files 1977-85" Box, "Interviews" File, "Interview – Dori Pelletier," 1979.

8 The administrative assistant did not think that there were many documents from Beendigen's early years because the activists did not keep records. Older records are stored in a storage unit that is not on-site, and I was not given permission to access those records.

9 Himani Bannerji, "Politics and the Writing of History," in *Nation, Empire, Colony: Historicizing Gender and Race*, ed. Ruth Roach Pierson and Nupur Chauduri (Bloomingdale: Indiana University Press, 1998), 287-301. For a critical discussion of diversity, see the chapter "The Paradox of Diversity: The Construction of a Multicultural Canada and 'Women of Colour,'" in Bannerji's *The Dark Side of the Nation: Essays on Multiculturalism, Nationalism, and Gender* (Toronto: Canadian Scholar's Press, 2000), 15-61.

0 Noel Dyck, *What Is the Indian "Problem"? Tutelage and Resistance in Canadian Indian Administration* (St. John's: The Institute of Social and Economic Research, 1991).

1 Royal Commission on Aboriginal Peoples, *Aboriginal Peoples in Urban Centres: Report on the National Round Table on Aboriginal Urban Issues* (Ottawa: Ministry of Supply and Services, 1993). James S. Frideres, "Aboriginal Urbanization," in *Aboriginal Peoples in Canada: Contemporary Conflicts*, 5th ed., ed. James S. Frideres (Scarborough: Prentice Hall, Allyn, and Bacon Canada, 1998), 235-56; Calvin Hanselmann, *Urban Aboriginal People in Western Canada: Realities and Policies* (Calgary: Canada West Foundation, September 2001).

2 In 1986, 32.8 percent of status women and 26.4 percent of status men lived off-reserve. Lilianne Ernestine Krosenbingk-Gelissen, "The Native Women's Association of Canada," in *Aboriginal Peoples in Canada*, 302.

3 Frideres, "Aboriginal Urbanization."

4 Royal Commission on the Status of Women in Canada, *Report of the Royal Commission on the Status of Women* (Ottawa: Information Canada, 1970), 238.

5 Edgar J. Dosman, *Indians: The Urban Dilemma* (Toronto: McClelland and Stewart, 1972).

6 Hugh Shewell, *"Enough to Keep Them Alive": Indian Welfare in Canada, 1873-1965* (Toronto: University of Toronto Press, 2004), 261.

7 Ibid., 258.

8 Andrew Armitage, *Comparing the Policy of Aboriginal Assimilation: Australia, Canada, and New Zealand* (Vancouver: UBC Press, 1995), 115.

9 Armitage, *Comparing the Policy of Aboriginal Assimilation*; Elizabeth Fournier and Ernie Crey, *Stolen from Our Embrace: The Abduction of First Nations Children and the Restoration of Aboriginal Communities* (Vancouver: Douglas and McIntyre, 1997); Christopher Walmsley, *Protecting Aboriginal Children* (Vancouver: UBC Press, 2005). For a discussion of the transfer of responsibility for child and family services to the First Nations community, see Peter Hudson and Sharon Taylor-Henley, "First Nations Child and Family Services, 1982-1992: Facing the Realities," *Canadian Social Work Review* 11, 1 (1994): 89-102.

0 Harold Cardinal, *The Unjust Society: The Tragedy of Canada's Indians* (Edmonton: M.G. Hurtig, 1969); George Manuel and Michael Posluns, *The Fourth World: An Indian Reality* (Don Mills: Collier-Macmillan Canada, 1974).

21 H.B. Hawthorn, *A Survey of the Contemporary Indians of Canada*, vol. 1 (Ottawa: Indian Affairs Branch, 1966). On the shortcomings of welfare policy, see chapter 15. On the importance of resolving jurisdictional disputes and including Aboriginal leaders in these discussions, see chapter 17.

22 Dyck, *What Is the Indian "Problem"?* especially chapter 7; J.R. Miller, *Skyscrapers Hide the Heavens: A History of Indian-White Relations in Canada* (Toronto: University of Toronto Press, 1991), 225-29.

23 For a discussion of the development of the White Paper and Native leaders' effective opposition to it, see Sally M. Weaver, *Making Canadian Indian Policy: The Hidden Agenda 1968-1970* (Toronto: University of Toronto Press, 1981).

24 Indian Chiefs of Alberta, *Citizens Plus* (Edmonton: Indian Association of Alberta, 1970), 1.

25 Ibid., 2.

26 Peters argues that although it was detrimental to off-reserve populations, Aboriginal organizations chose to focus on land-based self-government to concentrate their priorities. Evelyn J. Peters, "Geographies of Aboriginal Self-Government," in *Aboriginal Self-Government in Canada: Current Trends and Issues,* ed. John H. Hylton (Saskatoon: Purich Publishing, 1994), 163-79.

27 Kathleen Jamieson, *Indian Women and the Law in Canada: Citizens Minus* (Ottawa: Advisory Council on the Status of Women, April 1978).

28 Silman, *Enough Is Enough,* especially chapter 3; Mary Two-Axe Early, "'The Least Members of Our Society': The Mohawk Women of Caghnawaga," *Canadian Woman Studies/ Les cahiers de la femme* 11, 2 (1980): 64.

29 In 1971, Jeanette Corbière Lavell and Yvonne Bedard, from the Wikwemikong Band and the Six Nations Reserve respectively, challenged the sexual discrimination in the Indian Act through court action. In 1973, the Supreme Court of Canada ruled against them, arguing that the Canadian Bill of Rights did not supersede the Indian Act. Four years later, Sandra Lovelace of the Tobique Reserve filed a complaint against the Canadian government with the United Nations Human Rights Committee. On 30 July 1981, the committee ruled that the Canadian government was in breach of the International Covenant on Civil and Political Rights. The Canadian government's response was slow because it did not want to anger Aboriginal leaders. Initially, they allowed individual bands to request that subsection 12(1)(b) did not apply to them.

30 The federal government repealed subsection 12(1)(b) in 1985 when it passed Bill C-31 to comply with its obligations to the Charter of Rights and Freedoms, which was passed in 1982. Although the legislation reinstated the status of women who had lost theirs under subsection 12(1)(b) and recognized band control over band membership, it did not meet Native women's demand for the full and equal restoration of the rights of all people of Native heritage. For a detailed discussion of the constitutional debates, see Sally Weaver, "First Nations Women and Government Policy, 1970-1992: Discrimination and Conflict," in *Changing Patterns: Women in Canada,* ed. Sandra Burt, Lorraine Code, and Lindsay Dorney (Toronto: McClelland and Stewart, 1993), 92-150. For analysis of the impact of Bill C-31 on women, see Joan Holmes, *Bill C-31: Equality or Disparity? The Effects of the New Indian Act on Native Women* (Ottawa: Canadian Advisory Council on the Status of Women, March 1987) and Audrey Huntley and Fay Blaney, *Bill C-31: Its Impact, Implications and Recommendations for Change in British Columbia – Final Report* (Vancouver: Aboriginal Women's Action Network, 1999).

31 Harold Cardinal, *The Rebirth of Canada's Indians* (Edmonton: Hurtig Publishers, 1977), 107-15; Two-Axe Early, "'The Least Members of Our Society.'"

32 Archives of Ontario (AO), RG 68, Series 6, Box 5, File 7151-1, "Native People in Northern Ontario: A Demographic Profile, Ministry of Northern Affairs," December 1981.

33 Bernice Dubec, interview by author, 26 July 2000, Thunder Bay, ON, tape recording.

34 Cardinal, *The Unjust Society*, chapter 6.

35 For discussions of the various contributions Aboriginal women made to the construction of urban Aboriginal communities and organizations, see Special issue: "Keeping the Campfires Going: Urban American Indian Women's Activism," *American Indian Quarterly* 27, 3 and 4 (2003), ed. Susan Applegate Krouse and Heather Howard-Bobiwash. Two articles in this issue discuss the importance of certain family homes as known gathering places for Aboriginal people and women's role in community centres: Susan Lobo, "Urban Clan Mothers: Key Households in Cities," 505-22, and Heather Howard-Bobiwash, "Women's Class Strategies as Activism in Native Community Building in Toronto, 1950-1975," 566-82.

36 Audrey Gilbeau, interview by author, 28 July 2000, Thunder Bay, ON, tape recording.

37 Terry Simard and Mary Liljestrom, comp., *Ontario Native Women's Association Resource Manual*,(Thunder Bay: ONWA, August 1977), 2.

38 Gilbeau, interview by author.

39 For a discussion of how Aboriginal women struggle to use indigenous teachings to counter their disempowerment by western patriarchal legislation and policies, see Kim Anderson, *A Recognition of Being: Reconstructing Native Womanhood* (Toronto: Second Story Press, 2000), especially chapter 2. She explains that this has been particularly difficult for women who live in cities because their connection to the land is more tenuous and because the urban traditional movement has been shaped by the pan-Indian movement, which combines many traditional teachings. Anderson argues that it is important to question how indigenous traditions have been framed in western patriarchy. See also Emma Laroque, "The Colonization of a Native Woman Scholar," in *Women and the First Nations: Power, Wisdom, and Strength*, ed. Christine Miller and Patricia Chuchryk (Winnipeg: University of Manitoba Press, 1996), 11-18. For a discussion of the importance of the traditional movement that is critical of those who misinterpret traditions, see Lee Maracle, *I Am Woman: A Native Perspective on Sociology and Feminism* (Vancouver: Press Gang Publishers, 1996), 36-42.

40 Simard and Liljestrom, *Ontario Native Women's Association Resource Manual*, 1977.

41 Ibid., 2.

42 For a discussion of the roles and responsibilities of women, see the special issue on Aboriginal women of *Canadian Woman Studies/Les Cahiers de la femme* 11, 2 (1980).

43 Ontario Native Women's Association (ONWA) Records, Board of Directors Meeting Minutes, 1972-89, Minutes 5 July 1972.

44 ONWA Records, "By-Laws #3 & #4" File, "ONWA By-Law #4, Article XXXI, Code of Ethics." At the first annual assembly of the Native Women's Association of Canada, delegates passed a motion defining a Native person as one "who is a descendant of the original inhabitants of this country, now known as Indian (Status and Treaty), non-Status, Metis, and Inuit." ONWA Records, "1st Annual Assembly" File, Minutes of the 1974 Annual Assembly of the Native Women's Association of Canada, 22-25 August 1974.

45 Reflecting on how Native women's goals were misconstrued by white audiences, Mary Ellen Turpel writes, "Equality is not an important political or social concept." Mary Ellen Turpel (Aki-Kwe), "Patriarchy and Paternalism: The Legacy of the Canadian State for First Nations Women," *Canadian Journal of Women and the Law* 6, 1 (1993): 179.

46 *ONWA Resource Manual* (Thunder Bay: The Association, 1981), cover.

47   Joan A. Weibel-Orlando, "Introduction," Special issue: "Keeping the Campfires Going: Urban American Indian Women's Activism," *American Indian Quarterly* 27, 3 and 4 (2003): 500.

48   For a discussion of the media's role in reshaping Aboriginal women's arguments, see Barbara M. Freeman, *The Satellite Sex: The Media and Women's Issues in English Canada, 1966-1971* (Waterloo: Wilfrid Laurier University Press, 2001), chapter 8.

49   Caroline Lachapelle, "Beyond Barriers: Native Women and the Women's Movement," in *Still Ain't Satisfied: Canadian Feminism Today*, ed. Maureen Fitzgerald, Connie Guberman, and Margie Wolfe (Toronto: Women's Press, 1982), 257-64.

50   Kathleen Jamieson, "Multiple Jeopardy: The Evolution of a Native Women's Movement," *Atlantis* 4, 2 (1979): 157-78.

51   Dubec, interview by author.

52   Ibid.

53   University of Ottawa Special Collections, Lisa Bengtsson Fonds, Box 276, "Thunder Bay Anishinabequek" File, "Evaluation of Native Women's Festival," 1975.

54   Dubec, interview by author. Anishinabequek's extensive list of social, fundraising, and social service activities were outlined in Simard and Liljestrom, *Ontario Native Women's Association Resource Manual*, 1977.

55   "Regional Report: Thunder Bay Anishinabequek," *Northern Woman* 2, 3 (1975), reprinted in *Canadian Women's Issues*, vol. 1: *Strong Voices: Twenty-Five Years of Activism in English Canada*, ed. Ruth Roach Pierson et al. (Toronto: James Lorimer, 1993), 60.

56   Studies by the Housing Committee of the Lakehead Social Planning Council (LSPC) found a severe shortage of affordable housing in Thunder Bay. Lakehead Social Planning Council "Brief to the Advisory Task Force on Housing Policy, February 1973," *Briefs, Statements, Presentations, etc.* (Thunder Bay: The Council, 1973-83); "Presentation to the Meeting of the Ontario Cabinet, 14 May 1975," *Briefs, Statements, Presentations, etc.* (Thunder Bay: The Council, 1973-83).

57   Gilbeau, interview by author.

58   For example, in a rare discussion of women, the Hawthorn report explains that Aboriginal women's resignation to poverty manifested in a "slatternly" appearance. It then states that this resignation explains why violence is so prevalent in Aboriginal communities and that law enforcement officials tend to ignore much of the violence. Hawthorn, *A Survey of Contemporary Indians in Canada*, vol. 1, 62.

59   It is not known how many Aboriginal women used the service because Community Residences did not keep accurate records. Lakehead Social Planning Council, *Breaking Point: An Evaluation of Community Residences of the Thunder Bay City Social Services* (Thunder Bay, May 1979), 33.

60   Beendigen Records, Fort William Reserve (BR), Board of Directors Meeting, 11 May 1978; FPTH, "Interview – Dori Pelletier," 1979.

61   Dubec, interview by author.

62   BR, "Supplementary Letter of Patent" File, "Application for Incorporation," May 1978; "Beendigen Proposal for Funding," 1978.

63   Dubec, interview by author; BR, "Incorporation History" File, Colborne and Tomlinson to Department of National Revenue, 27 June 1978; Colborne and Tomlinson to Registrar Charitable Organizations, 5 January 1979.

64 The Canada Works grant was $45,203; the secretary of state grant was $4,397. BR, "Incorporation History" File, "Final Report to Secretary of State," 4 December 1978 to 26 January 1979; "Secretary of State Project Income and Expenses," 1 May 1978 to 1 December 1978.

65 FPTH, "Interview – Dori Pelletier."

66 Anne McGillivray and Brenda Comaskey, *Black Eyes All of the Time: Intimate Violence, Aboriginal Women, and the Justice System* (Toronto: University of Toronto Press, 1999), 45; Miller, *Skyscrapers Hide the Heavens*, 233-36.

67 BR, "Beendigen Proposal for Funding," 1978.

68 Both Gilbeau and Dubec remembered opposition to Beendigen on the grounds that it targeted Aboriginal woman.

69 Gilbeau, interview by author. For a critique of empathy in feminist organizing that examines how expressions of empathy obscure unequal power relations, see Sarita Srivastava, "'You're Calling Me a Racist?' The Moral and Emotional Regulation of Antiracism and Feminism," *Signs: Journal of Women in Culture and Society* 31, 1 (2005): 15-16.

70 Dubec, interview by author. For other discussions of the negative impact of child apprehension that are based on personal experiences, see Tamara Kulusic, "The Ultimate Betrayal: Claiming and Re-Claiming Cultural Identity," *Atlantis* 29, 2 (2005): 23-30; Shandra Spears, "Strong Spirit, Fractured Identity: An Ojibway Adoptee's Journey to Wholeness," in *Strong Women Stories: Native Vision and Community Survival*, ed. Kim Anderson and Bonita Lawrence (Toronto: Sumach Press, 2003), 81-94.

71 Andrew Armitage argues that the transfer of responsibility of services for Aboriginal children to the provinces was more disruptive than the residential school system because although children in the residential schools were isolated from their families and forced to disclaim their ancestry, they were surrounded by their peers and siblings. More important, residential school students knew that they would return to their parents for annual visits and when they finished school. Child apprehension practices terminated the relationship between First Nations Aboriginal children and their parents and, more often than not, separated siblings. See Armitage, *Comparing the Policy of Aboriginal Assimilation*, 120-21; Patricia Monture-Angus, "A Vicious Circle: Child Welfare and the First Nations," *Canadian Journal of Women and the Law* 3, 1 (1989): 1-17.

72 BR, "Beendigen Inc. History" File, "Crisis Home," n.d.

73 BR, "Beendigen Proposal for Funding," 5.

74 Ibid., 14.

75 Northwestern Ontario Women's Centre Archives (NWCA), Margaret Phillips, *Transition House Services in Northwestern Ontario*" (Thunder Bay: Northwestern Ontario Decade Council, July 1984), 3, 9.

76 If there was space at Beendigen, non-Aboriginal women could stay there when Faye Peterson Transition House was full.

77 Gilbeau, interview by author.

78 For example, Aboriginal women organized Kaushee's Place in Whitehorse, Yukon, in 1975. When white women joined the project, they refused to adhere to Aboriginal women's theories of violence and adopted a violence against women framework instead. Audrey McLaughlin, *Kaushee's Place: Yukon Women's Transition House: Final Report of a Three Year Demonstration Project* (Whitehorse: Kaushee's Place, 1983). For a discussion of one

activist's defence of adopting a gender-based analysis of male violence against women at Kaushee's Place, see Jan Forde, "True North, True Solutions?" in *Listening to the Thunder: Advocates Talk about the Battered Women's Movement,* ed. Leslie Timmins (Vancouver: Women's Research Centre, 1995), 93-108.

79 ONWA, *Breaking Free: A Proposal for Change to Aboriginal Family Violence* (Thunder Bay: The Association, 1989). Patricia Monture-Okanee's criticism of feminist definitions of violence against women that focused exclusively on gender and of the marginalization of First Nations women's analysis of family violence were a response to this report. Patricia A. Monture-Okanee, "The Violence We Women Do: A First Nations View," in *Challenging Times: The Women's Movement in Canada and the United States,* ed. Constance Backhouse and David H. Flaherty (Montreal and Kingston: McGill-Queen's University Press, 1992), 193-200.

80 ONWA, *Breaking Free,* 9.

81 Ibid., ii.

82 Monture-Okanee, "The Violence We Women Do," 199.

83 ONWA, *Breaking Free,* 43-49.

84 Ibid., 71.

85 Gilbeau, interview by author.

86 Dian Million, "Telling Secrets: Sex, Power and Narratives in the Social Construction of Indian Residential School Histories." Unpublished paper presented at "What Difference Does Nation Make?" Canadian/American Cultures of Sexuality and Consumption, The Weatherhead Centre for International Affairs and the Department of Women's Studies, Harvard University, 10 March 1999. A revised version of this paper is published in *Canadian Woman Studies/Les cahiers de la femme* 20, 2 (2000): 92-104.

87 For a discussion of maternal discourses in First Nations women's organizing, see Jo-Anne Fiske, "The Womb Is to the Nation as the Heart Is to the Body: Ethnopolitical Discourses of Canadian Indigenous Women's Movement," *Studies in Political Economy* 51 (1996): 65-95.

88 Claude Denis, *We Are Not You: First Nations and Modernity* (Peterborough: Broadview Press, 1997), 111.

89 Bonita Lawrence and Kim Anderson argue that articulations of sovereignty that prioritize "'sovereignty' (men's concerns) [over] 'community healing' (women's concerns)" are not useful because they fail to recognize that gender discrimination has been central to colonization. Bonita Lawrence and Kim Anderson, "Introduction to 'Indigenous Women: The State of Our Nations,'" *Atlantis* 29, 2 (2005): 1-8.

90 Andrea Smith, *Conquest: Sexual Violence and American Indian Genocide* (Boston: South End Books, 2005).

91 Maracle, *I Am Woman*; Patricia Monture-Angus, *Thunder in My Soul: A Mohawk Woman Speaks* (Halifax: Fernwood, 1995); Grace J.M.W. Ouellette, *The Fourth World: An Indigenous Perspective on Feminism and Aboriginal Women's Activism* (Halifax: Fernwood, 2004).

92 Kimberle Crenshaw, "Mapping the Margins: Intersectionality, Identity Politics and Violence against Women of Color," *Stanford Law Review* 43, 6 (1991): 1241-99; Smith, *Conquest.*

93 Bonita Lawrence, *The Exclusion of Survivors' Voices in Feminist Discourse on Violence against Women* (Ottawa: Canadian Research Institute for the Advancement of Women, 1996), 24. For a discussion of the struggles with government and traditional service agencies, see Gillian Walker, *Family Violence and the Women's Movement: The Conceptual Politics of Struggle* (Toronto: University of Toronto Press, 1990).

94 Lawrence, *The Exclusion of Survivors' Voices,* 21.

CHAPTER 2: FAYE PETERSON TRANSITION HOUSE, 1972-85

1 Archives of Ontario (AO), RG 29, Series 45, Box 4, "Design for Development – Northwestern Ontario" File, "Ontario's Regional Planning Program," n.d. For criticism of the province's regional plans, see AO, RG 29, Series 45, Box 11, "Lakehead Social Planning Council" File, "Initial Statements of Concern Relating to the Throne Speech," 1974. For the province's response, see AO, RG 29, Series 45, Box 14, "Social Planning – Research Branch Proposal"; AO, RG 29, Series 45, Box 14, "Planning for Social Planning – Thunder Bay District," November 1974.

2 Lakehead Social Planning Council (LSPC), "Critique of Northwestern Ontario: Strategy for Development, Ministry of Treasury, Economics, Intergovernment Affairs," 4 June 1978, *Briefs, Statements, Presentations, etc.* (Thunder Bay: The Council, 1973-83).

3 Gert Beadle, "North Western Ont," in *The Resisting Spirit* (self-published, n.d.).

4 Joan Baril, interview by author, 11 October 1999, Thunder Bay, ON, tape recording. For examples of the debates of the Thunder Bay Women's Liberation Group, see the Thunder Bay Women's Liberation Newsletters, Joan Baril Personal Papers.

5 Nancy Adamson, "Feminists, Lefties, Libbers, and Radicals: The Emergence of the Women's Liberation Movement," in *A Diversity of Women: Ontario, 1945-1980*, ed. Joy Parr (Toronto: University of Toronto Press, 1995), 265.

6 Julie Fels, interview by author, 22 July 2000, Thunder Bay, ON, tape recording.

7 Pamela Krichem, "A Home for Women's Centre," *Lakehead Living*, 7 November 1974, p. 1; "About Us: Northern Women's Centre," *Northern Woman* 2, 4 (1975): 8; Sharon Younger, "Northern Women's Centre Opens Doors to Public," *Thunder Bay Chronicle Journal*, 11 November 1974.

8 I discuss feminist criticisms and strategic use of these funding programs in "Feminist Initiatives, Government Limitations: Feminist Services, Politics and Voluntarism, 1970-1985," in *Women and Leadership*, ed. Audrey MacNevin et al. (Ottawa: CRIAW/ICREF, 2002), 57-75.

9 "About Us: Northern Women's Centre," *Northern Woman*. Their work was not remunerated until 1980, after the women's centre asked for operating funds from the city. See Northwestern Ontario Women's Centre Archives (NWCA), "Correspondence, Minutes, AGMs, Annual Reports, 1975-1990" Box, "Presentation to the Standing Committee on the Secretary of State," 31 March 1987.

10 Fels, interview by author. Doreen Boucher and Leni Untinen recalled that the city perceived feminists as "crazy" and "nuts." Doreen Boucher, interview by author, 3 August 2000, Thunder Bay, ON, tape recording; Leni Untinen, interview by author, 13 November 1999, Thunder Bay, ON, tape recording.

11 Fiona Karlstedt, interview by author, 26 July 2000, Thunder Bay, ON, tape recording.

12 The Thunder Bay Sexual Assault Centre, an organization founded at the women's centre, was funded by the city. That collective decided not to promote itself as a feminist organization in the community to keep municipal funding. The collective did organize and provide services according to feminist tenets. Boucher, interview by author.

13 The earliest statistics I found are from 1978. In that year, the women's centre noted an increase in calls from battered women. Between January and June, they recorded forty-four requests for crisis housing. NWCA, "Projects, 1977-1980" Box, "Employment and Immigration Canada 1978" File, "Women's Centre Interim Report," 1 September-30 September; "Projects 1977-1980" Box, "Women Sharing Applications" File, "Record of phone calls and requests for information," January-June 1978.

14 Chris Kouhi, "Women's Centre: Support Offered," *The Argus, Lakehead University's Student Newspaper,* 5 June 1974. Fels, interview by author, and Margaret Phillips, interview by author, 10 November 1999, Thunder Bay, ON, tape recording.

15 Lakehad Social Planning Council, *Breaking Point: An Evaluation of Community Residences of the Thunder Bay Social Services* (Thunder Bay, May 1979); "Report: Northwestern Ontario International Women's Year Co-Ordinating Council, March 1975," *Northern Woman* 2, 2 (1975): 6, and, in the same issue, "Thunder Clap," 44.

16 A women's organization had donated $3,000 to the women's centre, and the collective allocated the money to opening a shelter. Leni Untinen, "Shelter for My Sisters: A History of the Shelter Movement in Northwestern Ontario," in *Listening to the Thunder: Advocates Talk about the Battered Women's Movement,* ed. Leslie Timmins (Vancouver: Women's Research Centre, 1995), 176.

17 Faye Peterson Transition House (FPTH), "Back Logs and Files 1977-1985" Box, "Minutes of Proceedings Committee on Health, Welfare, and Social Affairs" File, "Report [for proposed] Community Residence (Family) (Crisis Housing)," 22 July 1975.

18 FPTH, "Back Logs and Files 1977-1985" Box, "Minutes of Proceedings Committee on Health, Welfare, and Social Affairs" File, Citizen's Committee on Crisis Housing to D.R. MacLeod, 14 August 1975.

19 Doreen Winko and Eve Pyderman, "Crisis Housing Report," *Northern Woman* 2, 5 (1975): 16.

20 Thunder Bay Archives (TBA), City Social Services Department Central Files, "Social Services Department Annual Report 1976." The city's records from this period have not been catalogued. As such, my research was restricted to those files the archivist cited as having pertinent information. Those records contained little information about the policies and protocols of the house. My analysis relies on the interpretation of those who observed it from the outside.

21 Lakehead Social Planning Council, *Breaking Point,* 49-51.

22 Winko and Pyderman, "Crisis Housing Report."

23 TBA, City Social Services Department Central Files, "Pamphlet for Community Residence," n.d.

24 "Crisis House Rules for Residences," appended to Lakehead Social Planning Council, *Breaking Point.*

25 Professional counselling was not available at all times. A social worker was available on Monday, Wednesday, and Friday to discuss family matters with the residents. The maximum stay was two weeks, although extensions could be granted if a woman applied to the Social Services Department.

26 Winko and Pyderman, "Crisis Housing Report," 16.

27 Ibid., 16.

28 Lakehead Social Planning Council, *Breaking Point,* 17.

29 Ibid., 19.

30 Winko and Pyderman, "Crisis Housing Report;" Fels and Karlstedt, interviews by author.

31 Boucher, interview by author.

32 Untinen, interview by author.

33 Phillips, interview by author.

34 For synopses of their efforts, see Fiona Karlstedt and Leni Untinen, *The History of the Battered Women's Movement in Northwestern Ontario* (Thunder Bay: Northwestern Ontario Women's Decade Council, Women against Violence Subcommittee, September 1989).

5 The city's reports did not provide statistics about the origins of the women. TBA, City Social Services Department Central Files, "Family Violence" File, City Social Services to NWO Women's Centre, 8 November 1983. Winko and Pyderman, "Crisis Housing Report."

6 FPTH, "Miscellaneous General Correspondence 1977-1985" Box, Crisis Homes Inc. to Mr. Hennesy, 18 April 1983.

7 NWCA, Minutes Binder 1982, "Report for Northwestern Ontario Women's Centre," 18 August 1982.

8 Beadle's poems are collected in three self-published volumes: *Salt and Yeast* (1977), *Rising* (1980), and *The Resisting Spirit* (n.d.). The proceeds of the first two collections were donated to *Northern Woman*, and funds from the last volume established an emergency fund for Crisis Homes Inc. shortly after the shelter opened.

9 Fels, interview by author. FPTH, Filing Cabinet, "Board Meeting Minutes" File, Minutes 10 January 1983; "Miscellaneous Correspondence 1977-1985" Box, "Letters Sent" File, Gert Beadle to Mr. Kallos, 21 February 1983. Beadle proposed that she would move into the home in mid-March, act as the house mother for the shelter, and pay the board a monthly rent of $225.

10 Leslie Papp, "Shelter from Abuse: Faye Peterson Home," *Lakehead Living*, 30 August 1983, pp. 1, 5.

11 Karlstedt, interview by author.

12 Untinen, interview by author.

13 Karlstedt and Untinen, *The History of the Battered Women's Movement*, 13.

14 Fels, interview by author.

15 Fels, interview by author. FPTH, "General Correspondence" Box, "References" File, "Pamphlet for Faye Peterson Regional Transition House," 1983.

16 Gert Beadle, "Report to Faye," in *The Resisting Spirit*, no page provided. When one enters the shelter, the first thing one sees is Peterson's portrait.

17 Fels, interview by author.

18 Volunteer (confidentiality requested), interview by author, 24 July 2000, Thunder Bay, ON, tape recording.

19 Brenda Cryderman, interview by author, 25 July 2000, Thunder Bay, ON, tape recording.

20 FPTH, "Miscellaneous General Correspondence 1977-1985" Box, "Statistics" File, "Statistics 1983." The majority of the women came from the region, although eight of the residents were from Thunder Bay. Two of the regional women had fled from a reserve. The collective also accepted one women from Alberta and two women from Toronto.

21 FPTH, "Miscellaneous General Correspondence 1977-1985" Box, "Clippings" File, Summer 1983, "Generosity Appreciated."

22 Papp, "Shelter from Abuse."

23 FPTH, "Miscellaneous General Correspondence 1977-1985" Box, "Per Diem Rates" File, Senior Policy Analyst, MCSS to FPTH, 13 May 1983.

24 FPTH, "Miscellaneous General Correspondence 1977-1985" Box, "Battered Briefs" File, "Proposal for FPTH," n.d.

25 FPTH, "Miscellaneous General Correspondence 1977-1985" Box, "Clippings" File, Summer 1983;, Gord McLaughlin, "Peterson Home Funding Held off by Council," Bruce Langer, "Funding Deferred for Transition House," *Thunder Bay Chronicle Journal;* Leslie Papp, "Transition Home Deserves Funding, not Council Delays," *Lakehead Living*, 9 August 1983.

56   Gillian Walker, *Family Violence and the Women's Movement: The Conceptual Politics Struggle* (Toronto: University of Toronto Press, 1990), 118.

57   Ibid., 183-85.

58   FPTH, Filing Cabinet, "Board Minute Meetings" File, 30 November 1983.

59   Untinen, interview by author.

60   Untinen, interview by author; Fiona Karlstedt, *Northwestern Ontario Status of Women Initiatives, 1973-1987* (Thunder Bay: Northwestern Ontario Women's Decade Council, 1987), 4

61   A house with ten to twelve beds would receive $142,000 per year to pay rent, food, ar salaries for three and a half staff and a supervisor. Each shelter was expected to rai $50,000 per year, and per diem arrangements would cover the remaining costs. In add tion, shelters would receive $50,000 per bed per annum for counselling. FPTH, "Misce laneous General Correspondence 1977-1984" Box, "Crisis Homes Inc. Board Meetin 1984" File, "Report on Toronto Meeting," 5 March 1984.

62   Fels, interview by author. The minutes recorded: "Gert Beadle reported that we may ha a new house in the proper zone ... An agreement to purchase has been made, depende upon zoning regulations." FPTH, "Miscellaneous General Correspondence 1977-198 Box, "Crisis Homes Inc. Board Meetings 1984" File, Minutes 5 March 1984.

63   FPTH, Filing Cabinet, "Personnel Committee Minutes Reports" File, Personnel Commi tee Minutes, 4 June 1985; FPTH, "Northwestern Ontario Decade Council – 1980s-1990 Box, "Northwestern Ontario Decade Council Violence Subcommittee" File, "Deca Council Violence Subcommittee Evaluation," 1987.

64   Fels and Baril, interviews by author.

65   Boucher, interview by author.

CHAPTER 3: KENORA WOMEN'S CRISIS INTERVENTION PROJECT, 1975-85

1   Women's Place Kenora Records (WPK), File 500-2, "Talking Package," 1978; "Keno Women's Crisis Intervention Project [KWCIP], 1975-1980" Box, "Family Resource Centr File, "Client Information Sheets 1979-1983."

2   I submit a caveat with my discussion of cross-cultural activism. I was not able to fir Aboriginal women who were involved with the project and have relied on the perceptio of non-Aboriginal women, the archival record, and written discussions of local coloni ing relations.

3   Grand Council Treaty No. 3, the Indian Friendship Centre, and the Kenora Nati Women's Association also provided emergency services for Aboriginal people in Kenor

4   Norman Giesbrecht and Joe Brown with Jan de Lint, *Alcohol Problems in Northweste Ontario, Preliminary Report: Consumption Patterns, Public Order and Public Health Pro lems,* Substudy no. 872 (Toronto: The Addiction Research Foundation, 1977).

5   Anastasia M. Shkilnyk, *A Poison Stronger Than Love: The Destruction of an Ojibwa Co munity* (New Haven and London: Yale University Press, 1985). Shkilnyk also argues th Kenora became heavily dependent on Aboriginal people in the 1950s and 1960s when go ernment administration became the second most important industry in town.

6   In response to discrimination, Aboriginal leaders organized a march in 1964 to rai awareness about the unfair treatment of Aboriginal people in Kenora. Giesbrecht ar Brown, *Alcohol Problems in Northwestern Ontario;* Shkilnyk, *A Poison Stronger Than Lo* 128.

7   A study conducted by Grand Council Treaty No. 3 found that close to 200 Indians died in Kenora between 1970 and 1974. Alcohol was involved in 70 percent of the cases, and two-thirds of the victims were younger than forty years old. Kenora Social Planning Council (Concerned Citizens Committee), *While People Sleep, Sudden Deaths in Kenora Area: A Study of Sudden Deaths amongst the Indian People of the Kenora Area, with Primary Emphasis on Apparent Alcohol Involvement* (Kenora: Grand Council Treaty No. 3, 1974).

8   Shkilnyk, *A Poison Stronger Than Love*; "Charges Withheld Pending Park Claim," *Kenora Daily Miner and News*, 22 November 1974, 1.

9   Eleanor M. Jacobson, *Bended Elbow: Kenora Talks Back, Part 1* (Kenora: Central Publications, 1975). The title was a play on the American Indian movement's stand-off at Wounded Knee; "bended elbow" referred to lifting drink. Upsetting to read, the book captures the derogatory stereotype of "the drunken Indian." Of 9,000 copies of the volume sold, 2,000 were sold in Kenora. The Ontario Human Rights Commission classified the pamphlet as hate literature.

10 WPK, "KWCIP, 1975-1980" Box, "Women's Conference" File, "Secretary of State Application: Kenora Women's Conference," 1975.

11 WPK, "KWCIP, 1975-1980" Box, "Women's Conference" File, "Kenora Women's Conference," 7 January 1975.

12 WPK, "KWCIP, 1975-1980" Box, "Women's Conference" File, "Secretary of State Application: Kenora Women's Conference," 1975; Minutes 12 November 1974; "Woman Power Conference Set," *Kenora Daily Miner and News*.

13 On the debates about racism in the women's movement, see Mary-Jo Nadeau and Sarita Srivastava, "Re-Writing the Borders: Nation, Race and the Narration of Canadian Feminism." (Unpublished paper presented at Feminism and the Making of Canada: Historical Reflections/Le féminisme et le façonnement du Canada: Réflexions sur l'histoire, McGill University, Montreal, QC, 7-9 May 2004).

14 Marilyn Fortier and Joanne Frost, interview by author, 30 October 1999, Kenora, ON, tape recording; WPK, File 500-2-2, "Memo from KWCI Project to KWCI Group," 1978.

15 Fortier and Frost, interview by author. Charlotte Holm concurred. She was not a member of the original group, but she argues that the training from the Thunder Bay Physical and Sexual Assault Centre probably incorporated a feminist analysis of rape that the women did not "latch on to" because their primary motive was "to help women through the system without being further traumatized." Charlotte Holm, interview by author, 22 October 1999, Kenora, ON, tape recording.

16 Dianne Singbeil, interview by author, 4 November 1999, Kenora, ON, tape recording.

17 For comparison, see Noreen Connell and Cassandra Wilson, ed., *Rape: The First Sourcebook for Women* (New York: New American Library, 1974).

18 Holm and Singbeil, interviews by author. There was a small lesbian community in Kenora. Kenora's lesbian community organized autonomously because it was not able to put lesbian issues on the local women's movement's agenda. A small group published a newsletter called *Images: A Survival Manual For Women* that discussed lesbian issues. However, most lesbians were not out in the community. Doreen Worden, interview by author, 29 October 1999, Kenora, ON, tape recording.

19 Holm, interview by author.

20 Barbara M. Freeman, *The Satellite Sex: The Media and Women's Issues in English Canada, 1966-1971* (Waterloo: Wilfrid Laurier Press, 2001), 17-20, 82.

21 WPK, "KWCIP 1975-1980" Box, "Minutes 1978-1979" File, Minutes 23 March 1978; "Presentation from the Rape and Sexual Assault Group to Kenora Council," 19 April 1978.

22 Fortier and Frost, interview by author.

23 Ibid. Frost remembered that the local rumours upset her husband.

24 None of the founding members was Aboriginal. In retrospect, the women who organized the service acknowledged that they should have given more thought to representation, but at the time they did not have a critical analysis of race. Fortier and Frost, Singbeil, interviews by author.

25 WPK, "KWCIP 1975-1980" Box, "Minutes 1978-1979" File, "Handwritten note re Incorporation" [1978].

26 Pat Jobb, "Centre Planning Moving Ahead," *Kenora Daily Miner and News* [November 1976]; WPK, File 500-2-2, Canada Works 1978, "Proposal" [1978].

27 WPK, "KWCIP 1975-1980" Box, "Progress Report, 1979-1980."

28 Holm, interview by author. All of the women whom I interviewed agreed that Copenace was an important member of the group.

29 The earliest statistics I found that identify the race of the clients are from 1980. In January 1980, 58 percent of the clients were Aboriginal. The statistics for 1983 are incomplete, but from April to June, 41 percent were Aboriginal, from July to September, 46 percent were, and from October to December, 35 percent were Aboriginal. WPK, "KWCIP 1975-1980" Box, "Family Resource Centre" File, "Client Information Sheets, 1979-1983."

30 WPK, Filing Cabinet, "Women's Place Kenora: Crisis Intervention Project" File, "Canada Works Application, 1978."

31 WPK, "KWCIP 1975-1980" Box, "Questionnaires 1978" File, "Some comments written on the questionnaire by women who had been battered" [1978].

32 WPK, "KWCIP 1975-1980" Box, "Native Health and Welfare" File, "Community Health Nurse," "Questionnaires from Agencies 1977-78, Statistics," "Probation and After Care Service," Doug Keshen (Legal Advisor, Grand Council Treaty No. 3) to KWCIP, 22 August 1979.

33 When Aboriginal women who worked as community health representatives on reserves began to report family violence to the Department of Indian Affairs, government bureaucrats advised them not to intervene because this did not fall under their mandate as health workers. Mary Jane McCallum, "The Early History of First Nations and Inuit Community Health Representatives, 1960-1970" (paper presented at the Northern Ontario History of Health and Medicine Group Lunchtime Seminar Series co-sponsored by the Northern Ontario School of Medicine and the Associated Medical Services Inc., Thunder Bay, ON, 6 October 2006).

34 WPK, "KWCIP 1975-1980" Box, "Questionnaires 1978" File. The following responses included comments on abused husbands and children: Ministry of Correctional Services, Kenora Jail, Native Health and Welfare Community Nurse, Child Stimulation Director.

35 WPK, "KWCIP 1975-1980" Box, "Talking Package and Questionnaire" File, "Notes on Visits with Agencies," n.d.

36 WPK, "KWCIP 1975-1980" Box, "Talking Package and Questionnaire" File, "Meetings with Community and Social Services, Mayor Romstedt, Kenora Social Services, and Kenora Detox," n.d.

47 WPK, "Women's Place Kenora 2" Box, "Reports to Native Community Branch" File, "Fact Sheets," April 1979-May 1982.

48 Holm, interview by author.

49 Shelter worker (confidentiality requested), interview by author, 1 November 1999, Kenora, ON, tape recording. An article in the local newspaper reported that the apartment could accommodate up to four or five women in crisis and their dependents. "Crisis Centre Opens Locally," *Kenora Daily Miner and Daily*, 2 August 1979.

0 WPK, Minutes Binder, Board Meeting 18 February 1981; Minutes 21 April 1981.

41 WPK, Box, "Reports to Native Community Branch" File, "Fact Sheet," April 1979-May 1982.

42 WPK, Minutes Binder, "Minutes of AGM 16 May 1984."

43 This view was shared by all of the women who worked as advocates. Holm, Singbeil, and shelter worker, interviews by author. See also Margaret Little's interviews with single mothers in Kenora in "A Litmus Test for Democracy: The Impact of Ontario Welfare Changes on Single Mothers," *Studies in Political Economy* 66 (2001): 9-36.

44 Singbeil, interview by author.

45 Ibid.

46 WPK, Minutes Binder, Minutes 6 December 1982.

47 Fortier and Frost noted this shift and stated that they left the group because they did not feel they had the skills to work with the more political women in the group. In 1981, two other members of the board left the organization because of the change in the direction of the group and the dynamics of the organization. WPK, "KWCIP 1975-1980" Box, "Canada Works Books" Envelope, "Officers and Occupations" n.d. [1979].

48 Copénace left her position as co-ordinator, although she did continue to assist the organization in an advisory capacity. It may be that she was the bridge between Aboriginal and non-Aboriginal women and that the collaboration weakened without her facilitation. White women were concerned by this development. WPK, Minutes Binder, Minutes 6 April 1981; Board Meeting Minutes, 15 June 1981.

49 Conversation with Charlotte Holm, 28 October 1999. For a discussion of the challenge of keeping cross-cultural boards together, see Audrey McLaughlin, *Kaushee's Place: Yukon Women's Transition Home: Final Report of a Three Year Demonstration Project* (Whitehorse: Yukon Women's Transition Home, February 1983), 65-67. McLaughlin does not consider how Aboriginal women were marginalized in the discussions of how to manage the shelter.

50 Bonita Lawrence, *The Exclusion of Survivors' Voices in Feminist Discourses on Violence against Women* (Ottawa: Canadian Research Institute on the Advancement of Women, 1996), 25.

51 WPK, "KWCIP 1975-1980" Box, "KWCIP" File, "Proposed Activities," n.d.

52 Holm, interview by author.

53 WPK, "KWCIP 1975-1980" Box, "Kenora Women's Intervention Crisis Group 1978-1979" File, Board Meeting Minutes 3 May 1978.

54 Standing Committee on Health, Welfare, and Social Affairs, *Report on Violence in the Family: Wife Battering* (Ottawa: May 1982).

55 WPK, Minutes Binder, Minutes 15 November 1982.

56 Ontario, *Hansard*, Standing Committee on Social Development, Tuesday, 14 June 1983, S-356.

57 WPK, "KWCIP 1975-1980" Box, "Family Resource Centre" File, "Family Resource Centres Information Package," August 1983.

58 Gillian Walker, *Family Violence and the Women's Movement: The Conceptual Politics of Struggle* (Toronto: University of Toronto Press, 1990).

59 WPK, "KWCIP 1975-1980" Box, "Family Resource Centre" File, "Family Resource Centres Information Package," August 1983.

60 Emphasis in original. Untinen, interview by author. She went on to criticize the southern presumptions of the report, noting that the average amount of her own hydro bills were higher than that proposed in the program's budget. OAITH was also critical of the minimum wage and argued that if the municipality operated the centre, the workers would be members of a union, which would oppose low wages for this work. WPK, "KWCIP 1975-1980" Box, "Family Resource Centre" File, "OAITH Response to Family Resource Centres in Northwestern Ontario," September 1983.

61 WPK, "KWCIP 1975-1980" Box, "Family Resource Centre" File, "Response to COMSOC re FRC" [1983].

62 Ibid. Sadly, the security of the Family Resource Centre became a concern after Liz Manella was murdered by her ex-husband in the centre on 14 March 1988. The key issue in the ensuing debate was over visitation by former spouses. Despite differences in ideological perspectives and practices, feminist organizations from across the province rallied behind the Kenora Family Resource Centre. "FRC Letters of Gratitude, and Appeal for Support," *Kenora Daily Miner and News*, March 29, 1988; Phil Cardella, "Coping with a Daughter's Murder: Alice Park's Campaign against Family Violence," *Kenora Daily Miner and News*, 3 November 1989.

63 For a critique of the dismissal by the battered women's shelter movement of the perspectives of women who use alcohol and drugs, see Lawrence, *The Exclusion of Survivors' Voices*, 21-23.

64 WPK, "KWCIP 1975-1980" Box, "Family Resource Centre" File, "Response to COMSOC re FRC" [1983] and "OAITH Response to Family Resource Centres."

65 WPK, Minutes Binder, Minutes 16 January 1984.

66 Their intervention was not welcomed by administrators, who argued that "radical elements" were disrupting negotiations. James Little, "Cost Sharing Decision Delaying Centre," *Kenora Daily Miner and News*, 5 June 1984, 1.

67 WPK, Minutes Binder, "Women's Place Kenora, Services in the Past Year," 19 October 1985; "Annual Report – Crisis Line 1984/85"; Christine Blackburn, "Family Resource Centre Opened by Provincial Minister," *Kenora Daily Miner and News*, 8 November 1985; Holm, interview by author.

68 "Women's Place Still Has a Valuable Place in the Community," *Kenora Daily Miner and News*, 9 January 1986.

69 Holm, interview by author.

70 Untinen, interview by author. She also argued that the government advised Family Resource Centre managers that OAITH opposed them.

71 For a detailed examination of how this competition affected relationships among community activists in a southern Ontario community, see Ruth M. Mann, *Who Owns Domestic Violence? The Local Politics of a Social Problem* (Toronto: University of Toronto Press, 2000).

72 WPK, File 1007-2, Ministry of Northern Development and Mines, Ontario, to Women's

Place Kenora, 12 March 1987; "Speech Delivered at Opening of Women's Place Kenora" [1987]; Holm, interview by author.

CHAPTER 4: THE NELSON SAFE HOME PROGRAM, 1973-89

1 For women's role in the student left, see *Women Unite! An Anthology of the Canadian Women's Movement* (Toronto: Canadian Women's Education Press, 1974). West Kootenay feminists discussed women's political and economic subordination and the need for radical social change in their newspaper *Images*, which they published from 1975 to 1983.

2 "Community Service Centre to Open in Nelson," *Nelson Daily News*, 8 January 1972, 2; "Manpower Approves Initiative Grants," *Nelson Daily News*, 17 January 1972, 2. In 1974, the NDP government in British Columbia passed the Community Resources Board Act. The legislation established twenty-three Community Resource Boards to co-ordinate local services. The program promoted citizen participation through volunteer mobilization and emphasized local authority in developing social programs. The provincial government funded experimental and innovative programs based on community need. The program was dismantled in 1977 when the Social Credit government formed the government. See Josephine Reckart, *Public Funds, Private Provision: The Role of the Voluntary Sector* (Vancouver: UBC Press, 1993).

3 Women's Place Kenora Records, "Kenora Women's Crisis Intervention Project, 1975-1980" Box, "Family Resource Centre" File, Northwestern Ontario Decade Council and OAITH, "The Safe Home Concept," August 1984.

4 This also happened in Vancouver. See Karlene Faith, "State Appropriation of Feminist Initiative: Transition House, Vancouver, 1973-1986," in *Seeking Shelter: A State of Battered Women*, ed. Karlene Faith and Dawn H. Currie (Vancouver: Collective Press, 1993); Leslie Kenny and Warren Magnusson, "In Transition: The Women's House Saving Action," *Canadian Review of Sociology and Anthropology* 30, 3 (1993): 359-78; Jan Barnsley, *Feminist Action, Institutional Reaction: Responses to Wife Assault* (Vancouver: Women's Research Centre, 1985).

5 Sam Simpson, interview by author, 19 May 2000, Winlaw, BC, tape recording. Bonnie Baker also remembered that the women's self-presentation was to some extent meant to challenge confining fashions. Bonnie Baker, interview by author, 19 May 2000, Winlaw, BC, tape recording. Articles in the local newspaper confirm Simpson's recollection of the impact the newcomers had in the region. "Valley Residents Concerned with Grants," *Nelson Daily News*, 14 January 1972, 2; "Valley Residents Veto Day Care Centres," *Nelson Daily News*, 17 January 1972, 2.

6 Peggy Pawelko, "Women's Lib More Than Just Burning Bras," *Nelson Daily News*, 6 February 1973; Nelson and District Women's Centre (NDWC), Box, "LIP Application, 1972-1973"; "Past Operating Grants (Secretary of State)" File, "Secretary of State Application," 1974. In 1975, *Images* asked non-feminist women for submissions so that the paper would speak to all women in the area. "Open letter," *Images* (February 1975): 7.

7 Baker, interview by author. Simpson remembered that this is how she was "shanghaied" into working for *Images*. Simpson, interview by author.

8 The Nelson and District Women's Centre still had a woman-only policy in 2000. In 1975, the West Kootenay Women's Association organized its first women's music festival, and for many years it was a women-only event.

9 NDWC, Box, File 10:4, "Pamphlet: Myths and Facts about Women's Centres" [1977]. See also the letters in response to the *Images* issues on women and relationships and on sexuality,

Images 5, 1 (January 1977) and 5, 2 (February 1977). A group of women who were outraged by the issue on sexuality lobbied the newsstand at the Kootenay Lake District Hospital to stop selling the local feminist newspaper. "Collectivial," *Images* 5, 3 (July 1977).

10 Bette Bateman, interview by author, 20 May 2000, Creston, BC, tape recording.

11 This is not to say that there was consensus on this issue. All of the women whom I interviewed explained that there was a lesbian/straight split in the feminist community. For a discussion of the divisive debates about sexuality in the British Columbia Federation of Women, see M. Julia Creet, "A Test of Unity: Lesbian Visibility in the British Columbia Federation of Women," in *Lesbians in Canada*, ed. Sharon Dale Stone (Toronto: Between the Lines, 1990), 183-97.

12 Diane Luchton, interview by author, 18 May 2000, Nelson, BC, tape recording.

13 Neil Websdale noticed similar patterns in his study of East Kentucky. He calls this solidarity amongst men and women's concomitant lack of anonymity in smaller centres "rural patriarchy." See Neil Websdale, *Rural Woman Battering and the Justice System: An Ethnography* (Thousand Oaks, CA: SAGE Publications, 1998) and Yasmin Jiwani, *Rural Women and Violence: A Study of Two Communities in British Columbia* (Vancouver: FREDA Centre for Research on Violence against Women and Children, June 1998).

14 "Rape: A Rural Problem Too," *Images* 7, 2 (June 1980): 5.

15 Carol Ross, interview by author, 10 May 2000, Nelson, BC, tape recording.

16 It is unknown how many battered women approached the women's centre because the organizers did not keep statistics, but organizers noted in funding applications that battered women came to the centre for advocacy. See NDWC, Box C-H, "Community Resources Board" File, "Grant application, Department of Human Resources, Community Programmes Division, 1974-1975."

17 Luchton, interview by author.

18 Baker, interview by author.

19 NDWC, Box, "West Kootenay Status of Women" File, "Women in Transition Newsletter," December 1973.

20 NDWC, Box, "Minutes WKWA [West Kootenay Women's Association] 1974-1979" File, General Meeting 27 February 1976; Minutes [March 1976]; Box, "Old Newsletters WKWA" File, Newsletter 27 February 1976. Transition houses appeared on the agendas for meetings in August and September 1979, but discussions were not recorded in the minutes. The West Kootenay Women's Association is the society feminists organized to sponsor the women's centre for funding purposes.

21 NDWC, Box, file containing grant applications, "Canada Works Program Application: Woman's Advocate," 1978-79; "Youth Job Corps Program Application: Feminist Services Training Program," 1979-80.

22 Bateman, interview by author. *Images* also reported on her experience with violence in "Rape – A Rural Problem, Too."

23 Bateman, interview by author. Taking women home also disrupted her family life because her husband would often stay elsewhere when she brought home women who were afraid of men.

24 NDWC, Box, "Minutes of Coordinating Collective Meetings" duotang, "Brainstorm re discussion topics," 14 July 1983.

25 Jillian Ridington, "Providing Services the Feminist Way," in *Still Ain't Satisfied: Canadian Feminism Today*, ed. Maureen Fitzgerald, Connie Guberman, and Margie Wolfe (Toronto: Women's Press, 1982), 93-107.

26 Sally Alexander, interview by author, 17 May 2000, Crescent Beach, BC, tape recording.
27 Ross, interview by author.
28 Emphasis in original. Cranbrook Women's Resource Centre, "CWRS Business" Box, "Constitutions – Other Groups" File, "Agreement between the Nelson Community Services Centre and the Minister of Human Resources," 27 August 1980.
29 Luchton, Simpson, and Ross, interviews by author.
30 Marilyn Callahan, "The Human Costs of Restraint," in *The New Reality: The Politics of Restraint in British Columbia*, ed. Warren Magnusson et al. (Vancouver: New Star Books, 1984), 232.
31 Simon Fraser University Archives, Katherine Hudson Vancouver Women's Book Store Fonds, Box 3, "The Current Funding Crisis – BC Coalition of Rape Centres," 26 January 1982. For other discussions of the impact of Social Credit social planning on feminist services, see Stella Lord, "Women's Rights: An Impediment to Recovery?" in *The New Reality*, 179-91; Christien St. Peter, "The Women's Movement," in *After Bennett: A New Politics for British Columbia*, ed. Warren Magnusson et al. (Vancouver: New Star Books, 1986), 336-51.
32 On the role of self-help groups in social movements, see Dieter Hoehne, "Self-Help and Social Change," in *Social Movements/Social Change*, ed. Frank Cunningham et al. (Toronto: Between the Lines, 1988), 236-51.
33 NDWC, Box C-H, "Family Violence" File, "Pamphlet: You Are Not Alone," n.d.
34 Alexander and Bateman, interviews by author. In Trail, the nurses from the psychiatric unit of the hospital initiated the organization of the Women in Need Society Transition House.
35 Simpson stated that not all battered women in Nelson were poor but that safe home users had fewer resources.
36 Ross, interview by author.
37 NDWC, Box P-R, "Resources – Violence" File, "NCSC Intervention Model," May 1983.
38 Nelson Community Services Centre (NCSC), Box, File 1.08 "Safe Home Reports," 1982; Box, "Safe Home – Current volunteers" File, "Applications, 1992." I found no application forms for safe home operators before 1992.
39 NCSC, Box, File 1:08, "Safe Home Reports," 9 August 1982, 29 March 1982, 3 December 1981, 29 September 1981, and 12 February 1981. I found safe home reports for only 1981 and 1982 in their records. In subsequent years, the community services centre kept only statistical records for funding.
40 Ross, interview by author; NDWC, Box A-B, "Battered Women" File, Sam Simpson, "Services Available to Battered Women and Their Children in the Nelson Area," April 1989.
41 Ross, Luchton, and Alexander, interviews by author.
42 Finding drivers to move women from safe homes to Trail posed a problem during the first years of the program. NCSC, "Crisis Line Safe Homes" Box, "Safe Home Contract Procedures" File, "Safe Homes" [1990]. Ross remembered that sometimes the police in Trail would meet the volunteer drivers half way.
43 NDWC, "Coordinative Collective Minutes, 1983-1984" duotang, Minutes 5 October 1983.
44 NCSC, "Crisis Line Safe Homes" Box, "Safe Home Contract Procedures" File, "Motel Policy," n.d. If they could not make arrangements with a restaurant, clients were referred to the Salvation Army.
45 NCSC, Box, File 1.08, "Safe Home Report," 19 March 1982.
46 NCSC, Box, File 1.08, "Safe Home Report," 29 March 1982.

47 The policies clearly stated that the volunteers' safety was paramount and instructed staff and volunteers not to go to the house if the assault was in progress. NDWC, Box P-R, "Resources – Violence" File, "Nelson Community Services Intervention Model," 1983.

48 NDWC, Box, "Nelson Women's Centre Reports" File, "Minutes of Community Services to Discuss Unemployment," 19 August 1984.

49 NCSC, "Crisis Line Safe Homes" Box, "From the Crisis Line Manual," n.d.

50 NCSC, Box, File 1.08, "Safe Home Report," October 1980.

51 NDWC, Box A-B, "Battered Women" File, Sam Simpson, "Services Available to Battered Women and Their Children in the Nelson Area," April 1989.

52 The transition house is named in memory of Aimee Beaulieu, who died in a suspicious fire along with her twin infants.

53 Baker, interview by author.

54 Conversation with Karen Newmoon, Nelson, BC, 22 June 1999.

CHAPTER 5: CROSSROADS FOR WOMEN/CARREFOUR POUR FEMMES, 1979-87

A version of this chapter was previously published in *Acadiensis* 35, 2 (2006).

1 Crossroads Records, Box, "Femmes Battues" File, "Causes of the Financial Problems of Crossroads/Carrefour," November 1985.

2 Yolande Saulnier, interview by author, 28 March 2003, Moncton, NB, tape recording; Rina Arseneault, interview by author, 3 March 2004, Fredericton, NB, tape recording.

3 In the late 1960s, Acadians became more political in their demand for the recognition of their language rights in the Maritimes. Moncton became the capital of the regional Acadian community because of the concentration of French-speaking Acadians, its well-publicized struggle with Mayor Leonard Jones to make the city bilingual, and its thriving cultural community. For an overview of the postwar Acadian rights movement, see Philippe Doucet, "Politics and the Acadians," in *Acadia of the Maritimes: Thematic Studies from the Beginning to the Present*, ed. Jean Daigle (Moncton: Chaire d'études acadiennes, Université de Moncton, 1995), 307-14.

4 Cécile Gallant, *Les Femmes et la renaissance acadienne/Women and the Acadian Renaissance* (Moncton: Les Éditions d'Acadie, 1992).

5 Acadian women also organized meetings to make a submission to the Royal Commission on the Status of Women. Corinne Gallant, interview by author, 29 March 2003, Moncton, NB, tape recording.

6 Gallant, interview by author. She later developed a course called the Philosophy of Feminism, which became part of the curriculum of the philosophy department at the Université de Moncton.

7 Elspeth Tulluch, *We, the Undersigned: A History of New Brunswick Women, 1784-1984* (Moncton: New Brunswick Advisory Council on the Status of Women, 1985), 392.

8 Gallant, interview by author.

9 Tulluch, *We, the Undersigned*, 69-79. The office was in Moncton rather than in Fredericton because the council thought that it was important to show that it was independent from government. The council also initially planned to move its offices to each new chairperson's community, and Moncton was Delaney-LeBlanc's hometown. Rosella Melanson, e-mail correspondence to author, 28 October 2005. Melanson worked at the New Brunswick Advisory Council on the Status of Women in 1979.

10 For a discussion of the role of the provincial advisory councils on the status of women in

the Maritime women's movement, see Janet Guildford, "A Fragile Independence: The Nova Scotia Advisory Council on the Status of Women," in *Mothers of the Municipality: Women, Work, and Social Policy in Post-1945 Halifax*, ed. Judith Fingard and Janet Guildford (Toronto: University of Toronto Press, 2005), 281-304.

11 The first federal report was published in 1980. Linda MacLeod, *Wife Battering in Canada: The Vicious Circle* (Ottawa: Canadian Advisory Committee on the Status of Women, 1980).

12 New Brunswick Advisory Council on the Status of Women, *Battue/Battered* (Moncton: The Council, 1979), 7.

13 Crossroads/Carrefour organizers took up this challenge. In 1983, they sponsored Options, a counselling program for abusive men. The service moved to Moncton Family Services in 1985.

14 Corinne Laplante, *A Spirited Woman*, trans. Sheila Boase and Irène Duchesneau (New Brunswick: Religieuses Hospitalières de Saint-Joseph, June 1999). The New Brunswick Association of Transition Houses was founded in 1987.

15 Crossroads Records, Filing Cabinet, "Canadian Advisory Council on the Status of Women" File, Susan Shalala, "No Turning Back: A Future for Battered Women: A Submission to the Standing Committee on Health, Welfare, and Social Affairs," 4 February 1982.

16 Huberte Gautreau and Beth McLaughlin, interview by author, 27 March 2003, Moncton, NB, tape recording. Gallant also recalled that she initially doubted Delaney-LeBlanc's assertion that Moncton needed a shelter.

17 Arseneault, interview by author; "Refuge for Moncton's Battered Women to Open in April," *Moncton Times-Transcript*, 28 January 1981.

18 Arseneault and Gallant, interviews by author.

19 Crossroads Records, Filing Cabinet, "Publicity" File, untitled list of events [1980].

20 Crossroads Records, Filing Cabinet, "Publicity (156)" File, press release, 12 May 1980; Box 772, Binder, Canada Works Application Form, 1979-80, and untitled information sheet, October 1980.

21 Crossroads Records, Box 772, Binder, press release [April 1980]. Other studies confirmed the incidence of wife abuse in the community. A study of the Moncton Family Court found that between December 1978 and December 1979, the court heard 112 cases in which violence was an issue and that the court prepared 70 peace bonds for women against their husbands. Crossroads Records, Filing Cabinet, "Public Speaking 1981-1988" File, transcript of a speech by Doris Gallagher [1981].

22 Crossroads Records, Box 772, Binder, untitled synopsis of responses from transition houses to Crossroads/Carrefour survey, 14 March 1980.

23 The programs were Canada Community Development Program, NEED, and Canada Works. Crossroads Records, Box 772, Binder, press release [April 1980]; untitled objectives of Crossroads/Carrefour, October 1980.

24 Crossroads Records, Box 772, Binder, City of Moncton Operational Grants to Organizations Application, 2 October 1982. The city also waived the sewage fees. Council decided to support the house after members went to the meeting to ask for $7,000. Mayor Dennis Cochrane explained that council offered the house because the presentation opened their eyes to the issue. Gautreau and McLaughlin, interview by author.

25 Crossroads Records, Box 772, Binder, "City of Moncton Operational Grants to Organizations Application," 2 October 1982.

26 Arseneault, interview by author. The logo was a butterfly flying over a rooftop. It represented women's transformation in a safe environment: "the roof and chimney ... symbolized the warmth and safety of the transition house and the butterfly symbolized women's escape from bondage." Sandra Arsenault, Doris Gallagher, and Treska Scheller-Robinson, *Information Handbook: Crossroads for Women, Inc.* (Moncton: Crossroads for Women/ Carrefour pour femmes, 1985), 58.

27 Lesley McMillan found similar patterns in a survey of refuge volunteers and workers in England. Many women became involved in the anti-violence work to give back to the anti-violence movement, but their involvement was also a sign of their political commitment to ending women's oppression. See Lesley McMillan, "'It's about Care as Much as It's about Feminism': Women's Personal and Political Motivations for Volunteering in Refuges and Rape Crisis Centres," *Atlantis* 28, 2 (2004): 126-37.

28 Crossroads Records, Box, "Newspaper Articles" File, "Transition House Full as Battered Wives Seek Help" [1981].

29 Crossroads Records, Filing Cabinet, "Minutes du personnel 1981-1982" File, undated notes [March 1982].

30 Crossroads Records, Box 772, Binder, Statistics attached to press communique [1982].

31 Crossroads Records, Box, "Newspaper Articles" File, "Transition house full as battered women seek help" [1981]; Filing Cabinet, "Statistics" File, Statistics 1981-82.

32 "Refuge for Moncton's Battered Women to Open in April."

33 Arseneault, interview by author.

34 Arsenault et al., *Information Handbook*; Crossroads Records, Filing Cabinet, "Public Speaking (1981-1988)" File, transcript of speech by Doris Gallagher, n.d.

35 Arseneault, interview by author.

36 Helene Robb, interview by author, 28 March 2003, Moncton, NB, tape recording.

37 Saulnier, interview by author.

38 Arseneault, interview by author.

39 Crossroads Records, Filing Cabinet, "Collective Meetings 1981-1988" File, Collective Minutes, 22 June 1983.

40 In June 1981, the collective agreed that staff would be knowledgable about the finances of the shelter. See Crossroads Records, Filing Cabinet, "Minutes du Personnel" File, Staff meeting minutes [June 1981]. The collective also invited former clients to the meetings to advise members on how to improve the services in the shelter. See Crossroads Records, Filing Cabinet, "Minutes du Personnel" File, Staff meeting minutes, 13 October 1981.

41 Gautreau and McLaughlin, interview by author.

42 Crossroads Records, Box, "Newspaper Articles" File, Advertisement of a meeting to promote Carrefour pour Femmes, Inc., *L'Evangeline*, 26 June 1981.

43 Saulnier, interview by author. All of the informants shared the view that "not having a boss" improved working conditions and presented an alternative to the clients.

44 Saulnier and Arseneault, interviews by author.

45 Fredericton Transition House and Hestia House in Saint John adopted modified collective structures; in its third year of operation, the Fredericton Transition House revoked the staff's voting privileges on the board. Campbellton maintained a traditional hierarchical relationship between the board and staff. See Crossroads Records, Filing Cabinet, "Transition Houses" File, "On Internal Structure (Decision making)," n.d.

46 Crossroads Records, Filing Cabinet, "Transition Houses" File, "On Internal Structure (Decision Making)", n.d.

47 Crossroads Records, Filing Cabinet, "Transition Centre – Coalition 166" File, Collective meeting minutes, 15 April 1982; Filing Cabinet, "Minutes du Personnel" File, Staff meeting minutes, 7 December 1983.

48 Crossroads Records, Filing Cabinet, "Transition Centre/Coalition" File, "Meeting Report, New Brunswick Coalition of Transition Houses," 30 September 1983.

49 Crossroads Records, Filing Cabinet, "Briefs (1983)" File, "Brief presented to the New Brunswick Working Group on the Problem of Wife Battering by Crossroads for Women," 12 October 1983.

50 Gautreau and McLaughlin, interview by author.

51 For a discussion of these programs, see Nancy Janovicek, "Feminist Initiatives, Government Limitations: Feminist Services, Politics and Voluntarism," in *Women and Leadership,* ed. Audrey MacNevin, Ellen O'Reilly, Eliane Leslau Silverman, and Anne Taylor (Ottawa: CRIAW, 2002), 57-75.

52 Gautreau and McLaughlin, interview by author.

53 Maureen MacDonald, "Chalk One up for Sisterhood," *New Maritimes: A Regional Magazine of Culture and Politics* 13, 6 (1995): 4-15, 17.

54 Crossroads Records, Filing Cabinet, "Minutes du Personnel" File, Staff meeting minutes, 22 March 1982.

55 Crossroads Records, Box, "Femmes Battues" File, untitled list of fundraising events, [1984]; Box 772, Binder, "Press release: Crossroads for Women, Inc. receives donation," July 1981. The cyclists were Pauline Bourque and Huberte Gautreau.

56 Arsenault et al., *Information Handbook,* 53.

57 Arseneault, interview by author.

58 Ibid.

59 Ibid.

60 Arsenault et al., *Information Handbook,* 62.

61 Arsenault et al., *Information Handbook.* Filing Cabinet, "Minutes du Personnel" File, Staff meeting minutes, 11 January 1982 and 8 February 1982.

62 Arseneault and Saulnier, interviews by author.

63 Arsenault et al., *Information Handbook,* 72.

64 Crossroads Records, Filing Cabinet, File 112, Department of Social Services and NBACSW, "Fact-finding Study Respecting Crossroads/Carrefour," May 1984.

65 Crossroads Records, Collective Minutes, 16 February 1981; Box 772, Binder, Crossroads/Carrefour to Richard Hatfield, 24 February 1984; Arsenault et al., *Information Handbook.*

66 Crossroads Records, Filing Cabinet, "Minutes du Personnel" File, Staff meeting minutes, 20 June 1984 and 8 August 1984; Filing Cabinet, "Fundraising, Identification and Description of Needs" File [1984].

67 Arsenault et al., *Information Handbook,* 77.

68 Crossroads Records, Box, "Femmes Battues" File, "Causes of the Financial Problems of Crossroads/Carrefour," November 1985.

69 This included three hours for staff meetings and two and a half hours of committee work. Crossroads Records, Box 772, "Employment Policies" File, "Terms and Conditions of Employment," September 1984; Box, "Femmes Battues" File, "Causes of the Financial

Problems of Crossroads/Carrefour," November 1985. The starting salary at Bryony House in Halifax was $16,000, and at the Transition House in Regina it was $21,000. The average salary for women working at Hestia House in Saint John was $18,000.

70 Crossroads Records, Box, "Femmes Battues" File, Crossroads to Richard Hatfield, 23 May 1985; "Causes of the Financial Problems of Crossroads/Carrefour," November 1985.

71 Robb, interview by author.

72 "Why the Obstructionism?" *Moncton Times-Transcript*, 10 October 1986. An editorial published a month earlier expressed the same opinion: "Help Is Warranted," *Moncton Times-Transcript*, 6 September 1986.

73 "Moncton Shelter Struggles to Survive," *Saint John Telegraph-Journal*, 18 October 1986.

74 Peter R. Boisseau, "Province Ensures Crossroads Will Continue, but No Frills," *Moncton Times-Transcript*, 1 December 1986. The provincial contribution increased to $145,000; the Crossroads/Carrefour budget was $181,401.

75 Crossroads Records, Filing Cabinet, File 105.5, Crossroads Collective to Nancy Clark-Teed, Minister of Health and Community Services, 11 June 1987.

76 Crossroads Records, Box 772, "Divers" File, "Historical Highlights, Crossroads for Women, Inc.", 1991. The United Way expected Crossroads/Carrefour to abandon its collective structure. The collective set up a "paper board" or a "two-faced model" to meet the funding requirements. McLaughlin and Gautreau, interview by author.

77 Crossroads Records, Box 772, Binder, President's report attached to collective meeting minutes, 3 December 1987.

78 Gautreau and McLaughlin, interview by author.

79 Arseneault, interview by author.

80 Saulnier, interview by author.

81 "Limited Funding Has Been a Continuing Problem for Staff," *Moncton Times-Transcript* [1986]. Organizers used the same words when they detailed the renovations to the house in an application for funding in 1982. Crossroads Records, Box 772, Binder, City of Moncton "Operational Grants to Organizations Application," 2 October 1982.

82 Crossroads Records, Filing Cabinet, "160.2 Statistics" File, Statistics 1981-87.

83 Gillian Walker, *Family Violence and the Women's Movement: The Conceptual Politics of Struggle* (Toronto: University of Toronto Press, 1990), 219.

CONCLUSION

1 Monda Halpern presents an excellent critique of the academic reticence to recognize rural women's politics as feminist. Monda Halpern, *And on That Farm He Had a Wife: Ontario Farm Women and Feminism, 1900-1970* (Montreal and Kingston: McGill-Queen's University Press, 2001), especially chapter 1.

2 Mary Jane McCallum, "The Early History of First Nations and Inuit Community Health Representatives," (paper presented at the Northern Ontario History of Health and Medicine Group Lunchtime Seminar Series co-sponsored by the Northern Ontario School of Medicine and the Associated Medical Services Inc., Thunder Bay, ON, 6 October 2006).

3 Lise Gotell, "A Critical Look at State Discourses on 'Violence against Women': Some Implications for Feminist Politics and Women's Citizenship," in *Women and Political Representation in Canada*, ed. Caroline Andrews and Manon Tremblay (Ottawa: University of Ottawa Press, 1998), 39-84.

4 Patricia A. Monture-Okanee, "The Violence We Women Do: A First Nations View," in *Challenging Times: The Women's Movement in Canada and the United States,* ed. Constance Backhouse and David H. Flaherty (Montreal and Kingston: McGill-Queen's University Press, 1992), 195.

5 Sherene H. Razack, *Looking White People in the Eye: Gender, Race, and Culture in Court-rooms and Classrooms* (Toronto: University of Toronto Press, 1998).

6 Andrea Smith, *Conquest: Sexual Violence and American Indian Genocide* (Boston: South End Press, 2005).

Bibliography

ARCHIVAL COLLECTIONS

Archives of Ontario (AO)
RG 29, Series 43, Task Force on Community Social Services, 1972-74
RG 29, Series 45, Northwestern Region Correspondence, 1970-75
RG 68, Ministry of Mines and Northern Affairs, Series 6, Director's files

Simon Fraser University Archives
Kathleen Hudson Vancouver Women's Book Store Fonds

Thunder Bay Archives (TBA)
City Social Services Department Central Files

University of Ottawa Archives and Special Collections/Archives et Collections Spéciales,
University of Ottawa Library Network
Lisa Bengtsson Fonds

University of British Columbia Library, Rare Books and Special Collections
Vancouver Status of Women Papers

Private Collections
Beendigen Records (BR)
Cranbrook Women's Resource Centre (CWRC)
Crossroads for Women/Carrefour pour Femmes (CR)
Faye Peterson Transition House (Crisis Homes Inc.) (FPTH)
Joan Baril Personal Papers
Nelson and District Women's Centre (NDWC)
Nelson Community Services Centre (NCSC)
Northwestern Ontario Women's Centre Archives (NWCA)
Ontario Native Women's Association (ONWA)
Women's Place Kenora (WPK)

OTHER SOURCES

Adamson, Nancy. "Feminists, Libbers, and Radicals: The Emergence of the Women's Lib-
    eration Movement." In *A Diversity of Women: Ontario, 1945-1980*, ed. Joy Parr, 252-80.
    Toronto: University of Toronto Press, 1995.
Adamson, Nancy, Linda Briskin, and Margaret McPhail. *Feminist Organizing for Change: The
    Contemporary Women's Movement in Canada*. Toronto: Oxford University Press, 1988.

Agnew, Vijay. *In Search of a Safe Place: Abused Women and Culturally Sensitive Services.* Toronto: University of Toronto Press, 1998.

Anderson, Kim. *A Recognition of Being: Reconstructing Native Womanhood.* Toronto: Second Story Press, 2000.

Anderson, Kim, and Bonita Lawrence. *Strong Women Stories: Native Vision and Community Survival.* Toronto: Sumach Press, 2003.

Armitage, Andrew. *Comparing the Policy of Aboriginal Assimilation: Australia, Canada, and New Zealand.* Vancouver: UBC Press, 1995.

Arsenault, Sandra, Doris Gallagher, and Treska Scheller-Robinson. *Information Handbook: Crossroads for Women, Inc.* Moncton: Crossroads for Women/Carrefour pour femmes, 1985.

Backhouse, Constance. *Petticoats and Prejudice: Women and the Law in Nineteenth-Century Canada.* Toronto: Women's Press, 1991.

Bannerji, Himani. *The Dark Side of the Nation: Essays on Multiculturalism, Nationalism and Gender.* Toronto: Canadian Scholars' Press, 2000.

–. "Politics and the Writing of History." In *Nation, Empire, Colony: Historicizing Gender and Race,* ed. Ruth Roach Pierson and Nupur Chauduri, 287-301. Bloomingdale: Indiana University Press, 1998.

–. "A Question of Silence: Reflections of Violence against Women in Communities of Colour." In *Scratching the Surface: Canadian Anti-Racist Thought,* ed. Enakshi Dua and Angela Robertson, 261-80. Toronto: Women's Press.

Barnsley, Jan. *Feminist Action, Institutional Reaction: Responses to Wife Assault.* Vancouver: Women's Research Centre, 1985.

Barrett, Michele. *Imagination in Theory: Culture, Writing, Words, and Things.* New York: New York University Press, 1999.

Beadle, Gert. *The Resisting Spirit.* Self-published, n.d.

Breines, Wini, and Linda Gordon. "The New Scholarship on Family Violence." *Signs: Journal of Women in Culture and Society* 8, 3 (1983): 490-531.

Brown, Michael P. *RePlacing Citizenship: AIDS Activism and Radical Democracy.* New York: Guilford Press, 1997.

Brownmiller, Susan. *Against Our Will: Men, Women, and Rape.* New York: Simon and Schuster, 1975.

Butler, Judith, Ernesto Laclau, and Slavoj Zizek. *Contingency, Hegemony, Universality: Contemporary Dialogues on the Left.* London: Verso, 2000.

Callahan, Marilyn. "The Human Costs of Restraint." In *The New Reality: The Politics of Restraint in British Columbia,* ed. Warren Magnusson, William K. Carroll, Charles Doyle, Monika Langer, and R.B.J. Walker. Vancouver: New Star Books, 1984.

Canada. House of Commons. *Debates,* 12 May 1982.

–. Standing Committee on Health, Welfare, and Social Affairs. *Report on Violence in the Family: Wife Battering.* Ottawa: May 1982.

Cardinal, Harold. *The Rebirth of Canada's Indians.* Edmonton: Hurtig Publishers, 1977.

–. *The Unjust Society: The Tragedy of Canada's Indians.* Edmonton: M.G. Hurtig, 1969.

Carroll, William K. "Social Movements and Counterhegemony: Canadian Contexts and Social Theories." In *Organizing Dissent: Contemporary Social Movements in Theory and Practice,* 2nd ed., ed. William Carroll, 3-38. Toronto: Garamond Press, 1997.

Clark, Lorenne, and Debra Lewis. *Rape: The Price of Coercive Sexuality.* Toronto: Women's Press, 1977.

Cohen, Marjorie Griffin. "The Canadian Women's Movement." In *Canadian Women's Issues*. Vol. 1: *Strong Voices: Twenty-Five Years of Activism in English Canada*, ed. Ruth Roach Pierson, Marjorie Griffin Cohen, Paula Bourne, and Philinda Masters. Toronto: James Lorimer, 1993.

Connell, Noreen, and Cassandra Wilson, ed. *Rape: The First Sourcebook for Women by New York Radical Feminists*. New York: New American Library, 1974.

Creet, M. Julia. "A Test of Unity: Lesbian Visibility in the British Columbia Federation of Women." In *Lesbians in Canada*, ed. Sharon Dale Stone, 183-97. Toronto: Between the Lines, 1990.

Crenshaw, Kimberle. "Mapping the Margins: Intersectionality, Identity Politics and Violence against Women of Color." *Stanford Law Review* 43, 6 (1991): 1241-99.

Cruikshank, Julie. "Oral Tradition and Oral History: Reviewing Some Issues." *Canadian Historical Review* 75, 3 (1994): 403-18.

Del Mar, David Peterson. *What Trouble I've Seen: A History of Violence against Wives*. Cambridge: Harvard University Press, 1996.

Denis, Claude. *We Are Not You: First Nations and Modernity*. Peterborough: Broadview Press, 1997.

Dobash, R. Emerson, and Russell P. Dobash. *Women, Violence, and Social Change*. London and New York: Routledge, 1992.

Dosman, Edgar J. *Indians: The Urban Dilemma*. Toronto: McClelland and Stewart, 1972.

Doucet, Philippe. "Politics and the Acadians." In *Acadia of the Maritimes: Thematic Studies from the Beginning to the Present*, ed. Jean Daigle, 307-14. Moncton: Chaire d'études acadiennes, Université de Moncton, 1995.

Dubinsky, Karen. *Improper Advances: Rape and Heterosexual Conflict in Ontario, 1880-1929*. Chicago: University of Chicago Press, 1993.

Dunk, Thomas. *It's a Working Man's Town: Male Working-Class Culture in Northwestern Ontario*. Montreal and Kingston: McGill-Queen's University Press, 1991.

Dyck, Noel. *What Is the Indian "Problem"? Tutelage and Resistance in Canadian Indian Administration*. St. John's: Institute of Social and Economic Research, 1991.

Faith, Karlene. "State Appropriation of Feminist Initiative: Transition House, Vancouver, 1973-1986." In *Seeking Shelter: A State of Battered Women*, ed. Karlene Faith and Dawn H. Currie. Vancouver: Collective Press, 1993.

Findlay, Sue. "Facing the State: The Politics of the Women's Movement Reconsidered." In *Feminism and Political Economy: Women's Work, Women's Struggles*, ed. Heather Jon Maroney and Meg Luxton, 31-50. Toronto: Methuen, 1987.

–. "Feminist Struggles with the Canadian State, 1966-1988." *Resources for Feminist Research/Documentation sur la recherche féministe* 17, 3 (1988): 5-9.

Fineman, Martha Albertson, and Roxanne Mykitiuk, ed. *The Public Nature of Private Violence: The Discovery of Domestic Abuse*. London and New York: Routledge, 1994.

Fiske, Jo-Anne. "By, For, or About? Shifting Directions in the Representations of Aboriginal Women." *Atlantis* 25, 1 (2000): 11-27.

–. "The Womb Is to the Nation as the Heart Is to the Body: Ethnopolitical Discourses of Canadian Indigenous Women's Movement." *Studies in Political Economy* 51 (1996): 65-95.

Flynn, Karen, and Charmaine Crawford. "Committing 'Race Treason': Battered Women and Mandatory Arrest in Toronto's Caribbean Community." In *Unsettling Truths:*

Battered Women, Policy, Politics, and Contemporary Research in Canada, ed. Kevin D. Bonnycastle and George S. Rigakos, 91-102. Vancouver: Collective Press, 1998.

Forde, Jan. "True North, True Solutions?" In *Listening to the Thunder: Advocates Talk about the Battered Women's Movement*, ed. Leslie Timmins, 93-108. Vancouver: Women's Research Centre, 1995.

Fournier, Elizabeth, and Ernie Crey. *Stolen from Our Embrace: The Abduction of First Nations Children and the Restoration of Aboriginal Communities*. Vancouver: Douglas and McIntyre, 1997.

Freedman, Catherine. "Anduhyaun: A Toronto Residence for Canadian Indian Girls Migrating to the City for Retraining." Master's thesis, York University, 1974.

Freeman, Barbara M. *The Satellite Sex: The Media and Women's Issues in English Canada, 1966-1971*. Waterloo: Wilfrid Laurier University Press, 2001.

Frideres, James S. "Aboriginal Urbanization." In *Aboriginal Peoples in Canada: Contemporary Conflicts*, 5th ed., ed. James S. Frideres, 235-56. Scarborough: Prentice Hall, Allyn, and Bacon Canada, 1998.

Gallant, Cécile. *Les Femmes et la renaissance acadienne/Women and the Acadian Renaissance*. Moncton: Les Éditions d'Acadie, 1992.

Giesbrecht, Norman, and Joe Brown, with Jan de Lint. *Alcohol Problems in Northwestern Ontario, Preliminary Report: Consumption Patterns, and Public Order and Public Health Problems*. Substudy no. 872. Toronto: The Addiction Research Foundation, 1977.

Gordon, Linda. *Heroes of Their Own Lives: The Politics and History of Family Violence, Boston 1880-1960*. New York: Penguin Books, 1989.

Gotell, Lise. "A Critical Look at State Discourses on 'Violence against Women': Some Implications for Feminist Politics and Women's Citizenship." In *Women and Political Representation in Canada*, ed. Carol Andrews and Manon Tremblay, 39-72. Ottawa: University of Ottawa Press, 1998.

Groves, Robert. *Urban Aboriginal Governance in Canada: Refashioning the Dialogue*. Ottawa: National Association of Friendship Centres, 1999.

Guildford, Janet. "A Fragile Independence: The Nova Scotia Advisory Council on the Status of Women." In *Mothers of the Municipality: Women, Work, and Social Policy in Post-1945 Halifax*, ed. Judith Fingard and Janet Guildford, 281-304. Toronto: University of Toronto Press, 2005.

Halpern, Monda. *And on That Farm He Had a Wife: Ontario Farm Women and Feminism, 1900-1970*. Montreal and Kingston: McGill-Queen's University Press, 2001.

Hanselmann, Calvin. *Urban Aboriginal People in Western Canada: Realities and Policies*. Calgary: Canada West Foundation, September 2001.

Hawthorn, H.B. *A Survey of the Contemporary Indians of Canada*. 2 vols. Ottawa: Indian Affairs Branch, 1966.

Hoehne, Dieter. "Self-Help and Social Change." In *Social Movements/Social Change*, ed. Frank Cunningham, Sue Findlay, Marlene Kadar, Alan Lennon, and Ed Silva, 236-51. Toronto: Between the Lines, 1988.

Holmes, Joan. *Bill C-31: Equality or Disparity? The Effects of the New Indian Act on Native Women*. Ottawa: Canadian Advisory Council on the Status of Women, March 1987.

Howard-Bobiwash, Heather. "Women's Class Strategies as Activism in Native Community Building in Toronto, 1950-1975." *American Indian Quarterly* 27, 3 and 4 (2003): 566-82.

Hudson, Peter, and Sharon Taylor-Henley. "First Nations Child and Family Services, 1982-1992: Facing the Realities." *Canadian Social Work Review* 11, 1 (1994): 89-102.

Huntley, Audrey, and Fay Blaney. *Bill C-31: Its Impact, Implications and Recommendations for Change in British Columbia – Final Report.* Vancouver: Aboriginal Women's Action Network, 1999.

Indian Chiefs of Alberta. *Citizens Plus.* Edmonton: Indian Association of Alberta, 1970.

Jacobson, Eleanor M. *Bended Elbow: Kenora Talks Back, Part 1.* Kenora: Central Publications, 1975.

Jamieson, Kathleen. *Indian Women and the Law in Canada: Citizens Minus.* Ottawa: Advisory Council on the Status of Women, April 1978.

–. "Multiple Jeopardy: The Evolution of a Native Women's Movement." *Atlantis* 4, 2 (1979): 157-78.

Janovicek, Nancy. "Feminist Initiatives, Government Limitations: Feminist Services, Politics, and Voluntarism, 1970-1985." In *Women and Leadership,* ed. Audrey MacNevin, Ellen O'Reilly, Eliane Leslau Silverman, and Anne Taylor, 57-75. Ottawa: CRIAW/ICREF, 2002.

Jiwani, Yasmin. *Rural Women and Violence: A Study of Two Communities in British Columbia.* Vancouver: FREDA Centre for Research on Violence against Women and Children, June 1998.

Karlstedt, Fiona. *Northwestern Ontario Status of Women Initiatives, 1973-1987.* Thunder Bay: Northwestern Ontario Women's Decade Council, 1987.

Karlstedt, Fiona, and Leni Untinen. *The History of the Battered Women's Movement in Northwestern Ontario.* Thunder Bay: Northwestern Ontario Decade Council, Women against Violence Subcommittee, September 1989.

Katz, Cindy. Foreword to *RePlacing Citizenship: AIDS Activism and Radical Democracy,* by Michael P. Brown. New York: Guilford Press, 1997.

Kechnie, Margaret, and Marge Reitsma-Street, ed. *Changing Lives: Women in Northern Ontario.* Toronto and Oxford: Dundurn Press, 1996.

Kenny, Leslie, and Warren Magnusson. "In Transition: The Women's House Saving Action." *Canadian Review of Sociology and Anthropology* 30, 3 (1993): 359-76.

Kenora Social Planning Council (Concerned Citizens Committee). *While People Sleep, Sudden Deaths in Kenora Area: A Study of Sudden Deaths amongst the Indian People of the Kenora Area, with Primary Emphasis on Apparent Alcohol Involvement.* Kenora, Ontario: Grand Council Treaty No. 3, 1974.

Kline, Marlee. "Complicating the Ideology of Motherhood: Child Welfare Law and First Nations Women." *Queen's Law Journal* 18, 3 (1993): 306-42.

Krosenbingk-Gelissen, Lilianne Ernestine. "The Native Women's Association of Canada." In *Aboriginal Peoples in Canada: Contemporary Conflicts,* 5th ed., ed. James S. Frideres. Scarborough: Prentice Hall, Allyn, and Bacon Canada, 1998.

Krouse, Susan Applegate, and Heather Howard-Bobiwash, ed. Special issue: "Keeping the Campfires Going: Urban American Indian Women's Activism," *American Indian Quarterly* 27, 3 and 4 (2003).

Kulusic, Tamara. "The Ultimate Betrayal: Claiming and Re-Claiming Cultural Identity." *Atlantis* 29, 2 (2005): 23-30.

Lachapelle, Caroline. "Beyond Barriers: Native Women and the Women's Movement." In *Still Ain't Satisfied: Canadian Feminism Today,* ed. Maureen Fitzgerald, Connie Guberman, and Margie Wolfe, 257-64. Toronto: Women's Press, 1982.

Lakehead Social Planning Council. *Breaking Point: An Evaluation of Community Residences of the Thunder Bay City Social Services*, May 1979.
–. "Brief to the Advisory Task Force on Housing Policy, February 1973." *Briefs, Statements, Presentations, etc.* Thunder Bay: The Council, 1973-83.
–. "Critique of Northwestern Ontario: Strategy for Development, Ministry of Treasury, Economics, Intergovernment Affairs. Thunder Bay, 4 June 1978." *Briefs, Statements, Presentations, etc.* Thunder Bay: The Council, 1973-83.
–. "Presentation to the Meeting of the Ontario Cabinet, 14 May 1975." *Briefs, Statements, Presentations, etc.* Thunder Bay: The Council, 1973-83.
Laplante, Corinne. *A Spirited Woman*. Translated by Sheila Boase and Irène Duschesneau. New Brunswick: Religieuses Hospitalières de Saint-Joseph, 1999.
Laprairie, Carol. *Seen but Not Heard: Native People in the Inner City*. Ottawa: Department of Justice, 1994.
Laroque, Emma. "The Colonization of a Native Woman Scholar." In *Women and the First Nations: Power, Wisdom, and Strength*, ed. Christine Miller and Patricia Chuchryk, 11-18. Winnipeg: University of Manitoba Press, 1996.
Lawrence, Bonita. *The Exclusion of Survivors' Voices in Feminist Discourse on Violence against Women*. Ottawa: Canadian Research Institute for the Advancement of Women, 1996.
Lawrence, Bonita, and Kim Anderson. "Introduction to 'Indigenous Women: The State of Our Nations.'" *Atlantis* 29, 2 (2005): 1-8.
Lewis, Debra J. *A Brief on Wife Battering with Proposals for Federal Action*. Ottawa: Canadian Advisory Committee on the Status of Women, January 1982.
Lister, Ruth. *Citizenship: Feminist Perspectives*. London: Macmillan Publishers, 1997.
Little, Margaret. "A Litmus Test for Democracy: The Impact of Ontario Welfare Changes on Single Mothers." *Studies in Political Economy* 66 (2001): 9-36.
Lobo, Susan. "Urban Clan Mothers: Key Households in Cities." *American Indian Quarterly* 27, 3 and 4 (2003): 505-22.
Lord, Stella. "Women's Rights: An Impediment to Recovery?" In *The New Reality: The Politics of Restraint in British Columbia*, ed. Warren Magnusson, William K. Carroll, Charles Doyle, Monika Langer, and R.B.J. Walker, 179-91. Vancouver: New Star Books, 1984.
Luxton, Meg. "Feminism as a Class Act: Working-Class Feminism and the Women's Movement in Canada." *Labour/Le Travail* 48 (2001): 63-88.
McCallum, Mary Jane. "The Early History of First Nations and Inuit Community Health Representatives, 1960-1970." Paper presented at the Northern Ontario History of Health and Medicine Group Lunchtime Seminar Series co-sponsored by the Northern Ontario School of Medicine and the Associated Medical Services Inc., Thunder Bay, ON, 6 October 2006.
MacDonald, Maureen. "Chalk One up for Sisterhood." *New Maritimes: A Regional Magazine of Culture and Politics* 13, 6 (1995): 4-14, 17.
McGillivray, Anne, and Brenda Comaskey. *Black Eyes All of the Time: Intimate Violence, Aboriginal Women, and the Justice System*. Toronto: University of Toronto Press, 1999.
McIvor, Sharon Donna. "Self-Government and Aboriginal Women." In *Scratching the Surface: Canadian Anti-Racist Feminism*, ed. Enakshi Dua and Angela Robertson, 167-86. Toronto: Women's Press, 1999.

McLaughlin, Audrey. *Kaushee's Place: Yukon Women's Transition Home – Final Report of a Three Year Demonstration Project* . Whitehorse: Kaushee's Place, February 1983.

MacLeod, Linda. *Battered but Not Beaten: Preventing Wife Battering in Canada*. Ottawa: Canadian Advisory Council on the Status of Women, 1987.

–. *Wife Battering in Canada: The Vicious Circle*. Ottawa: Canadian Advisory Council on the Status of Women, 1980.

McMillan, Lesley. "'It's about Care as Much as It's about Feminism': Women's Personal and Political Motivations for Volunteering in Refuges and Rape Crisis Centres." *Atlantis* 28, 2 (2004): 126-37.

Magnusson, Warren, William K. Carroll, Charles Doyle, Monika Langer, and R.B.J. Walker, ed. *The New Reality: The Politics of Restraint in British Columbia*. Vancouver: New Star Books, 1984.

Magnusson, Warren, Charles Doyle, R.B.J. Walder, and John DeMarco, ed. *After Bennett: A New Politics for British Columbia*. Vancouver: New Star Books, 1983.

Mahon, Rianne. "Child Care as Citizenship Right? Toronto in the 1970s and 1980s." *Canadian Historical Review* 86, 2 (2005): 285-315.

Mann, Ruth M. *Who Owns Domestic Abuse? The Local Politics of a Social Problem*. Toronto: University of Toronto Press, 2000.

Manuel, George, and Michael Posluns. *The Fourth World: An Indian Reality*. Don Mills: Collier-Macmillan Canada, 1974.

Maracle, Lee. *I Am Woman: A Native Perspective on Sociology and Feminism*. Vancouver: Press Gang Publishers, 1996.

Martin, Dianne L., and Janet E. Mosher. "Unkept Promises: Experiences of Immigrant Women with the Neo-Criminalization of Wife Abuse." *Canadian Journal of Women and the Law* 8, 1 (1995): 3-44.

Martin, Fern. *A Narrow Doorway: Women's Stories of Escape from Abuse*. Burnston, ON: General Store Publishing House, 1996.

Miller, J.R. *Skyscrapers Hide the Heavens: A History of Indian-White Relations in Canada*. Toronto: University of Toronto Press, 1991.

Million, Dian. "Telling Secrets: Sex, Power, and Narratives in the Social Construction of Indian Residential School Histories." *Canadian Woman Studies/Les cahiers de la femme* 20, 2 (2000): 82-104.

–. "Telling Secrets: Sex, Power, and Narratives in the Social Construction of Indian Residential School Histories." Unpublished paper presented at "What Difference does Nation Make?" Canadian/American Cultures of Sexuality and Consumption, The Weatherhead Centre for International Affairs and the Department of Women's Studies, Harvard University, 10 March 1999.

Monture-Angus, Patricia. *Thunder in My Soul: A Mohawk Woman Speaks*. Halifax: Fernwood, 1995.

–. "A Vicious Circle: Child Welfare and the First Nations." *Canadian Journal of Women and the Law* 3, 1 (1989): 1-17.

Monture-Okanee, Patricia A. "The Violence We Women Do: A First Nations View." In *Challenging Times: The Women's Movement in Canada and the United States*, ed. Constance Backhouse and David H. Flaherty, 193-200. Montreal and Kingston: McGill-Queen's University Press, 1992.

Morrow, Marina Helen. "Feminist Anti-Violence Activism: Organizing for Change." In

Reclaiming the Future: Women's Strategies for the 21st Century, ed. Somer Brodrib, 237-58. Charlottetown: Gynergy Books, 1999.

Morton, Suzanne. "Gender, Place, and Region: Thoughts on the State of Women in Atlantic Canadian History." *Atlantis* 25, 1 (2000): 119-28.

Murray, Bonnie, and Cathy Welch. "Attending to Lavender Bruises: A Dialogue on Violence in Lesbian Relationships." In *Listening to the Thunder: Advocates Talk about the Battered Women's Movement*, ed. Leslie Timmins. Vancouver: Women's Research Centre, 1995.

Nadeau, Mary-Jo, and Sarita Srivastava. "Re-Writing the Borders: Nation, Race and the Narration of Canadian Feminism." Unpublished paper presented at Feminism and the Making of Canada: Historical Reflections/Le féminisme et le façonnement du Canada: Réflexions sur l'histoire, McGill University, Montreal, 7-9 May 2004.

Napoleon, Val. "Aboriginal Self-Determination: Individual Self and Collective Selves." *Atlantis* 29, 2 (2005): 31-45.

National Women's Aid Federation. *Battered Women: Refuges and Women's Aid*. London: The Federation, 1977.

New Brunswick Advisory Council on the Status of Women. *Battue/Battered*. Fredericton: The Council, 1979.

Ontario. *Hansard*, Standing Committee on Social Development, 14 June 1983.

Ontario Native Women's Association. *Breaking Free: A Proposal for Change to Aboriginal Family Violence*. Thunder Bay: The Association, 1989.

–. *ONWA Resource Manual*. Thunder Bay: The Association, 1981.

Ouellette, Grace J.M.W. *The Fourth World: An Indigenous Perspective on Feminism and Aboriginal Women's Activism*. Halifax: Fernwood, 2004.

Perks, Robert, and Alistair Thompson, ed. *The Oral History Reader*. New York: Routledge, 1998.

Peters, Evelyn J. "Geographies of Aboriginal Self-Government." In *Aboriginal Self-Government in Canada: Current Trends and Issues*, ed. John H. Hylton, 163-79. Saskatoon: Purich Publishing, 1994.

–. "Subversive Spaces: First Nations Women and the City." *Environment and Planning D: Society and Space* 16, 6 (1998): 665-85.

Phillips, Margaret. *Transition House Services in Northwestern Ontario*. Thunder Bay: Northwestern Ontario Decade Council, July 1984.

Pierson, Ruth Roach. "The Politics of the Body." In *Canadian Women's Issues*. Vol. 1: *Strong Voices: Twenty-Five Years of Activism in English Canada*, ed. Ruth Roach Pierson, Marjorie Griffin Cohen, Paula Bourne, and Philinda Masters, 98-122. Toronto: James Lorimer, 1993.

Pierson, Ruth Roach, Marjorie Griffin Cohen, Paula Bourne, and Philinda Masters, ed. *Canadian Women's Issues*. Vol. 1: *Strong Voices: Twenty-Five Years of Activism in English Canada*. Toronto: James Lorimer, 1993.

Pizzey, Erin. *Scream Quietly or the Neighbours Will Hear*. Harmondsworth, Middlesex: Penguin Books, 1974.

Pleck, Elizabeth. *Domestic Tyranny: The Making of Social Policy against Family Violence from Colonial Times to the Present*. New York: Oxford University Press, 1987.

Razack, Sherene. "Domestic Violence as Gender Persecution: Policing the Borders of the Nation, Race, and Gender." *Canadian Journal of Women and the Law* 8, 1 (1995): 45-88.

–. *Looking White People in the Eye: Gender, Race, and Culture in Courtrooms and Class-rooms.* Toronto: University of Toronto Press, 1998.

Rebick, Judy. *Ten Thousand Roses: The Making of a Feminist Revolution.* Toronto: Penguin, 2005.

Reckart, Josephine. *Public Funds, Private Provision: The Role of the Voluntary Sector.* Van-couver: UBC Press, 1993.

Ridington, Jillian. "Providing Services the Feminist Way." In *Still Ain't Satisfied: Canadian Feminism Today,* ed. Maureen Fitzgerald, Connie Guberman, and Margie Wolfe, 93-107. Toronto: Women's Press, 1982.

Ristock, Janice L. *No More Secrets: Violence in Lesbian Relationships.* New York: Routledge, 2002.

Ross, Becki L. *The House That Jill Built: A Lesbian Nation in Formation.* Toronto: University of Toronto Press, 1995.

Roth, Benita. *Separate Roads to Feminisim: Black, Chicana, and White Feminist Movements in America's Second Wave.* Cambridge: Cambridge University Press, 2004.

Royal Commission on Aboriginal Peoples. *Aboriginal Peoples in Urban Centres: Report on the National Round Table on Aboriginal Urban Issues.* Ottawa: Minister of Supply and Services, 1993.

Royal Commission on the Status of Women in Canada. *Report of the Royal Commission on the Status of Women.* Ottawa: Information Canada, 1970.

Sanders, Douglas. "Indian Women: A Brief History of Their Roles and Rights." *McGill Journal of Law* 21, 4 (1975): 656-72.

Sangster, Joan. "Masking and Unmasking the Sexual Abuse of Children: Perceptions of Violence against Children in 'the Badlands' of Ontario, 1916-1930." *Journal of Family History* 25, 4 (2000): 504-26.

–. *Regulating Girls and Women: Sexuality, Family, and the Law in Ontario, 1920-1960.* Toronto: Oxford University Press, 2001.

–. "Telling Our Stories: Feminist Debates and the Use of Oral History." *Women's History Review* 3, 1 (1994): 5-28.

Schecter, Susan. *Women and Male Violence: The Visions and Struggles of the Battered Women's Movement.* Boston: South End Press, 1982.

Schreader, Alicia. "The State Funded Women's Movement: A Case of Two Political Agen-das." In *Community Organization and the Canadian State,* ed. Roxana Ng, Gillian Walker, and Jacob Muller, 184-99. Toronto: Garamond Press, 1990.

Shewell, Hugh. *"Enough to Keep Them Alive": Indian Welfare in Canada, 1873-1965.* Toronto: University of Toronto Press, 2004.

Shkilnyk, Anastasia M. *A Poison Stronger Than Love: The Destruction of an Ojibwa Com-munity.* New Haven and London: Yale University Press, 1985.

Silman, Janet. *Enough Is Enough: Aboriginal Women Speak Out.* Toronto: Women's Press, 1987.

Simard, Terry, and Mary Liljestrom, comp. *Ontario Native Women's Association Resource Manual.* Thunder Bay: Ontario Native Women's Association, August 1977.

Smith, Andrea. *Conquest: Sexual Violence and American Indian Genocide.* Boston: South End Press, 2005.

Smith, Dorothy. *Writing the Social: Critique, Theory, and Investigations.* Toronto: University of Toronto Press, 1999.

Spears, Shandra. "Strong Spirit, Fractured Identity: An Ojibway Adoptee's Journey to

Wholeness." In *Strong Women Stories: Native Vision and Community Survival*, ed. Kim Anderson and Bonita Lawrence, 81-94. Toronto: Sumach Press, 2003.

Srivastava, Sarita. "'Immigrant Women' Meet 'Canadian' Feminism: Transnationalism Encounters Muliculturalism." Paper presented at Rethinking Women and Gender Studies: Transnational Conditions and Possibilities, A Colloquium, University of Toronto, Toronto, ON, 28-30 September, 2006.

–. "'You're Calling Me a Racist?' The Moral and Emotional Regulation of Antiracism and Feminism." *Signs: Journal of Women in Culture and Society* 31, 1 (2005): 29-62.

St. Peter, Christien. "The Women's Movement." In *After Bennett: A New Politics for British Columbia*, ed. Warren Magnusson, Charles Doyle, R.B.J. Walder, and John DeMarco, 336-51. Vancouver: New Star Books, 1986.

Stirling, Mary Lou, Catherine Ann Cameron, Nancy Nason-Clark, and Baukje Miedema, ed. *Understanding Abuse: Partnering for Change*. Toronto: University of Toronto Press, 2004.

Stone, Sharon D. "Getting the Message Out: Feminists, the Press and Violence against Women." *Canadian Review of Sociology and Anthropology* 30, 3 (1993): 377-400.

Timmins, Leslie, ed. *Listening to the Thunder: Advocates Talk about the Battered Women's Movement*. Vancouver: Women's Research Centre, 1995.

Tulluch, Elspeth. *We, the Undersigned: A History of New Brunswick Women, 1784-1984.* Moncton: New Brunswick Advisory Council on the Status of Women, 1985.

Turpel, Mary Ellen (Aki-Kwe). "Patriarchy and Paternalism: The Legacy of the Canadian State for First Nations Women." *Canadian Journal of Women and the Law* 6, 1 (1993): 174-92.

Two-Axe Early, Mary. "'The Least Members of Our Society': The Mohawk Women of Caghnawaga." *Canadian Woman Studies/Les cahiers de la femmes* 11, 2 (1980): 64-66.

Untinen, Leni. "Shelter for My Sisters: A History of the Shelter Movement in Northwestern Ontario." In *Listening to the Thunder: Advocates Talk about the Battered Women's Movement*, ed. Leslie Timmons, 173-86. Vancouver: Women's Research Centre, 1995.

Ursel, Jane. "Considering the Impact of the Battered Women's Movement on the State: The Example of Manitoba." In *The Social Basis of Law: Critical Readings in the Sociology of Law*, 2nd ed., ed. Elizabeth Comack and Shelley Brickey, 261-88. Halifax: Garamond, 1991.

Valverde, Mariana. "A Post-Colonial Women's Law? Domestic Violence and the Ontario Liquor Board's 'Indian List,' 1950-1990." *Feminist Studies* 30, 3 (2004): 566-88.

Walker, Gillian. *Family Violence and the Women's Movement: The Conceptual Politics of Struggle*. Toronto: University of Toronto Press, 1990.

Walmsley, Christopher. *Protecting Aboriginal Children*. Vancouver: UBC Press, 2005.

Weaver, Sally M. "First Nations Women and Government Policy, 1970-1992: Discrimination and Conflict." In *Changing Patterns: Women in Canada*, ed. Sandra Burt, Lorraine Code, and Lindsay Dorney, 92-150. Toronto: McClelland and Stewart, 1993.

–. "The Hawthorn Report: Its Use in the Making of Canadian Indian Policy." In *Anthropology, Public Policy, and Native Peoples in Canada*, ed. Noel Dyck and James B. Waldram, 75-97. Montreal and Kingston: McGill-Queen's University Press, 1993.

–. *Making Canadian Indian Policy: The Hidden Agenda, 1968-1970.* Toronto: University of Toronto Press, 1981.

–. "The Status of Indian Women." In *Two Nations, Many Cultures: Ethnic Groups in Canada*, 2nd ed., ed. Jean Leonard Elliot, 56-79. Scarborough: Prentice-Hall, 1983.

Websdale, Neil. *Rural Woman Battering and the Justice System: An Ethnography.* Thousand Oaks, CA: SAGE Publications, 1998.

Weibel-Orlando, Joan A. "Introduction." Special issue: "Keeping the Campfires Going: Urban American Indian Women's Activism." *American Indian Quarterly* 27, 3 and 4 (2003): 500.

Women Unite! An Anthology of the Canadian Women's Movement. Toronto: Canadian Women's Education Press, 1974.

Index

Aboriginal people: and alcohol, 36, 37, 38, 63-4, 71, 139n7; Cree, 61; Cree language, 36; definition of, 121n1, 131n44; impact of colonization, 23, 24, 36, 39, 63, 114; Ojibwa, 61, 63-64, 67; Ojibwa language, 21, 36, 128n1. *See also* government policy on Aboriginal people

Aboriginal people, urban migration, 24-27, 129n12, 130n26; impact on children and family, 36; to Thunder Bay, 29; to Toronto, 21-22

Aboriginal rights, 26-28, 37, 64, 77; debates about collective and individual rights, 22, 27, 29, 32-33, 115, 134n89

Aboriginal women: community organization, 22, 30; leadership and self-government, 24, 31-32, 113-14; loss of Indian status, 1, 22, 25, 29 (*see also* Indian Act); negative depictions of, 132n58; scholarship on, 126n34; urban migration, 1, 13, 21, 25, 32. *See also* Native Women's Movement

abused women: attitudes toward, 3, 4, 6, 34; drug and alcohol addiction, 75, 142n63; experiences, 89-92; feminist advocacy for, 2, 5, 36, 47, 55, 71, 76, 77, 80, 85, 86; lack of services for, 1, 5, 34, 36, 38, 43, 47, 68-69, 87, 93, 98-99; legal protection, 3, 4; rural isolation, 83-84, 136n24. *See also* violence against women; wife battering

abusive men, 15, 91, 92, 97, 127n50; counselling services for, 3, 39, 40, 41, 69, 97, 115, 147n13; theorization of Aboriginal men's abuse, 39-40; theorization of male abuse, 10

Acadian: rights movement, 6, 96, 146n3; women, 95, 96-97, 146n5

Accueil Sainte-Famille (Tracadie), 97

Adamson, Nancy, 45

Addiction Research Foundation, 63

Aimee Beaulieu Transition House (Nelson), 5, 93, 146n52

Alexander, Sally, 86, 88, 119

Anduhyaun (Toronto), 21-22; meaning of, 128n3

anti-racism, 11, 77; marginalization of anti-racist critique, 12; in women's movement, 64

Arseneault, Rina, 100, 101, 102, 106, 107, 111, 119

Atikokan Crisis Centre, 51, 57-58

back-to-the-land movement, 79, 81-82

Baker, Bonnie, 82, 84, 93, 119, 143n5

Baril, Joan, 4, 45, 59, 119

Bateman, Bette, 83, 85, 119-20, 144n23

battered women. *See* abused women

battered women's shelter movement, 2-3; abused women's involvement in, 15, 54-55, 100, 111, 148n27; history of, 9, 115; urban/rural differences, 2, 5, 8, 83-84

Beadle, Gert, 44, 52, 53, 54, 58, 137nn38-39, 138n62

Beendigen, 5, 16, 21-42, 60, 63; community support for, 23, 40; founding of, 35-38; funding, 35-38, 133n64; meaning of, 21; statistics, 38; and urban migration, 21, 36-39

Bended Elbow: Kenora Talks Back. See Jacobson, Eleanor

Bennett, William, 80

Bernier, Leo, 58
Bill C-31, 28-29, 130n30
Bird, Florence, 4
Boucher, Doreen, 50, 59, 120, 135n10
Breaking Free: A Proposal for Change in Aboriginal Family Violence, 12, 23, 39-42, 116, 126n39. *See also* Ontario Native Women's Association (ONWA)
British Columbia Ministry of Human Resources, 87, 92
British Columbia Ministry of Women's Equality, 93
British North America Act, 25, 27
Byrony House (Halifax), 106, 127n48, 149n69

Canada, Standing Committee on Health, Welfare, and Social Affairs, 6, 56, 98; *Report on Violence in the Family: Wife Battering*, 73
Centr'aide Leroyer (St. Basile), 97
child welfare 1, 12, 92; Aboriginal alternatives to, 21, 32, 37; apprehension of Aboriginal children, 12, 37, 133n71; provincial policy, 12, 26; "sixties scoop," 12, 26
children, 97; abuse of, 10, 92; needs of, 36, 92, 102
Children's Aid Society, 37
Citizens Plus, 28
class relations, 10, 11, 15, 18, 47, 50, 89, 115
collective organizing, 46, 52, 58, 59, 81, 84-85, 95, 102, 103-5, 107, 108, 112, 114, 148n40, 148n45, 150n76
Community Resource Boards (British Columbia), 143n2
consciousness-raising, 3-4, 54, 84, 96
Copenace, Rosalind, 67, 140n28, 141n48
criminalization of woman abuse, 14, 18, 116; critique of, 40
Crisis Homes, Inc. (Thunder Bay), 51-56, 126n38. *See also* Faye Peterson Transition House
Cryderman, Brenda, 55, 120
Crossroads for Women/Carrefour pour

femmes, 5, 15, 17, 95-112; community support for, 99-102, 110; founding of, 98-99; funding, 95, 100-1, 106-9, 110; government opposition to feminist service-provision, 105, 108; statistics, 100, 111

Davis, Angela, 18
Delaney-LeBlanc, Madeleine, 97, 98
Department of Indian Affairs, 21, 25, 27, 30, 35, 115, 140n33
Denis, Claude, 41
domestic violence. *See* wife battering
Drea, Frank, 73
Dubec, Bernice, 30, 33, 35, 37, 39, 120, 133n68
Dryden, 51

ethics, 17-18, 119
ethnicity, 11

family, 87; Aboriginal, 12-13, 35; feminist critique of, 3, 10, 79, 81, 103; impact of government policy on Aboriginal families, 32, 37; protection of Aboriginal families, 3, 37-38, 39-41
family resource centres, 5, 57, 60; Family Resource Centre Program, 73-74; feminist critiques of, 74-76, 81, 142n60. *See also* Kenora Family Resource Centre
family violence: Aboriginal theorization of, 3, 12-13, 17, 21-42, 113-14, 117; Aboriginal theorization marginalized, 3, 12, 62, 72, 116-17, 133n78, 134n79, 141n49; feminist critiques of, 8, 10; gender-neutral definitions of, 8, 56, 69, 80, 87, 88-89, 94, 116; history of, 9. *See also* violence against women; wife battering
Faye Peterson Transition House, 5, 17, 42, 43-60, 63; community support for, 53, 55; founding of, 51-56; funding, 52, 55-58; opposition to feminist service-provision, 52, 58; statistics, 55

Fédération des dames d'Acadie, 96
Fellowship Centre of the Presbyterian
    Church (Kenora), 62, 75; support for
    KWCIP, 69, 71
Fels, Julie, 46, 47, 52, 53, 54, 58, 59, 120
feminism, 4, 11, 15, 82, 115; development of
    feminist consciousness, 2, 70, 82, 114;
    negative depictions of, 47, 66, 82;
    reluctance to identify as, 2, 10, 54, 61,
    65-66, 82-83, 102, 113-14, 135n12,
    139n15. *See also* women's movement
feminist services: feminist debates about,
    4, 45-46, 80-81, 84-85, 93, 94, 114;
    municipal government opposition
    to, 46-47, 67; philosophy of, 49, 55,
    86, 102-3; wages for workers, 95 (*see
    also* transition houses)
Fort Francis, 51
Fortier, Marilyn, 65, 67, 120, 141n47
Fredericton Transition House, 98, 99, 110
Freeman, Barbara, 32, 66
friendship centres, 13, 30-31, 34, 138n3
Frost, Joanne, 67, 120, 140n23, 141n47
funding: fundraising and donations, 35,
    51, 53, 66-67, 100, 101-2, 106, 110,
    136n16, 137n38; government funding
    (*see* government funding of women's
    movement); lack of and inconsis-
    tency of, 5, 81, 95, 107-10, 116; per
    diem, 6, 7, 52, 55, 70, 73, 88, 105, 107-
    8, 138n61; stabilization of funding of
    transition houses, 45, 55-58, 138n61

Gallagher, Doreen, 111
Gallant, Corinne, 96-97, 120, 146n6
Gautreau, Huberte, 98, 103, 120, 149n55
gendered racial violence, 23, 39, 117
Geraldton, 51
Gilbeau, Audrey, 30-31, 34, 36, 38, 39, 40, 121
Gordon, Linda, 9
government policy on Aboriginal people,
    11, 12, 23, 41; Aboriginal responses to,
    26-27; debates about jurisdiction,
    24-27; federal, 12; municipal, 13;
    provincial, 12-13, 26, 36; women and,
    7, 13, 32, 42

government funding of women's move-
    ment, 86; BUILD, 73; Canada Com-
    munity Development Program, 101,
    147n23; Canada Housing and Mort-
    gage Corporation, 7, 73, 75; Canada
    Works, 35, 67, 133n64; Department of
    Employment and Immigration, 99;
    job creation programs, 7, 46, 52, 73,
    99, 105-6; Local Education Action
    Program (LEAP), 46; Local Initia-
    tives Project (LIP), 46; Manpower
    Canada, 46, 79; Opportunities for
    Youth (OFY), 46; Status of Women
    Canada, 7
Grand Council Treaty No. 3, 61, 138n3,
    139n7
Griffin Cohen, Marjorie, 16

Hatfield, Richard, 110
Hawthorn Report, 26-27, 132n58
Hestia House (Saint John), 98, 110,
    148n45, 149n69
Holm, Charlotte, 68-72, 76, 121, 139n15
hostels for Aboriginal women, 22, 32
housing: affordable, 1, 132n56; subsidized,
    34, 73

INCITE Women of Color Against Vio-
    lence, 117
Images, 16, 84, 143n1, 143n7, 143n9
Indian Act, 1, 27-28, 29; Aboriginal
    women's opposition to, 22, 28-29, 33,
    130n29; impact of section 12 (1)(b)
    on women, 7, 22, 28-29, 130n30
Indian Chiefs of Alberta, 28
Indian Rights for Indian Women, 28-29
International Women's Day Coalition, 18
International Women's Year, 33, 64
intersectionality, theory of, 117; and local
    politics, 8, 115

Jacobson, Eleanor, 65, 139n9
Jamieson, Kathleen, 28
John Howard Society, 108
jurisdiction: Aboriginal women and 1, 8,
    13, 133n68; debates about federal,

provincial, and municipal responsibility 7, 13, 24, 27, 72-76, 100-1, 107-8, 124n15; in northwestern Ontario, 43, 55, 61, 69

Karlstedt, Fiona, 52, 121
Katz, Cindy, 9
Kaushee's Place (Whitehorse), 133n78
Kenora Detox Centre, 62, 69
Kenora Family Resource Centre, 5, 62, 73-77, 142n62
Kenora Native Women's Association, 67, 138n3
Kenora Rape Crisis Line, 15, 61
Kenora Rape and Sexual Assault Group, 65-67. *See also* Kenora Women's Crisis Intervention Project
Kenora Women's Crisis Intervention Project, 17, 61, 64, 67-70; and Aboriginal women, 67-68; community support, 68-69; founding of, 67; funding, 67 (*see also* Kenora Rape and Sexual Assault Group); opposition to feminist service-provision, 62, 69; statistics, 68, 69. *See also* Women's Place Kenora
Kootenay Lake Hospital, 88

Lakehead Social Planning Council, 35, 44, 132n56
Lawrence, Bonita, 42, 72
lesbians: in the anti-violence movement, 14; and intimate violence, 10, 14, 15; in Kenora, 15, 139n18; marginalization in women's movement, 14, 83; negative depictions of, 15, 66, 82-83; in Nelson, 14, 82-83, 144n11
LES FAM (Liberté, Egalité, Sororité – Femmes Acadiennes de Moncton), 96
Les Sœurs de Notre-Dame du Sacré-Cœur, 101
Lethbridge, 87
L'Évangéline, 103
Lion's Club, 102
Lister, Ruth, 19

Luchton, Diane, 83, 84, 121
Luxton, Meg, 15

McCarthy, Grace, 87
MacDonald, Maureen, 106
McLaughlin, Beth, 121
MacLeod, Linda, 5
Maracle, Lee, 11
Memramcook, 96
Métis, 29
Million, Dian, 40
Mitchell, Margaret, 6, 56
Moncton Times-Transcript, 110
Monture-Angus, Patricia, 12, 116, 134n79

Nakusp District Homemaker Service, 88
National Action Committee on the Status of Women, 29, 116
National Film Board, 8
National Indian Brotherhood, 28
Native People of Thunder Bay Corporation, 34, 35
Native rights movement; development of services, 2, 13, 21-22, 36, 39; in Kenora, 138n6; self-government, 22, 28; in Thunder Bay, 30; traditional movement 30-31, 131n39; treaty rights, 22, 28; and violence against women, 39
Native Women's Association of Canada, 131n44
Native women's movement, 12-13, 22-23, 24. *See also* Ontario Native Women's Association (ONWA); Thunder Bay Anishinabequek
 – relationship with Native rights movement, 22-23, 28-29, 33, 41, 114; in Thunder Bay, 31, 40
 – relationship with women's movement 11, 13, 29, 32-33, 36-37, 38, 41-42, 114-15; in Kenora, 13, 42, 60, 62, 63-73, 138n2, 140n24, 141n48; in Thunder Bay, 23, 42, 63, 128n7, 133n76
Nelson Community Services Centre, 79-80, 87-94

Nelson and District Women's Centre, 14, 17, 81-86, 143n8
Nelson Safe Home Program, 5, 17, 80, 86-93, 146n47
New Brunswick Advisory Committee on the Status of Women (NBACSW), 97, 98, 108, 146n9
New Brunswick Association of Transition Houses, 98, 104, 147n14
New Brunswick Department of Social Services, 105, 107-9
New Brunswick Working Group on the Problem of Wife Battering, 105
Northern Woman, 16, 23, 49, 50, 137n38
Northern Women's Centre, 45-46, 52
northwestern Ontario, 2, 16-17, 18, 24, 93; lack of services, 43-44; relationship to provincial government, 43-44, 57-58; women's movement in, 6, 13, 43, 51-60, 74-76
Northwestern Ontario Women's Decade Council (Decade Council), 51, 56, 74-75, 76

Ontario Association of Interval and Transition Houses (OAITH), 7, 45, 50, 51, 55-58, 73-74, 76, 142n60, 142n70
Ontario Ministry of Northern Development, 76
Ontario Ministry of Social Services, 35, 55, 58
Ontario Native Women's Association (ONWA), 13, 16, 17, 21, 22, 23, 24, 28, 30-33, 39-40, 41, 45, 113, 114, 126n39, 128n1; founding of, 31-32
Ontario Standing Committee on Social Development, 56

Penticton, 87
Peterson, Faye, 53-54, 137n46
Phillips, Margaret, 50, 121
Pizzey, Erin (*Scream Quietly or the Neighbours Will Hear*), 9, 39, 125n23
police, 7, 14, 61, 65, 68, 69, 71, 91-92, 99, 110, 116, 145n42; treatment of minority groups, 14, 40

poverty, 44, 106, 116; in Aboriginal communities, 12, 24, 27, 28, 34, 132n58; and abused women, 111, 145n35
Public Legal Information Services (New Brunswick), 97

race, 6, 10, 11, 13, 18, 61-62, 63, 115, 140n29; and social assistance, 63, 71; and violence, 23, 39, 42, 72, 77
racism, 1, 11, 14, 17-18, 21, 39, 72; in Kenora, 13, 62, 63, 64, 76; in women's movement, 17-18, 127n47. *See also* anti-racism
regional differences, 6, 11, 61, 126n36
Religieuses Hospitalières de Saint-Joseph, 97-98
Renault, Sister Cécile, 97-98
residential schools, 12, 40-41, 133n71
rape. *See* sexual assault
Regina Transition House, 149n69
reserves, 12, 73, 115, 140n33; conditions on, 64; lack of services, 25-27, 34, 40; relocation of, 63-64
Ristock, Janice, 14
Robb, Helene, 102, 109, 122
Ross, Becki, 14
Ross, Carol, 84, 86, 89, 92, 122, 145n42
Roth, Benita, 11
RCMP. *See* police
Royal Commission on the Status of Women, 4, 32, 66, 96, 146n5

safe homes, 88; in Aboriginal communities, 34; feminist critique of, 80; informal, 4, 47, 52, 85, 144n23. *See also* Nelson Safe Home Program
Saint-John Telegraph-Journal, 110
Salvation Army, 51, 88, 145n44
Saulnier, Yolande, 102, 103, 107, 111, 122
second-stage housing, 39
sexual assault, 2, 3, 45, 65; theorization of 3, 65. *See also* gendered racial violence; Kenora Rape and Sexual Assault Group
shelters for battered women. *See* transition houses

Shewell, Hugh, 25
Shkilnyk, Anastasia, 63
Simpson, Sam, 81, 122, 143n5, 143n7, 145n35
Singbeil, Dianne, 65, 71, 122
Smith, Andrea, 17
social assistance, 43, 46-47, 49, 50, 60, 61, 63, 67, 77, 89, 114; in Aboriginal communities, 12, 25-26, 138n5; and Aboriginal women, 1, 12, 13, 21, 71; municipal control of, 6, 7-8, 43, 44, 55, 69-70, 75; Ontario General Welfare Act, 73; treatment of abused women, 7, 8, 48, 61-62, 71
Social Credit, 7, 80, 84, 143n2; cutbacks to social services, 80-81, 87-88, 93, 94
solidarity movement, 87-88
Srivastava, Sarita, 11

Thunder Bay Anishinabequek, 13, 17, 21-42, 113, 132n54; meaning of Anishinabequek, 128n1
Thunder Bay Community Residences, 17, 43, 44, 45-51, 52, 58-59; Aboriginal women at, 35, 132n59; statistics, 48. *See also* Thunder Bay Social Services
Thunder Bay Indian Friendship Centre, 30-31
Thunder Bay Sexual Assault Centre, 50, 135n12, 139n15
Thunder Bay Social Services, 43, 44, 45-51. *See also* Thunder Bay Community Residences
Thunder Bay Women's Liberation Group, 4, 45
Toronto Interval House, 5, 9
transition houses, 2-3, 17, 113; conditions in, 54, 69-70, 99-101, 108-9, 141n39; development of, 5, 115; experiences of women in, 16; origins, 5, 9; philosophy of, 5-6, 49, 54-55, 103-4; staff, 95, 103-4, 107, 115; wages, 17, 35, 105-12, 149n69
Trudeau, Pierre Elliot, 27

United Way, 10, 110, 150n76

Untinen, Leni, 50, 53, 57, 58, 74, 76, 122, 135n10, 142n60, 142n70

Vallée Lourdes (Bathurst), 97
Vancouver Transition House, 5, 9, 91
Vancouver Women's Centre, 4
violence against women. *See also* family violence; gendered racial violence; wife battering
– Aboriginal theorization of, 3, 10-11, 17, 22-23, 38-42, 113, 116; white feminist responses to, 11, 38-39, 41, 62, 72, 114, 116
– feminist theorization of, 3-4, 113
– framework, 10, 14, 72, 77, 133n78; critique of, 10-11
– lesbian theorization of, 14
Voices: A Survival Manual for Women, 15
volunteerism, 55, 57, 66, 67, 74, 79-81, 85, 87, 90, 93, 94, 143n2

Walker, Gillian, 9, 56, 74, 111
welfare. *See* social assistance
White Paper on Indian Policy (*Statement of the Government in Indian Policy*), 13; Aboriginal opposition to, 27-28
wife battering
– denial of, 2, 59, 83-84, 147n16
– feminist theorization of, 4, 10, 88, 97, 113
– incidence of, 1, 56; in Aboriginal communities, 39, 68; in Kenora, 68-69; in Moncton, 99, 147n21; in Nelson; in Thunder Bay, 47
– politicization of, 1, 8, 39, 41, 96, 98, 101-2
– reports on, 5, 6, 8, 10, 12, 89, 97, 116
– resistance to politicization, 4, 5-6, 116; in Kenora, 66; in Moncton, 98, 109, 111; in Nelson, 87; in Thunder Bay, 48-49, 59
women: immigrant, 10, 14, 115; inequalities among, 11, 14, 117 (*see also* lesbians); women of colour, 14, 117. *See also* Aboriginal Women

Women against Violence against Women (WAVAW), 3
Women in Need Society (Trail), 86-87, 88, 90, 91, 145n34
women's centres, 4, 46; records, 15-16, 129n8
women's movement, 9; marginalization of Aboriginal women and minority groups, 11, 42, 114, 117; regional, 6, 17, 23, 43-44, 49, 50-53, 58, 59-60, 76; United States, 11; urban/rural differences, 9-10, 113-14, 123nn2-3; women's liberation movement, 18, 82, 97
women's movement, relationship with the state, 7, 8-9, 74, 113
– relationship with municipal government, 7, 44; in Kenora, 62-67, 114; in Moncton, 99, 109-10, 147n21, 147n24; in Thunder Bay, 46-51, 53, 58-60, 114;
– relationship with provincial government, 56-57, 87,88, 95, 102-3, 105, 107-10
Women's Place Kenora, 70-77; and Aboriginal women, 70, 71, 72; community support for, 71; funding, 76 (*see also under* Kenora Women's Crisis Intervention Project); municipal opposition to, 75-76
Worden, Doreen, 122

YWCA, 21

Printed and bound in Canada by Friesens

Set in Minion by Robert and Shirley Kroeger, Kroeger Enterprises

Copy Editor: Lesley Barry

Proofreader: Dianne Tiefensee